THE MANY FACES OF CRIME

THE MANY FACES OF CRIME

A TRUE DETECTIVE'S CHRONICLE

DENNIS W. McGOOKIN

The History Press

Jacket illustrations
Front: Kenneth Noye (PA Images/Alamy Stock Photo); Man walking away
(Peter Wollinga/Shutterstock); Perry Wacker (Shutterstock)
Back: Memorial to the victims of the 2000 Dover human trafficking incident
(Paul Martin/Alamy Stock Photo)

First published 2024

The History Press
97 St George's Place, Cheltenham,
Gloucestershire, GL50 3QB
www.thehistorypress.co.uk

British Library Cataloguing in Publication Data.
A catalogue record for this book is available from the British Library.

ISBN 978 1 80399 596 0

Typesetting and origination by The History Press
Printed and bound in Great Britain by TJ Books Limited, Padstow, Cornwall.

Trees for Life

CONTENTS

1

THE MANY FACES OF CRIME

I have an excellent memory for faces. I recall the face of every dead body I have ever seen. Every murder victim, every suicide, every cot death and every death reported as unexplained. Some faces stand out more than others, of course.

The clock in the mortuary had just touched 1800 hrs, but there was still one body on the examination table under a white sheet. The child's tiny corpse had laid in-waiting for four long hours, whilst my exhausted mortuary team – their faces pale and drawn, their eyes soft and sad – examined the child's young mother. She had died from multiple stab wounds.

I watched the mortician lift a corner of the sheet, pulling it back gently to expose the sweet face of a young girl with long, dark hair. She looked like she was in a peaceful sleep, but she was dead, of course, and her moment of death had been far from peaceful.

She was around the same age as my own daughter. She had the same olive skin, the same long, dark hair. I swallowed. In all my thirty years in the force, I had never been quite so impacted as I was in that moment. Another victim of a horrendous knife attack. Her slight frame was still fully clothed but heavily bloodstained. She had a stab wound on the right side of her skull. She gripped in her right hand a fistful of what would turn out to be her own hair. I didn't want to be there. I wanted to see my children but it was my business to stay. To ensure that even the smallest piece of evidence was taken, recorded and managed correctly.

A suspect was in custody. All I could hope for was that, under my leadership, everybody would do their job correctly (which, as you will see, is not always the case), that justice would ultimately be served. A justice too late for this little girl and her mum – innocent victims whose faces will stay with me forever.

Victims of horrendous crimes start as strangers but, case after case, I have been drawn into the intimate details of their fate. Whilst working on each case, their features, eye colour, likely complexion whilst living, are brought to life in stark detail, reminding me that each victim was once a person with dreams, a future, a life. Someone's brother, sister, daughter, mother, son, father, friend, uncle, aunt. Crime leaves a trail of victims in its wake. Even fifty-eight Chinese immigrants, dead in the back of a lorry at the Port of Dover, were so much more than numbers to me. Each one had a story I would have to investigate. Each linked back to a family, across the other side of the world, who I hoped to meet in order to glean enough insight into their lives from their loved ones, anything which might help me solve the case.

It is not only the snapshots of the victims which live in my mind's eye.

All the investigative stories in this book are based on fact. The names of several officers and witnesses are excluded for a variety of reasons, predominantly out of respect for those involved and especially because, after personal and traumatic events are placed in the public eye, only a scant degree of privacy remains.

I will show you how the investigation into the now famous 'M25 Road Rage' killing developed. We will follow the details about the hunt for, and subsequent conviction of, the notorious criminal Kenneth Noye, who was responsible for that brutal murder. Criminals such as Noye run, but they cannot hide from justice.

I am often asked why I had the urge to take up a career in which I would inevitably witness so much misery. After all, I grew up in a loving, stable family home and my childhood was a happy one. During the summer of 1969, however, Belfast (the capital city of Northern Ireland) saw the first of the now historic disturbances, which came to be known around the world as 'The Troubles'. The Irish Republican Army (IRA) supported a campaign of civil disobedience, predominantly carried out by Republican communities, which resulted in unprecedented attacks on the Royal Ulster Constabulary (RUC). Some Loyalist communities carried out similar protests, which resulted in further attacks on the RUC.

It didn't take long before the IRA waged a counter attack. They launched a campaign of violence against the RUC in which former street violence was replaced with firearm and bomb attacks on police stations and individual officers.

The arrival of the British Army – who were brought in to support the RUC – and the resulting media stories were my first introduction to terrorism. My parents were supporters of law and order and we lived on the south side of the city where we, as a family, were mostly sheltered from what was happening in other parts of the province.

I had wanted to be a police officer since I was knee-high to a grasshopper. Perhaps it was my maternal uncle Ed who inspired me, as he was a serving officer in the RUC. He was quite a character and I was very close to him. Much to the horror of our family, he was targeted by the IRA. His house on the south-west side of the city was the subject of an IRA bomb that had been planted minutes after he, his wife and my two cousins had left their home. Thankfully, no one was injured in this attack, but it brought it home to our family just how serious the situation was. No one was safe. The perpetrators of such attacks used any method they could to achieve their goals, based on what we considered to be misguided beliefs.

With this incident and such political unrest as a backdrop, I decided I wanted to be a police officer.

'I'm going to apply to join the RUC straight after my 18th birthday,' I declared. My parents were deeply concerned about this after the attack on my uncle's home.

After those few tense days, we finally had an open discussion and my Uncle Ed was present. After some wrangling, and with Uncle Ed's endorsement, I finally agreed to go to England and join a police force there instead of at home. I was forever grateful to my uncle for acknowledging and respecting my dream.

After the decision had been made, I went directly to my bedroom, where I studied the map of England in my atlas. I shut my eyes and placed my finger on the map at random. It landed on Dartford. I then applied for and was subsequently accepted into the Kent County Constabulary.*

I only returned home occasionally, but my parents did regularly holiday in England so that they could visit me. Some forty years later, however, my mum was well into her 80s and I went home to Belfast to see her. Dad had passed away some years before.

This was when my mum took my hand and said, 'I thought you would come back home after only a few years in England.'

She had never mentioned this before, but it was then that I realised what a great source of sadness my absence must have been for her, despite me telephoning her every week without fail.

I never did return to live in Northern Ireland.

When I first left school, I was still too young to join the Police Service in England, so I took a job as a laboratory technician in a local school. The year was 1971, and I had nine months to wait until I was permitted to join the Kent Police.

My first steady girlfriend, at that time, was the only one of my friends who drove her own car. One evening, we went out together and stopped in a country lay-by to kiss goodnight. Within minutes, I saw blue lights in the darkness, approaching our location. Very shortly afterwards, two military jeeps pulled up – one in front and one behind our car. I established very quickly that they were the newly formed Ulster Defence Regiment. They had obviously designated our location as a key position for a motor vehicle checkpoint.

---

* The Kent County Constabulary is referred to as Kent Police. After 2002, the name officially changed to Kent Police. I will refer to the Chief Constable as the Chief Constable of Kent.

It was concerning for such a young man (desperate to impress his girl-friend) to watch this bunch of soldiers decamp from their Land Rovers and stride across the tarmac with such determination.

I wound down the window and said, in what must have been a very shaky voice, 'Sorry, officer, we're not doing anything.'

To which he replied, 'Well, get out of the way, son, and let a real man in there.'

I half smiled – I didn't know what to do. It suddenly dawned on me that I wasn't as grown up as I thought I was.

Thankfully, this situation was quickly resolved. We drove off into the darkness and my girlfriend took me home. In hindsight, I find the soldier's line amusing, and he certainly meant no harm, but little did I know then how many times I would be held at gunpoint in my career when the potential stakes would be much higher than they were that evening.

One particular day in November will always stay in my mind: Tuesday, 2 November 1971. I had finished work at the school in the late afternoon, when I started to make my way home. As I approached the Ormeau Road, which was close to our home on Jamison Street, there was a large explosion. I rounded a corner and stared down the road towards the local police station.

A cloud of dust and smoke rose into the air some 300yd away from where I stood. I ran towards the scene, hoping to help. Initially, I thought the police station had been the target of a terrorist attack, but as I moved closer, I realised it was the Red Lion Public House and a small shop, both of which sat on either side of the police station, which had been bombed.

People were screaming and wailing, and within minutes the military, police, fire service and ambulances arrived at the scene. I tried to be of some use but, in truth, all I was good for was clearing rubble, together with many other community members.

Later that day, I returned home to discover on the news that three people had died and some thirty others were wounded in the blast. Ironically enough, the police station was not seriously damaged.

Terrorism was now on my own doorstep but, much to my parent's relief, I was headed for a career in policing in England.

My career swiftly developed and after my two-year uniformed probation period, my desire to become a detective grew. I was initially appointed as a Temporary Detective Constable (T/DC), where I put my investigative skills into practice. These early days exposed me to the workings of local media. It never occurred to me, at that time, to what extent I would end up being exposed to the world press and other such international media services.

As a young Detective Sergeant (DS), I was involved in one investigation which followed a police officer being stabbed to death. I was present when a senior officer interviewed a suspect for this killing, and after that interview was finished, I thought I would never see the man again. Some fifteen years later, however, he and I would come to meet across a bullet-proof courtroom in Madrid.

Major crime investigations are rarely resolved quickly. Throughout my career, several of them overlapped with other ongoing investigations. At any one time, I could be running half a dozen cases: several murder investigations, a missing person investigation, reviewing an unnatural death in an adjoining police force, plus receiving notification of a DNA identification in a rape enquiry. For a Senior Investigating Officer (SIO) it was common to have to fit all these into the diary simultaneously. Something that further complicated the work was the fact that they were always at different stages of the investigation.

In addition to this, I was involved in training detective officers at all levels of their service, and at various stages of their careers. Chief Officers of different ranks had to have an understanding of what would be required of them if and when they were appointed to lead a series of serious linked crime investigations and major disasters on local, regional, national and international levels.

I also became involved in work with the European Commission in Palestine. During that experience, I was held at gunpoint by Israeli soldiers as I entered Gaza.

As a Detective Chief Inspector (DCI), I had to contend with all manner of tragedy in any given month. There is a poignant chapter in this book which shows how I could be dealing with the death of a child in tragic circumstances one day, whilst the very next day I'd have to handle the disappearance and subsequent death of an adult – no less a tragedy, for it was still a loving parent's child.

I came to discover the truth behind the infamous disappearance of the common-law wife of a multi-millionaire. I dealt with the police response and investigation following the death of fifty-eight Chinese nationals found in the back of an articulated lorry at the world-famous Port of Dover. My journey as a detective also took me far away from Kent to the Pitcairn Islands, deep in the Pacific Ocean where, once again, I found myself being held at gunpoint – this time on the island of Tahiti on my return journey home.

Police forces in the United Kingdom have to deal with many serious, undetected crimes. They are often linked forensically through DNA, fingerprints, fibre-matching, etc., sometimes by the same offender(s) and other times linked from crime scene to crime scene. You may, for instance, find a tool-mark, or perhaps the bullet casing from a gun which has been discharged, and link it to another crime. These series of crime investigations inevitably, and more often than not, cross several different police force boundaries. The Critical Research Index (CRI) is one example of a methodology we follow, which brings the computer databases for critical crimes together.

Some die at the hands of an offender, whilst others survive the crime. There are, however, always families, friends and associates who are still deeply affected. Does this mean that they are also victims in their own right? I believe they are.

Most of my stories relate to victims who did not survive. One must bear in mind, however, that there are individuals left behind, many of whom have a long journey through a difficult healing process, particularly when they have actually witnessed a violent incident perpetrated on a loved one. In these cases, the terms victim and survivor can be interchangeable. The families and loved ones left behind have to carry on living, despite the extreme circumstances of their loss, and their lives are truly changed forever.

Trying to bring offenders to justice is my way of setting out to do my best for all the victims, including the surviving victims. I know I am not alone when I say that officers serving in the police force are changed forever by every single story we are drawn into through our work. Every victim who crosses our paths, touches us and changes our lives in some way.

Remembering faces can be both a blessing and a curse. I never forget a victim – never – but other faces are imprinted on my mind. Not only those of the dead, but faces of the living – those left behind to suffer the fallout of crime. Such faces shouldn't be forgotten, and I hope they find even a small degree of comfort knowing they are not.

Then there are the faces of perpetrators – the roughly sketched-out identikits or criminal profiles which come to life in 3D technicolour and whose faces I am also destined to live with, in my mind's eye, all my living days.

2

THE EARLY YEARS

My new career began when I arrived at Kent Police Headquarters on Bank Holiday Monday, 28 August 1972. This day marked the launch of a career which would span thirty amazing years.

'Black humour' or 'Dark humour' is defined in the Oxford Dictionary as 'A kind of humour characterised by the morbid or provocative treatment of subjects like death and disease' and in the Cambridge Dictionary as 'a humorous way of looking at or treating something that is serious or sad'.

Such humour was, and probably still is, a vital coping strategy in my line of work. As the adage goes, 'If you don't laugh you cry.'

Let's face it, neither the victim nor the family ever want to see a police officer sobbing in their lounge. It therefore follows that despite the horrors police officers such as myself, and police staff around the world, must face each day, we are often forced to see the funny side of tragedy.

The best investigators draw off years of experience, logical thinking, knowledge of the law, and above all, the ability to keep a cool head. One can only arrive at that stage of seniority and competence, however, after acknowledging that before you arrive at such a point, you will first, undoubtedly, be forced to learn from an array of mistakes.

In order to reassure any aspiring detective, I must admit that I stumbled through plenty of difficult lessons myself. Provided you admit to your mistakes and deal with them professionally, without trying to cover them up, then you can learn from them. When you do try to cover them up, that's when unforeseen circumstances have the greatest chance of becoming serious.

Don't be embarrassed, or ashamed when you catch yourself seeing a more amusing side of events. Time and time again, your laughter is likely to be set off at what you deem to be the most inappropriate moments. This is, more often than not, merely a coping mechanism, and perfectly understandable.

I have included a few such anecdotes in this chapter, which recount times when naïve errors were made by me, or my colleagues, and where dark humour prevailed. Hopefully, this will allow a little laughter into what could otherwise be regarded as a very serious book. Allow me to regale you with a couple of my more amusing tales before moving on to the graver stuff.

On a miserable, grey Tuesday afternoon in January 1973, I found myself, fresh out of the Police Training Centre, on uniformed patrol in Gravesend. It was my first posting. I was in the 999-emergency car with an experienced officer, PC Peter Eggleston, when we responded to a call from a concerned neighbour.

An elderly gentleman had not been seen for several days and his house had been shrouded in complete darkness for all that time. Being young and fit, I was the one instructed to climb through the fanlight window in the lounge and open the front door from the inside.

It was starting to get dark but I had left my torch in the police car, so I really could not see what I was doing and had to scramble about to find a light switch. The living room had a strange, damp and somewhat disgusting smell about it. Terrified of tripping over a dead body, my heart was pounding.

I managed to get to the door, tripping only once, over a small table. I found the light switch but it did not work – the electricity seemed to have been disconnected.

It was all too much for me really, so I ended up retreating out the front door to grab some fresh air and regain my composure. I informed Peter that the man was not in the lounge, before retrieving my torch from the car. Peter rebuked me and ordered me to return to the house and search the premises upstairs at once.

As I crept up the stairs, I was overpowered by the pungent stench of what smelt like a mixture of death and filth to me. There was no sign of life – I was terrified of what I might find. I checked the bathroom but there was nothing there. The smell got worse the closer I got to the darkened back room. I shone my torch across the floor, catching sight of the legs of the bed. I raised the light higher and saw the outline of a body lying underneath a small sheet. If this was the man we were looking for, then he seemed quite dead.

I darted out of the room. 'He's up here, Peter,' I shouted down the stairs. 'He's dead.'

Peter came up the stairs and I gallantly directed him into the bedroom, shining my torch on to the corpse.

Within one split second, the darn thing came to life!

'Fuck off,' it shouted, sitting bolt upright. 'Get out of my house, you bastards.'

I screamed.

I can't remember exactly what I said, but whatever expletives I did employ at that moment will never be published here. I was shocked to high heaven and exited that room in a cold sweat.

Peter took control of the situation and, quite rightly, made it his priority to reassure the old man, who obviously thought we were intruders in his home.

Once Peter had done apologising to the gentleman on my behalf, he left the house to find me, this young, inexperienced PC, still trembling from shock. Peter was old-school and a very experienced officer. He scooped the wreck of me up off the pavement where I stood and returned with me to the car.

We drove in silence all the way back to the police station.

The scene we had just left kept spinning round and round in my head. The stench I had assumed was death was probably the result of poor living standards in a house which had surely not been cleaned or aired for years.

It was upon our return that Peter taught me not only a few tricks in the art of good storytelling, but also the knack of laughing at things which might otherwise make you cry. I was the butt of many jibes later that night and fortunately I was able to take the situation in my stride and handled the endless jokes at my own expense, but despite all the laughter, the look on that old man's face will stay with me forever.

My time spent with Peter and another experienced colleague, PC Mick O'Rourke, were filled with insight into how to deal with all manner of situations.

I was out on a night shift with the two of them when we responded to a fight outside an Indian restaurant in the centre of Gravesend. We pulled up at the scene and were out of the car very fast.

One of them told me to get after a youth who had started to run off. I had never apprehended anyone before, so this would potentially be my first formal arrest.

With not a second to spare – not even to throw my cap on – I drew my wooden truncheon with my right hand in what is called the upward, striking position and bolted, in chase, after the youth.

Officers weren't tied down by the abundance of equipment they have to carry nowadays. No stab-resistant vest, no issued handcuffs, just a notebook in my back pocket and a radio in my left hand.

There I was, brandishing my truncheon aloft, and though it felt like the real thing to me, in honestly, it must have looked like something out of the Keystone Cops. The youth ran down a narrow alleyway with me in close pursuit, wearing my smart, cloth uniformed. I was gaining on him fast when he eventually gave up.

I felt rather proud at that moment when, truncheon in hand, I arrested and cautioned the criminal. Several individuals were taken into custody that night.

Back at the police station, I was told to report to the duty sergeant, Police Sergeant (PS) Arthur Kelso. I was still feeling so proud to have made my first arrest and, since PS Kelso had also originated from Belfast and was a fellow Ulsterman, I was sure he would be pleased for me and praise me both for my fitness and for having made my first arrest. This was not what I was being called in for, however. Quite the contrary.

Sergeant Kelso was in the process of rolling a cigarette when I walked in.

'Why did you have your truncheon out, boy?' he asked.

(Just as an aside: the lads, Peter and Mick, had obviously seen me running down the street with my truncheon in the air and reported it to the Sergeant.)

Sergeant Kelso was a rather dour individual because of his Belfast accent and dry delivery, and I genuinely couldn't take him seriously. Certain that he was joking, I tried my best to hold back my smirk, but to no avail.

'But Sarge,' I said, 'they taught us at training school that if you need to arrest someone for public disorder then you should use your truncheon.'

'This is not a joke,' he replied sternly. 'You should only use your truncheon if you are being threatened and you were not being threatened.' He went on to give me more fatherly advice about when to use it and when not — which is almost never, in fact!

It hit me between the eyes to discover he wasn't kidding, and this tick-off clearly had a lasting effect on me because over the following thirty years, I never once used or even produced my truncheon again. I also learnt that the main use of a truncheon is to break the glass in a door when gaining entry to a house when there is a concern for an elderly resident. So, if you ever see a battered-looking wooden truncheon, the policeman using it is unlikely to be a violent thug and much more likely to be helping the vulnerable in distress.

On a Friday evening in March 1975, I was exposed to my first murder scene. The battered body of a local priest, Father Anthony Crean, was found in his bath at his home in the grounds of a convent in Shorne village on the outskirts of Gravesend. I established that the body had been found by two nuns who lived in the convent.

I had no prior training, nor was I given any advice or guidance beforehand but, regardless, Sergeant Kelso instructed me to stand guard at the front door and await the arrival of scene of crime officers (SOCOs).

Any officer left alone with a dead body for the first time will tell you what an unnerving experience it is. It was cold and wet outside, and, despite my apprehensions, I decided to stand inside the house rather than outside. Not knowing the necessity of crime scene management, I went ahead and turned the radiator by the front door on. After all, the late priest and myself were the only ones there.

I was present when senior officers, led by DCI Lew Hart and DI Ken Tappenden, arrived at the house to survey the scene, which simply involved looking at the body. They didn't touch anything because every touch leaves a trace, of course, which means contamination of a crime scene. To this very day, I preach the gospel about crime scene contamination during all my training sessions.

Everybody always stopped what they were doing once the detectives arrived, back in those days.

'Step back. Step back. The detectives have arrived!'

It was as if the detectives knew everything when, in fact, they most certainly did not. For a start, they didn't wear gloves or white suits like they do these days. Even in the middle of the night they would turn up at the scene 'suited and booted' – with suits and ties on – as if headed for the office at 0800 hrs.

Logic now tells me what guarding such a scene involves; making sure that no one comes in without proper authority and disturbing nothing whatsoever at the scene, no matter how cold you may be. I didn't know this then, however, and although I didn't disturb anything other than the radiator valve, I did wander into the hallway, from where I could see straight into the bathroom where the body of Father Crean lay fully clothed in the bath. Father Crean's was only the second dead body I had ever seen and I will never forget it. His face and head were covered in blood. I didn't go any closer to the bathroom but I do remember thinking what a horrible, frightening way to die. The first was when I was about 8 years old. My father had told my brother and I that we should say goodbye to Grandad, who was a First World War veteran and a very special man. I wasn't at all prepared to see my grandfather's face, which seemed like a waxwork to me, lying in a coffin in that small room at my aunt's house. I can still see his face today.

It was a sparsely furnished one-bedroom bungalow, more like a gatehouse than a home. I was drawn to a small, slightly ajar cupboard inside the hallway and I peered in. I was just being nosey, I guess.

There, right before my eyes, was a long-handled axe. On the head of the axe was what appeared to be human hair, stuck in blood, which I assumed was from the injuries sustained from the blade.

I was careful not to touch it but I assumed that it would be helpful to tell the SOCOs about it, so once they arrived, I said, 'I think you will find the weapon you're going to be looking for is in that cupboard.'

These two officers were not at all grateful for information of this nature to come from such a young PC.

'You should not be looking in any cupboards,' they rebuked me in no uncertain terms.

Oooh, I've just been told off, I thought.

I reassured them that I had not touched a thing and, thankfully, they didn't tell Sergeant Kelso.

I handed the guarding of that scene over to my colleague, PC Peter Norman, who was a young officer himself at the time. Many, many years later we laughed when he told me for the first time about how terrified he had been that the murderer might return to the scene, and that he sat gripping his truncheon throughout the entire night.

The media ended up reporting that after a large-scale search for a murder weapon, the SOCOs were the ones who recovered the weapon hidden in the house. They were highly commended for discovering it when, of course, I was the one who had seen it and told them where it was.

In the years that followed, these men became close colleagues in the same Criminal Investigation Department. Although they knew about my looking into the cupboard that night, what they didn't know was that I had turned on a radiator too – something else I should not have done. Fortuitously for all involved, neither spotting the weapon nor turning on the radiator affected the outcome of this investigation, and the suspect was quickly apprehended. Nonetheless, this early experience has informed the way I train to this day, because I never forget to include how important good crime scene management is, so young PCs have certainly gained the benefit of my mistakes. Whenever a young in-service officer is present, I wonder if they will remember each face of the deceased as clearly as I do.

When young PCs were guarding murder scenes, I always asked them, 'Have you been properly briefed as to what your role is?' Thankfully, it seems that the message has gotten across to sergeants and supervisors. I also asked them as often as I could and when the situation allowed it, 'Have you ever been inside and seen the crime scene of a murder?'

'Never,' is what the vast majority reply. In which case, I would instruct them that, if the time was right, they could come into a crime scene with me so I could explain the scene to them – identifying key areas of evidential importance and how they would be dealt with.

When they did come into crime scenes with me, I made sure they were suited in the white overalls, masks, gloves, with their head and feet covered. I'd always made sure that a SOCO was with me and even if it was a junior SOCO, I would stand at the crime scene with them, whilst surveying the scene myself, and ask for their input.

'Right,' I'd say, 'what do you see here? Because it's important that if you are going to be working at this scene and you've got an idea or a hypothesis of what's happened here, then tell me what you're thinking.'

Giving young PCs the opportunity to see how they should treat murder scenes this way is part of their basic training, it's very good learning for them.

'If you're the first on the scene,' I emphasise, 'don't worry about crime scene management. You are disrupting a crime scene any time you come into it but the whole point of getting there quickly is for the preservation of life, so if entering the scene saves someone's life then you can, by all means, disrupt it. If, however, it is obvious that the person is dead, then – and only then – you should step back and simply guard the scene. In other words, at the outset, don't ever imagine you should not rush into a scene – saving lives is your priority.'

Patrick David Mackay admitted to the killing of Father Crean along with a series of other killings of elderly women in London, known as the Chelsea Pensioner Murders. He was sentenced to life imprisonment, not for murder but manslaughter. The trial judge made an Order which would ensure that Mackay remained in secure custody 'unless and until' he ceased to be the menace to society that he clearly was. He is now regarded as one of Britain's longest-serving prisoners.

Later in my career, when I was the on-call SIO for the force, I was called to the scene of a lady who had been found dead in her bedroom. What I did not know, and was not told at the time, was that the PC who had initially attended the scene had gone off duty and been replaced. He had made no disclosures to the officer who took over the scene from him.

This resulted in treating the death as unexplained.

The victim's common law husband voluntarily attended the police station. He was not under arrest. He was very accommodating and stayed with us that night. He offered an alibi, which would be investigated as quickly as practicable.

When we all returned to the police station the following morning, I was in the process of briefing the SOCOs who had been at the scene and the interview teams who were going to be speaking to the man, when a PC walked in.

'Excuse me,' he said, 'who is in charge of the lady's death last night?'

'That's me, Superintendent McGookin,' I replied, 'and guess what? I am in charge. Who are you?'

'Oh, I was the first officer at the scene last night,' he said, removing a document from his clipboard. 'I think this might be useful for you.'

'What is it?' I asked.

'It's her suicide note.'

'What?' I asked. 'We've had a man here all night, and you bring me a bloody suicide note now? What the hell do you think you've been up to?'

I was flabbergasted at such poor communication. I imagined that fellow from *Line of Duty*, Superintendent Hastings – who is played by the actor Adrian Dunbar and speaks with a Belfast accent – he would have been furious. He probably would have said something like, 'For the sake of Mary, Joseph and that wee donkey, what do you think you were doing?' Together with a few more expletives, no doubt.

This PC had the best part of twenty years of service but he was a rural bobby and so that was all he was used to. It is ridiculous that he made such a stupid mistake – to go off duty when you're holding somebody's suicide note – it just beggars belief, but hopefully it is something that would not happen again. At least he had thought to put the suicide note in a plastic sleeve.

The lady had given clear details about why she was about to take an overdose. She'd fallen out of love with her boyfriend and was now in love with another of his work colleagues. She had been unfaithful to him with yet another one of his work colleagues and decided to take the easy way out.

As a result of this PC's actions, a lot of police time had been wasted that night. What's more, an innocent man had stayed with us overnight and all because an officer didn't do his job properly. This incident formed the foundation of my training lectures – an officer must never underestimate the importance of their own personal role and responsibility in the overall process.

In another incident, a police officer from our force had murdered his wife and three of his children, including a newborn baby. He then went to the garage and hung himself. It was a very clear case of murder/suicide but, of course, there were families and other individuals, including police colleagues, who knew the victims personally and still had to try and cope with this dreadful situation professionally.

I went in and surveyed the scene. By the early 1980s, crime scene preservation had come ahead in leaps and bounds. Everyone wore white suits, overshoes, gloves and head coverings. It was then that I saw a lovely photograph of the children of the family up above the mantelpiece. I thought how tragic this story was, but at the end of the day, we must be professional and get on with the job.

When our Chief Constable (CC) came to the scene, his first words were, 'Well, Dennis, I take it you're not going to let me into the crime scene?'

To which I replied, 'Sir, definitely not.'

We both smiled.

The scene was guarded all through that night. The scene of crime team were then left to gather forensic evidence and prepare for the post-mortem examination of the five deceased, whilst my detectives prepared for the next day's briefing.

I left my home at 0800 hrs the following morning. It took about fifteen minutes to get into my office. I had stopped to get petrol just beside Police Headquarters, and after I had filled up and walked inside to pay, I was stopped dead in my tracks. That photo of those children, which had been on the mantelpiece, was now in every single newspaper on the stand in front of me.

I hit the roof and phoned the DCI who would be dealing with this on behalf of HM Coroner, at once.

'Colin,' I said, 'my office immediately.'

'What is it, guv?' he asked.

'My office now. I will be there in two minutes,' I said.

We met in my office and I asked him, 'Colin, have you seen the newspapers this morning?'

'No, guv, not at all.'

I said, 'Well, best you go take a look and tell me who is responsible for taking that photograph off the wall at the crime scene and giving it to the press last night.'

He was back in my office within ten minutes. 'Governor, I have no idea at all,' he said.

'Right,' I replied. 'Well, find out straight away and come back to me. It looks like somebody is going to lose their job today.'

Within ten to fifteen minutes he told me that it was the head of our Media Services Department. He had been called out by their own media officer and attended the scene after most of us had left. Somewhere along the line, someone had told him about the photograph. He had then gone to the PC who was guarding the scene, given the PC his details and said, 'I am authorised to come into this scene.'

Bless the young PC who let him in. From his training he knew that if anybody produced authority, they could enter the scene and (in fairness to the PC) there is no way he could have anticipated such deceit. This media guy simply regarded himself as a senior, civilian colleague and believed he had a god-given right to do whatever he wanted. He was able to produce an identification card stating that he was Head of Media Services. The PC logged him in properly, then timed him in and timed him out.

This man went into that scene, took that photograph off the wall and brought it back to Headquarters to give it to the press without anybody's authority. In the process of collecting that photo, he would have had to step into a scene where a mother and three of her children had been brutally murdered.

I wanted him suspended immediately but the force wouldn't do it.

'At the end of the day,' I instructed the SIOs and Senior SOCOs (S/SOCOs) under my command, 'he is not to come to any crime scene, whatsoever, without my personal permission. Even if I am out of the country, you must get hold of me, no matter where I am!'

He was reprimanded for going into the crime scene and taking that photograph off the wall but he kept his job, something I find unbelievable to this very day.

Years later, this same man came to the scene of the dead Chinese immigrants at Dover and walked into my crime scene with reporters. That was the type of man I was dealing with. Thankfully, I was there that day and I threw them out.

'Get out,' I told them.

'All we want is a photograph of the lorry,' they said.

'You're not getting that photograph,' I replied, 'and you never will, because you can't be trusted. That is a certain piece of evidence which could relate to organised crime in Holland, Belgium, across Europe and all the way back to China. So, get out.'

I had first been exposed to the media when I was still a young and inexperienced T/DC. I had been handed an investigation into a decapitated cat which had been found on a large council estate in Gravesend. I didn't have a clue how the poor creature came to lose its head but when a second similar incident occurred, a weekly local newspaper started to take an interest.

I took a telephone call from a female reporter who was desperate to write a story about these poor creatures. She started suggesting that the deed might be the work of some evil cult.

'I cannot not rule anything out,' I said (stupidly enough).

It was to be predicted really. The following week, the newspaper headlines read 'Police Seek Cult Cat Killer'.

My full name featured in the story! Oh dear.

My Superintendent was not best pleased, that's for sure, the article implied that police were not doing enough to save cats! Which is ridiculous, of course.

I simply thought I was being helpful. In any case, it taught me an important lesson: to be careful what you say, especially to the press.

There were other occasions in my life as a Detective Constable (DC) on a Major Crime team that had their funny side. Around the start of the 1980s, burglaries and thefts of (and from) motor vehicles were rising throughout the country. Chief Officers expected resources to be focused on catching those responsible, so we were often required to carry out surveillance on suspects.

Several colleagues and I were called out to follow a suspected car thief in a rural part of the county. The individual had driven to a large, wooded area where walkers parked their cars. This spot typically attracted car thieves. The suspect left his car and walked into the woods and, with my colleagues nearby in support, I was tasked to follow him.

The suspect walked through the trees, whilst I followed at a discreet distance. I was watching him in the distance when he suddenly turned around and began walking back in my direction. It was crucial I keep my surveillance secret but there was absolutely nowhere for me to turn and, in my haste, it seemed that only safe and expedient thing to do was to climb up a sycamore tree.

I switched off my radio so he wouldn't hear it and, stricken with panic, I watched him as he continued to wander back towards me. Certain that he would sense me near him, I climbed higher and higher up the tree.

By the time he arrived at the base of 'my tree', my heart was thumping. What on earth would I do if he looked up? I was in plainclothes, so I was not readily identifiable as a police officer, but a fully-grown man up a tree would be hard to explain in any case. I reassured myself that as long as he carried on walking, he would pass by soon enough. Imagine my horror then, when he decided to stop directly beneath me. He hovered there for no apparent reason, for several minutes, before wandering off towards my colleagues.

Once he was a safe distance away, I turned my radio back on to pre-warn my colleagues that he was now heading towards the car park. In a bid to ascertain how close he was, they asked for my exact location. I didn't have the heart to tell them that I was thirty feet up a tree. Whether the man knew (or feared) that he was being followed, I will never know, but what we do know is that he returned home and remained there for the rest of the day.

The following day, we tailed him to a nearby set of private garages, from which he emerged in a stolen car. We directed uniformed officers to stop and arrest him. Soon after, he admitted to taking possession of the car, knowing it to be stolen, together with a series of thefts from motor vehicles. He never mentioned our surveillance, and I must admit that I never mentioned my tree-climbing escapades to anyone (until now).

Whilst working on the Major Crime Team as a DC, a few colleagues and I were required to travel to the Battersea area of London one evening, to identify and arrest a suspect called 'Stallman', who was wanted for the murder of his landlord in East Malling in Kent.

We tracked Stallman to a flat which he was sharing with a Catholic priest, although they had no connection other than their need for cheap accommodation. The owner of the property gave us access, where we awaited the arrival of our suspect. The flat had a small hallway which led into the lounge area. The door to the flat opened inwards and when opened, it covered a small area where coats were hanging. I stood in that coat area whilst my colleague crouched behind the settee in the lounge. Anyone who has ever played hide-and-seek knows the nervous apprehension you feel whilst waiting in your hidey-spot. Well, believe me, waiting to jump on a suspected murderer brings the fear on ten-fold. It's certainly no child's play.

My adrenalin was rising incrementally and I am sure my colleague was the same. Any sound we heard could be our man. After twenty minutes, we heard the front door to the building shut and someone thumped their way up the stairs towards the flat.

The door opened and a male entered the flat. As he stepped inside, I pushed the door shut and in the same instant I jumped upon the individual's back. My colleague came out from behind the settee.

We then realised that it was the priest not our suspect and, as you can imagine, the poor man was shocked beyond belief. We reassured him as quickly as we could as to why we were there and he told us that the man we wanted was bound to be back in the flat at any moment. He then went quietly into his bedroom to keep out of our way, whilst we waited in anticipation of the next visitor.

I would not be surprised if the poor priest suffered from what we now call post-traumatic stress disorder, and I apologise unreservedly if this is the case. Of course, this is not the face of a dead man, but I remember that man's expression, a mixture of shock and terror, so clearly.

Our adrenalin jumped back up when those keeping observation on the front of the property warned us that a man who fitted the suspect's description was approaching the building. Sure enough, he entered via the front door, and even heavier footsteps than before approached the flat. This had to be our man. Time seemed to stop whilst the suspect was unlocking that door. The tension in the room was palpable.

As soon as the male entered the flat, we sprang out and quickly overpowered him. At times like this, you don't want to give someone even the vaguest opportunity to run off, so we held him down firmly as we arrested him.

'You are under arrest for the murder of Hank Stallman,' I stated clearly, before cautioning him, which in those days went like this:

'You are not obliged to say anything unless you wish to do so but anything you do say may be taken down and may be given as evidence against you.' (This wording of the caution has since been updated and rephrased, and is included in the Police and Criminal Evidence Act Codes of Practice.)

Anyone who's watched any television cop show will know that the response to an arrest should be noted down. Imagine my horror when he yelled, 'Bloody hell! I am Hank Stallman but I am *not* bloody well dead!'

Although I rectified my error at once, the embarrassment of arresting a man for his own murder would stay with me for the rest of my career and well beyond. My colleague took great pleasure in telling the rest of the team about my mistake and those colleagues have repeated my words back to me on a regular basis over the years, revelling at every opportunity to remind me that my career hasn't always been so successful. For my part, such taunting probably helped keep my feet on humble ground.

Hank Stallman stood trial for the murder of his landlord but was eventually acquitted. Neither he, nor the priest, made any complaints against either myself or my colleagues.

The faces in all these true stories are as clear to me today as they were at the time. There is, however, one exception – that of the car thief whom we followed to the wood. I recall his exact silhouette. If you were to place him in a line-up with his back to me, I would identify his shape, size, hair and the style of his black leather jacket. I would have no problem accurately identifying him. Perhaps I was so anxious he would spot me that I never dared look into his face. Perhaps I was so terrified of falling out of that tree, as if he were some circling lion whose jaws I was about to fall prey to, that I only needed to hold the shadow of him in mind to do what needed to be done (in this case, to simply hold on tight to that trunk).

Many of the following stories are tragic and upsetting, not only because of the cold brutality of the crimes executed but because of my tendency (at times, I wonder if it is a curse) to recall the features of so many people, in so many roles. There is no erasing the faces of crime for me. It is possibly enough for you, the reader, to hear the stories and your own imaginations will no doubt fill in the gaps enough to conjure up a face or two. Imagine what it is like to live with the real-life faces from the following tragedies.

3

DEATH OF A CHILD

All acts of violent crime are disgraceful but there is an added dimension of sadness in cases which involve the death of a young child. Of course, it makes no difference to a grieving parent whether their deceased child is a grown adult or not – the hurt, pain and loss is still there.

Domestic violence is a tragic indictment of our society and, sadly, it is something which takes place all around the world every single day. Such events are brought on by alcohol, drugs, jealousy, or for no apparent reason. The tragedy is heart-breaking enough when something snaps within an individual's head to trigger a violent act against someone they are supposed to love – a partner, parent, spouse or their own child/children within their care (especially when children are seriously injured in the process) – but it is even more harrowing for all involved in a case when the victims die and other children at the scene witness the killings.

The same holds true in missing person cases. Whether it is a child or any person regarded as vulnerable, the Police Service responds with a sense of urgency. Sadly, however, when someone who is classed as 'non-vulnerable' disappears without a trace, they can fall into the category of 'ordinary person' and, unless there is an apparent risk to that person,* the police do not always respond as quickly.

As a Sub-Divisional Detective Inspector in Margate (and again, when I later became Area DCI at Swale) I oversaw numerous investigations into acts of violence involving someone's child and, in all these cases,

---

* See Risk Assessment Table - Missing Persons Process Chart overleaf.

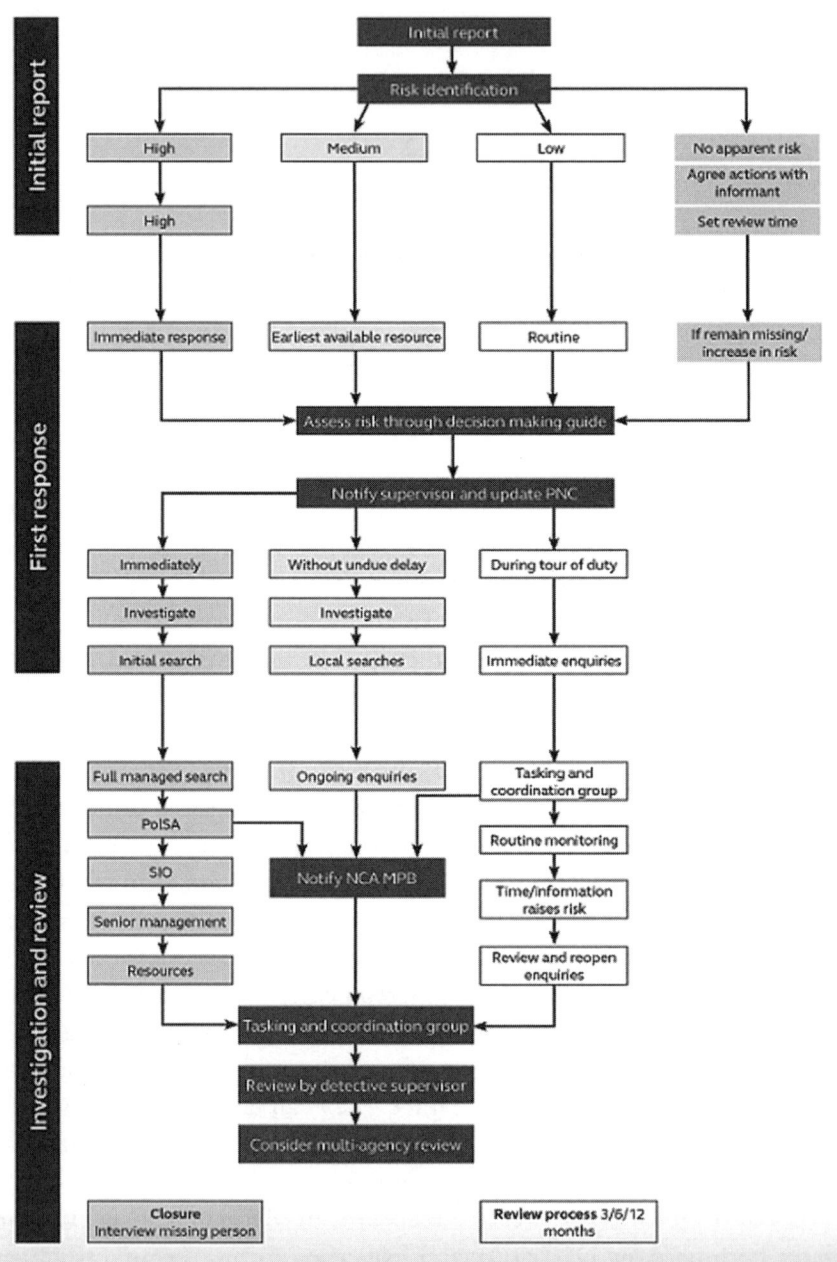

Missing persons process chart (The College of Policing)

what lived constantly in the forefront of my mind was the grief and suffering of the parents and extended families. I have selected three such deaths which highlight this for me. The first two cases took place in the Swale District of Kent.

A Son Called Darren

I was shocked to read a newspaper article in October 1989, about a young boy called Darren who was killed whilst riding his bicycle on Sittingbourne High Street. He had just left his parents' shop in town, when a thirty-tonne truck hit him. We are all aware that accidents happen, of course, but in this incident, the behaviour of the truck driver became the focus of a major police investigation because when he hit Darren, he failed to stop.

The driver's name was Taylor. He was a 33-year-old local, at the time. Horrified witnesses described in detail how they watched helplessly, as the driver ran over the child's body and drove off. Several witnesses attended to the child but there was little they could do. Others watched the lorry hurtle down the High Street, knocking down a bollard before swerving into an oncoming vehicle containing a lady and her children.

Emergency services arrived promptly at the scene and police officers arrested Taylor on suspicion of dangerous driving. He was taken to the nearby Sittingbourne police station where he was further arrested for causing the death of the young boy, Darren.

Whilst he was in custody, officers established that Taylor had never held a driving licence. He had a long criminal record, stretching back to his teenage years, which included several driving offences and acts of violence. Several years earlier, he had lost one eye after being shot in a family feud. The loss of an eye does not bar a person from holding a license, but they must meet other visual requirements before obtaining a license from the DVLA. Taylor had never bothered to consider such regulations, which are obviously created to keep the roads as safe as possible. Quite simply, he should never have been driving.

After many years of campaigning, the sentences for injuring or killing a person whilst driving a vehicle have become more stringent. In retrospect, the rules at the time of this incident could only be regarded as shockingly lenient. Taylor appeared in court and was only sentenced to eighteen months' imprisonment. He ended up being released after serving only twelve months.

This was by no means the end to this tragic story, it was merely the beginning.

Darren came from a hardworking, loving family on the nearby Isle of Sheppy. The grief his family and friends endured was beyond comprehension. Over a period of several months, his mum and dad, Marilyn and Stephen, faced the horror, not once but on four occasions, of finding their child's grave vandalised. No one was ever identified as being responsible for these acts of vandalism but the spotlight fell on Taylor and his associates, because they had harassed Stephen when they passed him on the street in Sittingbourne, by mocking him about the damage to their child's grave. These matters were not reported to the police, at that time, so we only found out about this harassment retrospectively, when we spoke with the family at a later date.

His parents eventually applied, and were granted permission, to move their son's remains to a secret resting place outside the county. They had no alternative. One can only begin to imagine the emotional upheaval of having to apply for the exhumation of your little boy from his resting place.

Most individuals and families are offered access to help, and do seek support in their efforts to come to terms with such tragic incidents. Too often, however, we find that no degree of counselling or support is enough. This most certainly turned out to be the case here.

By the spring of 1992, I had been promoted to DCI. I was at home, enjoying a quiet Saturday evening in the company of my family, when I took a telephone call from our Police Headquarters Operation Room. It was the duty Inspector.

'Sorry to disturb your evening, boss,' he said, 'but there has been a shooting in Sittingbourne and the duty SIO has asked for you specifically to attend the scene.'

'I will get there as soon as I can,' I said. I was living in Broadstairs, though, so it would take at least fifty minutes to get there. 'In the meantime, can you give me more details of the incident?'

I remember his response word for word.

'It's a strange one,' he said. 'A bloke called Taylor has been shot outside his house by some guy he knows, and his girlfriend is wounded too. Apparently, Taylor killed this guy's son about eighteen months ago in an RTA. It looks like a revenge hit.'

'Is the gunman in custody?'

'No, he has disappeared,' the Inspector replied.

I finished the telephone call and within minutes I was in my car making my way to Sittingbourne police station.

On arrival, I spoke to the duty uniform Inspector who had been organising the police response to the incident. He had kept a record of the locations to which officers had been deployed, and everything they were doing to find Darren's dad, Stephen. This was when the Inspector related the story to me, regarding the accident involving Darren's death. Even though it had happened before I was appointed to the area, I recalled the incident at once, since I had read about it many months prior.

Over the following few hours, local officers searched Stephen's home but there was no trace of him. His wife, Marilyn, told officers that Stephen had not coped well with the trauma of Darren's death and that the continual desecration of his son's grave had finally driven him to utter and total despair. Despite her begging him not to, Stephen had acquired a shotgun and gone out to track Taylor down.

A forensic search of their family garage found iron-filings which indicated that the barrel of a gun had very likely been sawn off. It turned out that Stephen knew where Taylor lived in Sittingbourne and went there to confront him. He waited in his car until Taylor and his girlfriend had left their house and then started walking towards Stephen's car. Stephen got out of his car and blasted Taylor twice at close range, wounding him seriously. Taylor survived the attack and his girlfriend, who'd been standing nearby, received a wound to her arm (which was not life threatening).

For the first time in my career, I realised I was going to be dealing with a crime bound to attract a lot of attention from national media. Unless we located and arrested Stephen post-haste, that very same night in fact, there would be a media frenzy for information. My real concern, however, was that Stephen be located, since he was clearly disturbed and there was the chance that he might harm himself.

Despite searching numerous properties all night across the force area, there was no trace of Stephen. The following morning, the incident was headline news on all radio and television channels. I will always remain grateful for the support of our duty Assistant CC, Keith Biddle. It was thanks to his advice that I learnt how to delegate and to have trust in our experienced and competent staff. There are times when you simply cannot do everything yourself, and his invaluable guidance on that score has remained with me for the rest of my career and beyond.

When Marilyn spoke with our officers that Saturday evening, she was still unaware of the details of the incident – it was the uniformed officers who broke the news to her. The following morning, I met with Marilyn, and through tears she relayed their tragic story to me in person. Their lives had been ruined after the loss of their son, Darren. Both she and her husband had felt suicidal over many months. Neither one of them could cope any longer.

Thankfully, she found a way to hold her emotions at bay that afternoon, and we managed to hold a joint press conference at the police station. I opened the conference by outlining the events of the previous evening and requested that any witnesses to the shooting, or anyone who had information regarding Stephen's whereabouts, contact the police immediately. Marilyn spoke next, and made an extremely stirring appeal to her husband to give himself up to my investigation team.

Nothing was forthcoming from the appeals, however. Despite extensive searches over the following twenty-four hours, there was no trace of Stephen. We could not rule out the possibility that Stephen had taken his own life.

Thankfully, the following day, a local solicitor contacted my office requesting an arrangement for Stephen to, quietly and without undue publicity, surrender himself to the police. I gave my word and arranged for my colleagues, DI Ray Cousins and DS Graham Driscoll, to visit the solicitor's office where Stephen was waiting.

The officers interviewed Stephen back at the police station, in the presence of his solicitor. He made a full confession in which he shared the background of his child's death. He told the officers that he had tossed the firearm into the sea. (The weapon has never been recovered.) It is the police's role to investigate such claims and, if someone must answer charges, the police must ensure that person is put before the court. Even if we sympathise with the actions of an individual, an officer of the law is simply that: an officer of the law.

Stephen was charged with:

- The attempted murder of Taylor
- Wounding Taylor's girlfriend
- Possession of a shotgun with intent to endanger life
- Assault on both Taylor and his girlfriend.

The following summer, Stephen stood trial at Maidstone Crown Court. At the outset, it seemed likely to be a simple, clear-cut case with a full confession, but Stephen pleaded not guilty to each of the offences. The horror of his son's death and Taylor's behaviour all formed part of the evidence during the trial. It came as no surprise to me, nor to any of my colleagues, when the jury of nine women and three men cleared Stephen of each of the charges.

Large crowds gathered outside the court to welcome the not guilty verdict. This acquittal made both national headline news on television that night and again, the following day, in every national newspaper.

I regret the fact that I was not able to attend court that day. I know for a fact that members of the jury were in tears. The judge's comments summarised this terrible tragedy for me perfectly:

Any father or mother, or member of a family – and we are all members of a family – must feel a sympathy and an understandable compassion for a father or mother who has lost a child. A child who loses his life from natural causes is, heaven knows, tragic enough, but if it is from a hideous death in an appalling road accident, the loss must be even worse. Any person who does not feel for these parents in their agony and anguish must be made of stone.*

---

* Sourced from Court Records and published publicly in the press.

Hard as it is, of course, the Police Service is obliged to remain totally impartial at all times. It is our responsibility to simply investigate crimes and to present the evidence to the Crown Prosecution Service (CPS). It is the CPS who decide to prosecute someone and bring the matter to court for it to be heard. Thereafter, it is for the jury to decide, based on the evidence presented before them, whether a person is guilty, or not guilty. In this case, strange as it may be, they found Stephen not guilty. Crowds outside the court cheered.

On the part of Stephen, this was essentially a vigilante revenge attack. When faced with such a tragedy as that of little Darren, and the behaviour of somebody like the driver, who didn't even stop at the scene voluntarily, and given the story behind the desecration of the little boy's grave, the fact that the parents had to take that little boy's body to rebury it outside the county in order to gain some solace, I wouldn't be entirely honest if I said I did not understand why Stephen was driven to do what he did. I still urge people, however, *never* to take the law into their own hands. It can under no circumstances be condoned. To put it quite simply, more often than not, a person is going to get caught – especially when the motive is so apparent – and be forced to go through the legal process of being arrested, interviewed, possibly locked up or at the very least remanded in custody.

A Son Called Andy

The second case I'd like to talk about in this context began with me leaving my office in Sittingbourne on a bright sunny day in mid-July, back in 1992. I was driving home along the A2 road, through the town of Faversham, at the border of our neighbouring police area of Canterbury.

I was passing a small news agency when my attention was drawn to a billboard used by the local press to advertise their weekly paper headlines. The notice read 'Murder fear as son vanishes'.

My immediate thought was that someone in Canterbury had messed up and if that statement turned out to be true, they would be in big trouble. I thought no more about it.

The following morning, when I saw the notice again, I realised it was a headline in the Sittingbourne newspaper. This put it in my area, as opposed to the Canterbury Area (which would have had no relevance to us), so I asked my secretary to research the local newspaper straight away, and reassure me that the report was not a matter for me to be troubling myself or our command team with.

The structure of command teams in most police forces in the UK consists of a selection of senior officers and senior civilian colleagues. A force command team is led by the CC, or an equivalent rank, in some larger forces. Most force areas are split into Areas or Divisions. They each have their own command team but are answerable to the Chief Constables Command Team. These Area Command teams are led by either a Chief Superintendent or, depending upon the size of the force, a Superintendent. The head of these local command teams is supported by a Uniform Chief Inspector, a senior detective (of Chief Inspector rank, at the very least) and the equivalent grade of civilian officer. Together, they identify priority actions and targets for officers under their command.

After my secretary had done her research, she informed me that the case referred to a family on the Isle of Sheppy. The reason it was in the newspaper was to make an appeal for information regarding their 22-year-old son called 'Andy', who had been missing for almost two weeks by now.

I subsequently liaised with my uniformed colleagues and, to my horror, I was told that a uniformed Inspector on the Isle of Sheppy was 'keeping an eye on that missing person enquiry'. I travelled over to Sheerness police station at once.

Whilst examining the missing person log, I noted that the report had been made by the young man's parents, and I felt that police may have overlooked one of the most important facts – someone who knew and loved this missing person was not being heard. In this case, it was the young man's mum. She had stated that she was certain, in her own mind, that something bad had happened to her son.

I liaised with our command team and referred the matter to the Major Crime Department at Force Headquarters who appointed a colleague, Detective Superintendent (DSU) David Birchall, to review the case. He, in turn, led a major investigation into the disappearance of Andy.

It was because of the ten-day time-lapse since Andy had last been seen that crucial evidential opportunities were missed. Andy's friends were very supportive of his parents as the investigation progressed, and visited them regularly. Two of his friends in particular claimed they had not seen Andy on the day that he disappeared, nor since.

Weeks turned into months, but there was still no trace of Andy. The major investigation had failed to establish what had happened to him, and the case was handed back to me. I visited Andy's parents, and tried to reassure them that we would continue the search for their son, and follow up every available lead. I got on reasonably well with them but our service had been so slow off the mark that the family felt we had already failed them in those early stages of the enquiry. It was because of this that they had difficulty trusting anything anyone said to them.

It took approximately three years to resolve the mystery regarding Andy.

I received a telephone call, out of the blue, from the solicitor, Mr Andrew McCooey, who had, in fact, been Stephen's solicitor (in Darren's story). Mr McCooey is quite a renowned individual. He has represented prisoners on death row in America and was also Myra Hindley's solicitor, after her conviction for the 'moors murders', up until the time she died in prison in 2002.

'We've got a young man here,' he said, 'who wants to tell you what happened to Andy.'

I sent the team around and the young man in question came to the police station accompanied by his solicitor. He was cautioned and taken straight into an interview room with a tape-recorder running. He then proceeded to tell us exactly where the body was and gave us an explanation as to what had happened.

This man was, ironically enough, one of the many friends who had supported Andy's parents during the original investigation – one of Andy's best friends. He had come forward to admit that he and another friend had killed Andy during an argument over a drug deal. The individual claimed that Andy had confronted them with a snooker cue after they had failed to settle a drugs debt.

They had hit Andy once over the head with a metal chest-expander and he had died instantly. In their panic, they wrapped his body in black plastic sacks and buried him just over the other side of a wall, in the back yard of an empty house beside their flat. They'd scrubbed the carpet thoroughly and, when questioned later, claimed that Andy had never been in their flat that day.

Despite the passage of time, a forensic examination of the flat found Andy's blood on the underneath side of the carpet. Of course, such details would have been captured much earlier if only we had gotten to grips enough to have listened to the parents in the first place, and done proper searches.

Andy's body was recovered shortly after this confession. The two individuals eventually pleaded not guilty to Andy's murder, but were found guilty of his manslaughter. They were also convicted, in regard to the unlawful burial, with obstructing HM Coroner.

This particular case highlighted for me the importance of listening properly to those who are close to the missing loved one. If they sense something out of the ordinary has happened, then their hunches and concerns really do need to be heard. Force policy and national guidelines have since been reviewed and amended as a direct consequence of over-sights in this very case. Nowadays, all concerns and suggestions brought forward by parents are given equal weight, particularly in the early part of an investigation. (See table below.)

'Force policies' deal with individual forces. These are all covered under the umbrella of the National Police College and the advice therein is constantly being updated. A history of the Missing Persons Bureau – initially set up by the Metropolitan Police in approximately 2005 – includes every review which has taken place over the years. Since 2013, this guidance falls under the remit of the National Crime Agency.

Under this remit, there is also a national missing children's team; a safeguarding team which includes social workers and probation services with experts in each department. The good thing about this is that every subject covered by the College of Policing will have in place a system to modify and review all different aspects of policing. It does not just sit on a shelf to be forgotten about. Cases like the abduction and murder of Sarah Everard on Clapham Common in the summer of 2021, for instance, and the conviction of the police officer, Wayne Couzens, of her abduction and murder, will have an enormous effect on Missing Persons Guidance. After an independent complaints review looks at every report covering behaviour of the relevant forces, then all advice and recommendations are considered and the national guidance is changed accordingly. In theory, we should get to a point where there is no hiding place for inefficiencies when dealing with missing persons.

Again, I have to point out how important it is for everyone involved in a case to listen to the hunches of those who knew a victim well. Not doing so has a domino effect down the line – so many oversights can be avoided when all parties are properly heard.

This brings to mind another story in England which is commonly referred to as the 'Stephen Port Murders' and has been widely publicised in all avenues of the media. Port is currently serving a whole life sentence for the murder of four young men; a spree which began at his home in Barking, London, in June 2014. The full circumstances surrounding these deaths was revealed at HM Coroner's Court, when an inquest into the deaths began in early October 2021. In normal circumstances where someone is convicted of murder, there is no requirement for a full inquest. This case, however, raised an important concern in which a fundamental question needed to be answered: could three lives have been saved if the police had investigated the first death differently?

The first victim was named Anthony, whose body was found propped up against a wall outside Port's home. Port claimed that he had discovered the body and called the 999 emergency services. Officers from the Metropolitan Police Service (MPS) and a London Ambulance Service (LAS) crew attended scene but, despite the ambulance crew saying they considered 'foul play', the MPS decided that an initial medical examination indicated it was probably non-suspicious, and they subsequently allowed the body to be removed to the local hospital mortuary.

The victim's family, located in the City of Hull, were informed of their son's death. Some seven years later, when there finally was an inquest, Anthony's mother told the inquest that she had told the police from the outset how certain she had been that her son had been murdered, but 'nobody would listen' to her. She also stated that, if the police had done their job properly, then the other three young men would still be alive.

The inquest was eventually told that each of these four young men had died from lethal quantities of anaesthetic gamma-hydroxybutyric acid (commonly referred to as GHB) found in their blood streams, and that they had all been sexually assaulted. Three of the young men's bodies (Gabriel died on 28 August 2014, Daniel died on 20 September 2014 and Jack died on 14 September 2015) were found in a local church graveyard, a short walk from Port's address.

When Port was eventually interviewed by the MPS, he admitted that Anthony had been in his flat when he died. He claimed that he moved Anthony's body outside because he did not want to get in trouble.

It was in the period after he was released on bail that he murdered Gabriel and Daniel. He was subsequently charged with perverting the course of justice and sentenced to a term of imprisonment. On his release, once he had returned home, he met and murdered Daniel in the same manner as the other victims.

Other family members and friends of the victims gave evidence throughout the inquest, and in all their statements they told the MPS that they believed their relative/friend had been murdered, but no one had listened to them.

Eventually, Jack's family started their own investigation and found new evidence, which they referred to senior police officers. It was this evidence which resulted in a new investigation team taking over the case, and they quickly linked all four deaths to Port.

The rest of this story is still ongoing, but the question I pose above was answered by the jury at the inquest when they said that '"fundamental failures" to investigate Port "probably allowed him to kill another three men" after his first murder in 2014'.★

Police officers simply must listen to the people who know these unfortunate victims of crime.

I now have a mantra: listen to the parents. More often than not, they know much more than police officers credit them with.

★ www.telegraph.co.uk/news/2022/08/30/
stephen-port-families-serial-killers-victims-compensated-met/

A Mother and Her Children

The spa town of Tunbridge Wells will always be close to my heart. As a newly appointed detective, I shared a flat in the town centre with a colleague, Nic Uglow, who is still a very close friend. We had so many laughs and good times when we were off duty. I find it sad now when I hear the town mentioned by the media – all our good times are over-shadowed by my memories of this third case I wish to share.

It occurred following my appointment as a SIO at FHQ Major Crime Department. I was about to embark on a review of a missing person when I received a telephone call from my boss, Nic Biddiss, at home at 0700 hrs on Monday, 13 November, asking me to go directly to Tunbridge Wells police station in order to take command of a double homicide which had occurred the previous evening.

He had very few details of the incident other than the fact that an adult female and her 8-year-old daughter had been killed by the child's estranged father. The male believed to be responsible for these deaths had been arrested at the scene and was in custody at the police station.

I cancelled my work plan for the day at once and headed to Tunbridge Wells, which was about a thirty-minute drive from my home. I vividly recall that journey, as this was my first (and second) murder which I was to deal with as an established SIO. My mind was racing, as I thought of everything I had to do. Thankfully, the advice I had previously had from ACC Biddle was still very fresh in my mind.

These were the concerns occupying my thoughts on that drive:

- Crime scene management – how many crime scenes would there actually be? Were SOCOs already working at the scene?
- Media – had anyone prepared an initial report for the media? If so, would that report fit into the media strategy which I would write up later?
- Suspect – who exactly was he? Was he fit to be interviewed? Had he had access to a solicitor? Had all his clothing been seized?
- Are there any other victims, or independent witnesses?
- Have the police officers who attended the scene made their witness statements?
- Has HM Coroner been informed?

The list was endless, but those were just some of the tasks I was faced with. This might, at the very least, offer you an idea of the extent of issues which had to be anticipated and dealt with as they cropped up.

Tunbridge Wells police station is renowned within the force as having the worst parking facilities of all police stations in the county. Spaces are limited and normally reserved for local senior officers and marked police vehicles, but since I was the SIO, I took the decision to park there. To my relief, no one challenged me.

I was met by the local DI, who had been working on the case the previous evening with the duty on-call senior detective. A staff briefing had been arranged for 0900 hrs. This gave me time to have a more in-depth briefing on the facts of the case as they were known at that time, which was of great assistance to me.

The sequence of events turned out to be absolutely horrendous. I went through all particulars at the briefing so that all officers and civilian staff were made aware of them, because full knowledge of the particulars, no matter how shocking they were to hear, would assist them once they each had work allocated to them.

The briefing began in a conference room at exactly 0900 hrs. As was my tradition, I introduced myself to everyone present, even though most of them knew me through my previous work as a young detective at that very police station. I then asked each individual to introduce themselves and what a 'good job' carrying out this simple task turned out to be.

The first female officer who introduced herself was the school liaison officer who would be going to the school (which all the children at the scene of the crime had attended) immediately after the briefing. I thanked her for the information but I failed to ask if someone had yet been in contact with the head teacher at the school. Unfortunately, no one in the force had thought of doing this the previous night. This oversight led to some criticism of the force down the track from the Child Protection Review Forum (formerly known as the Child Safeguarding Practice Review).

> Where any child is injured, unless it is very clearly accidental, there is a process which must be followed. Every agency who has had dealings with the child or the family must review their own actions in relation to that child or family. They must respond in writing to the Children Protection Review Forum, who will then publish a report with recommendations and comments.

As the briefing continued, it was established that the family consisted of:

- The mother (Victim No. 1)
- Her 8-year-old daughter (Victim No. 2)
- Her 7-year-old son (Victim No. 3), who witnessed the events but survived unharmed
- Her 5-year-old son (Victim No. 4), who had a life-threatening knife wound to his throat
- Her 4-year-old son (Victim No. 5), who also had a life-threatening knife wound to his throat
- The neighbour's child (Victim No. 6), who was unharmed
- The mother's close friend and uncle to Victim No. 6, who was unharmed. This man was 19 years old and was present in the house when the offender (the children's father) arrived unexpectedly.

It transpired that the mother, who was British, and her children had moved away from the family home in the East End of London due to her failing relationship with the children's father. They had been given a council house on the outskirts of Tunbridge Wells in an area known as Southborough. The estranged father had visited this house on previous occasions but the relationship with his wife had broken down completely.

When the father entered the house, the mother's friend (uncle of Victim No. 6) grew extremely fearful, due to the look of evident rage in the father's eyes. According to the friend, the father simply ignored his own children and stormed into the kitchen, where his wife was washing up at the sink.

Within a very short period of time, the friend heard raised voices coming from the kitchen. He described how it grew worse and worse, with the children's mother screaming back at her husband. The yelling intensified, and as the 19-year-old friend stood up, the husband appeared in the kitchen doorway, holding a bloodstained knife. He stared straight at the friend, who screamed, and the father turned back toward the kitchen. The friend grabbed hold of his nephew (leaving the other three boys frozen to the spot), ran out of the house and up a set of steps to his own family home two doors away. He shouted out to his mother to open the door and call the police, which she did.

It was later established that, in this short period of time, the husband had stabbed his wife at least seventy times, leaving her to die on her kitchen floor. He returned to his three sons in the lounge area, where he slashed the throats of his two youngest sons, telling his eldest son that his punishment was to live forever with the horror he had just witnessed. Despite their horrific injuries, the little boys were still alive, albeit seriously injured.

The man left his sons and returned to the kitchen, where he slashed his own wrists. This fact was determined because his blood was distributed directly above the skirt his wife was wearing.

He came out of the kitchen, still ignoring all his sons, and moved towards the front door which was located beside the stairs of the house. It was here that his young daughter, on hearing all the screaming, came downstairs from her bedroom and was confronted by her father, who was still holding a large kitchen knife.

He turned to his daughter and stabbed her in the side of the head. As she fell to the floor, the mother of the friend, who had called 999, appeared in the entrance to the house and, in an amazing feat of courage, pushed the father away. She picked up the little girl, to carry her outside and up the steps, just as police and ambulance crews appeared on the scene.

The swift actions of the attending uniformed officers and ambulance crews are embedded in my mind as being utterly heroic. Uniformed officers entered the property and a female officer (just recently having finished her initial police training) took immediate action. She had the foresight to hold together the slash wounds which had been inflicted upon the throats of each of the little boys. Paramedics soon took over but there is no doubt that it was her swift action which helped save the lives of these two children.

All these little children were taken to hospital where, tragically, the little girl was pronounced dead. The eldest son was safe, but the two younger boys underwent emergency surgery – their lives were hanging in the balance.

The father was immediately arrested but, due to his self-inflicted injuries on his wrists, he too had to be taken to hospital. After a short period of time, his wounds were stitched and dressed and he was deemed to be fit to be detained at the police station.

The children's aunt was quickly identified, and because she lived close-by, the eldest son was released from hospital into the care of his aunt and uncle.

May God bless each of the victims. From the outset, as a family liaison exercise, the police handled this case extremely well. The strong support provided to them by way of witness support, the ensuing court process, funerals and the Crown Court trial, continued for many months before we started to implement what we call the 'exit strategy'. How we 'break away' from the victims is just as important as the support we provide along the way.

As the briefing continued, I asked a colleague to get an update from the hospital on the condition of the two little boys. I was subsequently able to tell the team that the boys had survived the night. The next twelve hours was a crucial period for these children.

My Senior Scene of Crime Officer (S/SOCO), Mick House, updated the team about the main crime scene, including the fact that the body of the mother remained in situ in the kitchen, pending the arrival of a Forensic Pathologist. I reviewed the actions I deemed necessary for the team, over the coming twelve hours. These included:

- House-to-house enquiries in the street where the family lived
- A search of each designated scene
- Liaison with the school
- A series of interviews of our suspect, who was the mother's estranged husband.

After this briefing I visited the crime scene, where I arrived to find television cameras and reporters standing around the police tapes which had been set up to protect the crime scenes. A member of our Media Services Department requested that I give a statement to the press immediately.

I took her out of earshot of the press and told her in no uncertain terms that they would simply have to wait until I had assessed the crime scenes.

Dressed in a crime scene suit, I carried out my assessment of the scenes with Mick House and we then discussed our forensic strategy for this investigation. Once I had completed this work, I made numerous notes in my incident log book (which was a red A4 hardback book) after which I gave the press statement, as promised. By this time, a large group of local residents had gathered, eager to hear what I had to say.

Wishing to keeping my account fairly general, I held back on many details. I told them when the incident had occurred, shared the fact that a lady and young girl had tragically died, and explained that two young boys from the same family had suffered life-threatening injuries but were now stable in hospital.

Finally, I told them that a man was in custody on suspicion of murder and that the police were not looking for any other suspects at that time. As I finished this statement, one of my officers asked if he could have a quiet word with me. We stepped away from the press gathering and he discreetly pointed out a lady in the crowd. She was the mother of the friend who had been in the house at the time of the attack; she was the lady who had rescued the little girl. I thanked him and made a mental note to visit the lady once the press had dispersed.

I went to see this lady in her home about twenty minutes later. I was still holding my red-covered notebook. She opened her front door as I descended the steps which approached her house and welcomed me inside.

A smile spread across her face whilst I was speaking with her, but it was a smile which did not quite match her eyes. She was clearly doing her best to appear respectful at such a tragic time, but finally, it seemed she could not hold it in any longer.

'With your accent and that book,' she blurted out, 'you remind me of Eamon Andrews and *This Is Your Life*!' This was a popular television programme in which the Irish-born broadcaster, Eamon Andrews, surprised people with their life stories which he recorded in his famous red book. She wasn't exactly laughing, but I could sense that her brain was trying to find some kind of normality amidst the horrific scenes she'd been forced to deal with. This lady had held a dying child in her arms and given her comfort and safety in her final moments.

Once the two of us had settled down, I took the opportunity to do what I had come for; that is, to commend her for what she had done the previous evening. Needless to say, throughout my career, I never used a red book again!

I returned to the police station and checked that all my staff were fully occupied before updating the Policy File that had been started the previous night. I also reminded the supervisors on the team to be aware of any stress or welfare issues which might occur amongst our staff, taking into account the tragic details of these crimes.

A Policy File in the Police Service is a document that is normally used in complex reactive and intelligence-led investigations (i.e. a cold scene murder or a major illegal drug supplying investigation) to record the Strategic & Tactical Decisions made by a SIO.

Where an investigation is likely to run for an extended period of time or if it requires a high volume of officers from various disciplines (i.e. surveillance team, search teams, firearms officers, etc.) it is considered good practice to separate the document to cover:

- All strategic and tactical decisions
- Administration decisions (including Health and Safety, Welfare, hours of duty, expenses, etc.)
- Sensitive Issues (Use of surveillance, witness protection, undercover police officer deployment, etc.)

With the exception of a 'Sensitive' document, all other sections of an SIO's Policy File should be available for staff working on that investigation to view. The document will also serve as a critical record of the management of an investigation.

Lunchtime was upon us before I knew it, and a message arrived telling me that the body of the mother was being taken to the mortuary at the local hospital. The forensic post-mortem of both mum and daughter were due to begin at 1400 hrs.

I arrived at the mortuary and joined the mortuary team just before it was due to start. Two bodies covered in white sheets lay side by side on mortuary slabs. Our pathologist, Dr Mike Heath, asked me if I had any preference as to which body should be examined first. It did not really matter so I simply said, 'Let's begin with Mum.'

At every stage of a forensic post-mortem photographs are taken for evidential purposes. When a case comes to trial it is extremely rare for these photographs to be shown to the jury, but they are essential for a pathologist to have, as a record of the examination. The injuries this poor lady had suffered were probably the worst I have ever seen. She was virtually decapitated and her body was covered in numerous stab wounds, several of which overlapped other gruesome wounds. The examination went on for several hours. I sensed that everyone was going to need a break before we looked at the little girl.

At this point, I took a telephone call from one of the Chief Officer's secretaries, whom I knew quite well.

'Ma'am,' she said, and I knew immediately that she was referring to the Chief Officer for Crime, 'has instructed that you are to attend a de-briefing at 2200 hrs tonight at Tunbridge Wells police station for the police officers who attended the deaths in Southborough last night, once they have finished their shift.'

Don't shoot the messenger, I thought as I hung up, and thanked her. It was evident at that stage that the senior officer had no concept of what I was dealing with.

The second post-mortem began at 1830 hrs. To say that I was shocked when that little girl was uncovered from the white sheet would be an understatement. She was the same size and build as my eldest daughter. She had the same olive-tinted skin and long dark hair as her as well. The first horrific stab wound I saw was to the side of her head. It was covered in blood and, what was most heart-breaking, was that there, in her little clenched hand, was a handful of her own hair. The pain in her head must have been so unbearable that she had tried to pull the pain away from her head by pulling out her hair.

Like the first post-mortem, this one also took several hours to complete so it was close to 2100 hrs by the time I returned to the police station. I checked in on my staff, and thankfully some of them had requested permission from their supervisor to get off home and left.

I checked with the interview team, who were about to start the third interview of the day with our suspect and his solicitor. The suspect had declined to answer any questions in his previous interviews, and authority had been obtained from the local Superintendent to extend his detention for twelve hours, so the prisoner was going to be with us for another night.

Eventually 2200 hrs came around and I felt exhausted, both emotionally and physically. The post-mortems really had taken their toll and I simply wanted to get home, but I headed for the debriefing. I mustered the section of officers into a conference room and awaited Ma'am's arrival.

Shortly after, she arrived in full uniform and the debriefing began. The 'welfare' briefing (or de-briefing, as it had been named) had stipulated that it would be me who was to give the officers an update on the investigation. Ma'am requested that I begin.

Firstly, I told the officers that they had each done a wonderful job under very difficult circumstances. I then updated them on the condition of the surviving children. I relayed the results of the post-mortem examinations and, finally, shared with them the results of the interviews with the suspect, along with the fact that he was to remain in custody at the police station that night.

I had nothing else to say and simply asked if anyone had any questions. None were forthcoming, so I excused myself and left the room.

I returned to the office I was using (which was, ironically enough, the same office I had used when I was a young detective at Tunbridge Wells) and practically collapsed into my chair with fatigue. I still smelt of the mortuary. All I wanted was to get home to see my two girls but I still needed to make sure that the 'i's were dotted, the 't's were crossed and that I had done all that needed to be done before I could go home. I checked for any messages, completed my Policy File for the day and had just started to tidy up when I heard the click-click sound of a lady's heels resounding, clearer and clearer, down the hall as they approached my office. Guess who appeared in the entrance to the office with a face of thunder?

It was Ma'am, yes, and she immediately let rip at me. 'Who do you think you are, leaving my briefing?' – or debriefing, she should have said!

I was already on my feet and ready to leave. 'Ma'am,' I stated calmly, 'I have been in the mortuary for eight hours today and for the last four hours I have been beside the body of a little girl who is very similar to my own daughter but with one single difference between them – that little girl is lying in the mortuary whereas, hopefully, my own little girl is fast asleep, and safe, in her own bed. I have had enough for today and I'm going home to see my girls.'

Ma'am looked at me and without saying a word, turned and walked out of the office. I left the office in a different direction and went home.

Ma'am never mentioned the episode again but it has always lived with me, as it is another one of those situations which prompts me to ask: who cares about the carer? Or, from my days at school, when we were forced to learn Latin: *quis curabit ipos curators?*

When I returned home, emotional and exhausted, I opened the bedroom doors of each of my beautiful girls and thanked God for their safety, knowing that the following day I would be dealing with a family whose lives had been decimated.

When I got back to the police station just after 0800 hrs the following morning, I was only too aware of the full day's work my entire team of staff had ahead of them, and sent out an instruction that there would be a team briefing at 1600 hrs that afternoon.

Over the course of the morning, I monitored the final interview with the suspect in which he'd been shown the murder weapons he had used to kill his wife and daughter, and seriously injure his two little boys. Since he had made no comment during all preceding interviews, we did not expect for him to say any more than that at this one and, as predicted, he did initially make no comment. The instant he saw the large bloodstained kitchen knife with the blade bent due to the pressure he had exerted on his victims, however, he screamed like a wild animal before curling up into a ball with his feet upon the chair he sat on.

His solicitor rightly asked for the interview to be terminated and he was returned to his cell.

Soon afterwards, in consultation with the Crown Prosecution Service and the Custody Sergeant, I authorised that the suspect be charged with two counts of murder and two counts of attempted murder. He was subsequently remanded in custody to await trial at Maidstone Crown Court.

The trial eventually took place and the suspect pleaded not guilty to each charge. The prosecution witnesses gave their evidence but he declined to give evidence in his own defence. The jury retired to consider their verdicts but, after barely enough time for one cup of tea, they returned to court to give their verdicts of guilty to each charge. The offender was sentenced to life imprisonment.

Incredibly but thankfully, the two younger boys made a full medical recovery and, together with their older brother, were formally adopted by their aunt and uncle. They will never know how often their mother and sister are in my thoughts. I can only hope they were able to find some sense of peace in their lives.

Strangely, whilst the pale, lifeless faces of both mother and daughter remain with me, two other images stored in my tenacious memory are the photographs taken by my S/SOC, Mark Walsh, during one of the emergency operations to save one of the boys. These photographs became a very important exhibit at the offender's trial, as they demonstrated the skills of the surgeon and staff at the hospital. The eyes of every jury member filled up with tears upon seeing them.

Some six months later, one final photograph was taken of the boys which showed a detailed closeup of the very fine scar which lined each of their throats. They will, no doubt, be able to hide those markings from view until they are able to talk about that horrible day when their family was destroyed, but they will live with the emotional wounds forever, the scars of which can surely never be entirely covered up.

On that very sad note, let me move on to an entirely different narrative. I never knew how many days I had off, nor how few sighs of relief I could take before the phone would ring again, alerting me to yet another gruesome case – another death, another crime, another spate of funerals – and all former, personal plans and projects would have to be cancelled. Here we go again.

4

FROM MISSING TO MURDER

Prologue

In the summer of 1994, Diana Goldsmith, an attractive 44-year-old single mother of two daughters and a younger son, was settled into her new home in the town of Sevenoaks in Kent. Diana was a sociable person, who tended to drink heavily and enjoy the company of various men and women in the town. The father of her two youngest children was Derek Goldsmith, an extremely wealthy businessman, so she had a comfortable lifestyle.

When the pair met, Diana was already pregnant with her first daughter, a child whom Goldsmith came to treat as his own. Goldsmith owned the family home and the small white Volvo saloon which Diana drove. Unfortunately, the relationship between Diana and Goldsmith failed, but he still loved the children. He wanted custody of his young son but after a lengthy legal dispute, Diana gained custody of the child.

Diana decided to take the children on holiday to Greece after the matter had been settled in court. Although she had a new partner in her life, a 59-year-old local government councillor called Charlie Hatt, Diana wished to get away and enjoy some time alone with her children, so she decided Charlie was not to accompany them on holiday. In an interview, Charlie told us that he was not too impressed with this decision and that, although they argued about it, Diana and the children did end up going on holiday without him.

Everything in the house appeared normal upon their return home after the holiday. Diana picked up the mail from the floor when she opened her front door, along with a spare set of her house-keys, which she immediately recognised as the keys she had previously given to Charlie. This didn't surprise her, it was simply Charlie's way of protesting after they had argued. Charlie was soon back in their lives in any case.

Later that year, Goldsmith and Diana agreed that it would be his turn to have the children for the coming Christmas. He planned to take them to his villa in Grand Canary, with his new wife, Sarah. Knowing that she would be alone, Diana invited her sister and family to join her in Kent for the Christmas period.

Christmas Eve arrived, and during the late afternoon, the children rang their mum from Grand Canary to wish her a merry Christmas. Diana was pleased to know the children were safe and enjoying Christmas with their dad.

Diana started getting excited about seeing her sister and family. She continually looked out her window in anticipation of their arrival. The road outside was reasonably quiet. The last time she glanced outside before her sister arrived, she noticed a white van driving slowly along the road. She assumed the driver and his passenger were lost, looking for a particular address, perhaps.

Diana ignored Charlie this Christmas, just as she had the last. By all accounts, she thoroughly enjoyed her sister's company over those days.

The children returned safely to the family home and life fell into its regular routine in the new year, with Diana taking her children to school, followed by shopping, picking the children up from school and finally, enjoying a drink with her boyfriend, Charlie, with friends.

Wednesday, 25 January 1995, was different, however. Diana took the kids to school, as usual, but she never came back to collect them, and at Sevenoaks police station later that evening the civilian support officer on duty at the front counter was greeted by an attractive, middle-aged lady who identified herself as Mrs Sarah Goldsmith.

Mrs Goldsmith wished to report a lady as missing. 'Because,' she said, 'she hasn't collected the children from their schools this afternoon and has not been home since.'

The missing lady in question was Diana Goldsmith.

Diana's car was also missing and her family feared that she may have been involved in an accident. An immediate search on the Police National Computer (PNC), however, showed no report of the car having been in an accident.

Sarah Goldsmith informed the officer that she was the school secretary at Diana's son's school. Her husband, Derek Goldsmith, was the son's father and he also owned the building in which the school was located. When Diana failed to collect her son, Sarah took the little boy to where his sisters were waiting, at their home. Diana's two daughters had decided to walk home when their mother failed to collect them. They did have their own back-door keys but the back door had been left unlocked that day – they did not find this so unusual since their mother had often forgotten to lock it in the past.

They waited together until 1700 hrs but when Diana still didn't return home, Mrs Goldsmith took all three children to her house, Orchard House, located in a nearby village, so they could be with their father.

Sarah further explained that she was aware of Diana's drinking problem. She knew Diana may well have been drunk somewhere and simply forgotten about the children.

The officer completed a Missing Person Report and Diana's car details were recorded on the PNC but not a great deal more was done that night. The police rarely take much notice of an adult who is not regarded as vulnerable and has been missing for less than twenty-four hours.

The following day, local DCI Alan Dann reviewed the limited amount of work which had been done, and instructed his staff to make enquiries with Diana's known acquaintances. There was still no sign of Diana or her car. Police spoke to her sister in Wiltshire, who told them that she had not seen or spoken to Diana since she and her family had visited Diana over the previous Christmas. Diana's sister confirmed that they had spent Christmas Eve and Christmas Day together because the children were abroad with their father in his villa in Grand Canary – Diana would otherwise have had to spend Christmas alone.

Later in the day, security staff at Lakeside Shopping Centre in Essex contacted their local police because a white Volvo car, which was securely locked, appeared to have been abandoned in one of their multi-storey car parks. A check on the PNC identified it as Diana's car, but there was no sign of Diana.

Lakeside Shopping Centre is a large out-of-town shopping centre located in West Thurrock, in the borough of Thurrock, Essex, just beyond the eastern boundary of Greater London. The complex is the one of the largest in Britain with 1,434,000 sq. ft available as retail floor space. There are over 250 shops, 50 cafes and restaurants, and a 26-acre lake, named Alexandra Lake, with a PADI certified diving school complex.

With the discovery of the car and still no trace of Diana, the matter was brought to the attention of DCI Dann at Sevenoaks police station and the investigation was stepped up. There were many unanswered questions. Where is Diana? How did her car get to Lakeside? Surely this was just a missing person? No one had yet considered that it may have been an abduction or a murder – probably because her lifestyle was so questionable – she could have just as easily been on a drinking binge with friends.

The vehicle was eventually searched by Essex Police before being recovered to a secure facility. This was the first opportunity police had to secure potentially crucial evidence which might have helped establish what had happened to Diana, and yet, investigators failed to ask all sorts of questions they should have asked before moving the car, not after.

For instance: what position had the driver's seat been in when the car was found? Had the rear-view mirror been altered? No one could remember if the seat or mirror had been adjusted before, during or after the vehicle was recovered to the security facility. The seat had been pushed back as far as it would go. The reason this was an issue was because Diana was not a tall individual, so pushing the seat back did not make sense. No property was found in the car – her keys and her handbag were missing.

To get to the Lakeside Shopping Centre from Sevenoaks, you have to take the nearby M25 motorway and then travel through the Dartford

Tunnel. The shopping centre is located near the exit of the tunnel. The journey takes about twenty minutes. When Diana's sister and the children were contacted again, this time to be updated about the car, they grew much more anxious, for they were certain that Diana would never have driven herself to Essex – she was afraid of tunnels.

The following day, the police investigation was stepped up. Officers made enquiries with her friends and in public houses she was known to frequent. Arrangements were made for Alexander Lake to be searched, just in case Diana had chosen to take her own life. CCTV footage at every possible location around the Lakeside complex was seized but when it was viewed, there were no sightings of Diana. Diana's home became the subject of a scene of crime examination but the forensic examination of the house proved unsuccessful. There was no evidence of a forced entry to the property, no sign of a disturbance and nothing appeared to have been stolen. The police did not feel it necessary to keep the house secure.

Charlie Hatt was questioned and he volunteered to stay in Diana's house in case she returned home. This request by Hatt to stay there was permitted, bizarrely enough. After remaining at the house for three days, and with no sign of Diana, Goldsmith ordered him to leave. Goldsmith took over the responsibility of the house, and the car he had let Diana have was returned to him. He also took over the care of the children.

As this initial investigation of what was still classed as a 'Missing Person' enquiry progressed, Derek Goldsmith, Sarah Goldsmith and the children were all interviewed but none of them could offer any explanation as to where Diana might be or why her car had ended up at Lakeside. When Goldsmith was interviewed, the officer noticed a large scratch mark on the side of his neck. Goldsmith claimed it was a shaving injury and it was not even photographed, so, unfortunately, this possible evidential opportunity was entirely overlooked. With little to no useful evidence identified at these early stages of the Missing Person enquiry, the matter was referred to the Force Headquarters (FHQ) and an SIO, Detective Superintendent Peter Philpott, was appointed to lead the enquiry, which was given the operational name Operation Boxer.

His initial lines of enquiry included a forensic examination of Diana's car and a review of who had been interviewed. Information from some of Diana's friends, including Charlie Hatt, suggested that Goldsmith was a vindictive individual who behaved like a man who'd get what he wanted by any means, so an Intelligence Profile on Goldsmith was prepared.

> An Intelligence Profile (also referred to as a Subject Profile) will include information on a person's family and relationship, lifestyle and habits, employment record details and their financial situation.

Intelligence Profile: Derek Goldsmith (b. 1936)

Goldsmith made his fortune as an inventor. He owned a company called 'Aqualisa' and he designed and developed a thermostatic spring used to provide water at a constant temperature in, what is known today as, the power shower. He sold the company for £23 million. He would go on to develop other companies but none of them were as successful as 'Aqualisa'. One enterprise included setting up his son-in-law, Michael Fitzpatrick, in a scrap metal business, located on a large housing estate in Bromley, Kent. He also designed firearms and was a registered firearms dealer. He was a shrewd businessman, used to fighting for what he regarded as his.

Goldsmith met Diana when she successfully applied for a job as his secretary. She was pregnant to another man at this time, but when their relationship developed into a love affair Goldsmith divorced his first wife, with whom he already had a son and daughter, and Diana moved into 'Orchard House'. They soon had a daughter and a son together. Goldsmith never married Diana but she changed her name by deed poll to Goldsmith, and all of the children took that surname.

When the relationship between them failed, they agreed that Diana and the children should vacate 'Orchard House'. Although he wanted to have custody of his young son, he was happy for Diana to have custody of the girls. Despite losing his application for custody, he was allowed access to the children but he was not permitted to be alone with his son. It was believed that he married Sarah in the hope that this would support his application for custody of his son.

'Orchard House' is a substantial 8/9-bedroom country residence dating from the late 1920s. It is set in 30 acres of land which also includes a large lake.

Whilst preparing this profile, it was noted that Goldsmith had started building a large, indoor swimming pool and he had ordered and received a final delivery of concrete for the base of the pool on the exact date that Diana was last seen by her children. In addition to this, he had been clearing several large trees and a large area of shrubbery on his grounds. All of this was being disposed of in a large fire pit that he had dug out.

Another line of enquiry included a search of the grounds of Orchard House for any evidence of Diana having been there. There was also a media appeal, asking the public for any information which might lead to her whereabouts. Nothing of any evidential value came from these actions.

After several weeks of this enquiry, there was still no evidence of where Diana might be, and as there was no activity on her bank account, the investigation ground to a halt, which meant officers and civilian staff working on the enquiry were redeployed to other major crime investigations.

Goldsmith's young son was subject to a High Court order at the time (as part of the custody battle) and Sarah insisted that Goldsmith notify the court that Diana was now officially 'Missing' whilst the police investigation was ongoing.

Much to Goldsmith's annoyance, the court ordered that the child was not permitted to be alone with his father and it was agreed that the child should reside with the family of Goldsmith's eldest son from his first marriage.

Ten Months Later
Up until 1995, I was an Area DCI. In October of that year, however, I was transferred to the Major Crime Department (MCD) at FHQ, where I became a Senior Investigating Officer (SIO). The MCD are a specialist team of experienced detective officers of varying ranks. The head of the department is a Detective Superintendent. The department specialises in major enquiries ranging from murders, serious sexual assaults, armed robberies to multiple deaths, etc. The officers are supported by a team of civilian colleagues who record all evidential material on a national computer system called HOLMES (Home Office Large Major Enquiry System).

HOLMES (Home Office Large Major Enquiry System) is a computer system which was developed after the publication of two reports into the 'Yorkshire Ripper' killer, Peter Sutcliffe. The first report was carried out after he was arrested and charged with the murders (Byford Report, 1982) and the second after his conviction and sentence to life imprisonment (Sampson Report, 1983).

Both reports highlighted the administration failures and the below quote from Lord Byford's report summarises this problem:

The ineffectiveness of the major incident room was a serious handicap to the Ripper investigation. While it should have been the effective nerve centre of the whole police operation, the backlog of unprocessed information resulted in the failure to connect vital pieces of related information. This serious fault in the central index system allowed Peter Sutcliffe to continually slip through the net as the evidence and details of clues against him, including the many interviews, were split up and divided between at least two separate name index cards, instead of one. Lost among thousands of other cards, they were never 'married' together. As well, also unintentionally, a file on Peter Sutcliffe was broken into different parts. These events prevented the clearest possible evidence against him from being presented through the card index system. The West Yorkshire police had considered using computers for the records of the major incident room, but, at the time, suitable facilities did not exist.

My first deployment on MCD was to carry out a formal review of the investigation into the disappearance of Diana Goldsmith. I was required to advise my senior officers on two specific issues, both relating to locating the body of Diana, if, in fact, she was dead:

- Should a new swimming pool, which Goldsmith was building at his home at the time of Diana's disappearance, be excavated in the search for Diana's body?
- Should a large fire pit, which Goldsmith had created on his land prior to Diana's disappearance and had since been filled in, be excavated?

As previously mentioned, Goldsmith had ordered an extra load of concrete for the foundation of the pool on the very day Diana disappeared. I could not definitively say whether or not there was anything sinister about this, but I had to consider the potential cost, staff hours, equipment, etc., for digging out the tons of concrete which formed the base of the swimming pool, when there was no known evidence that Goldsmith was in any way involved in Diana's disappearance. I ended up taking the view that I could not recommend the pool be dug up. I made a similar recommendation about the fire pit – my thought process being that if you dig out one, then you should be prepared to dig out both.

I further recommended that on the first anniversary of Diana's disappearance, a new media appeal should be made, supported with new posters appealing for information and circulated at all key locations in Sevenoaks, shopping malls in Kent, Essex and south-east London. I also recommended that all relevant witnesses be re-interviewed and asked if they would voluntarily supply DNA samples and fingerprints. Each of these recommendations were accepted by the force, with one extra one added by the Head of the CID – I was to take on the role of SIO for Operation Boxer with immediate effect.

In the build-up to the anniversary, I assembled a small team of officers, which included Detective Sergeant Graham Driscoll as the team supervisor, Police Constable Bob Kelly, who would be my Office Manager and HOLMES computer supervisor, and Detective Constable Lenny Johnson, who had been and would continue to be the Family Liaison Officer for the Goldsmith family.

> The primary purpose of a Family Liaison Officer (FLO) is that of an investigator. Their role is to gather evidence and information from the family to contribute to the investigation and preserve its integrity. The FLO also provides support and information, in a sensitive and compassionate manner, securing confidence and trust of families of victims of crime (primarily homicide), road fatality, mass disaster or other critical incident, ensuring family members are given timely information in accordance with the needs of the investigation.
>
> National Police Chief's Council*

---

* library.college.police.uk/docs/NPCC/2_Management_Structure_for_Family_Liaison.pdf

When the anniversary of Diana's disappearance arrived, we had excellent support from the local and regional media. We identified some interesting issues when the Investigation Team re-interviewed people. Diana's ex-boyfriend (but still a friend), Charlie Hatt, admitted that in the year prior to Diana's disappearance, during the latter part of the summer, he had been annoyed with her when she had gone to Greece on holiday without him. He remembered telling her that he was ending their relationship because of her behaviour when drunk. When Diana showed no remorse and left on holiday, he went to her house and put his set of keys to her house through her letterbox.

Charlie then told the interviewing officer that, whilst Diana was away, he bumped into Goldsmith in Sevenoaks High Street, by chance. When Goldsmith engaged him in conversation, Charlie told Goldsmith about having put his keys through the letterbox.

Whilst Hatt was giving us this information, we received an anonymous phone call. One of our civilian administrators in the Major Incident Room (MIR) picked up the call.

'I have some information,' the caller said, 'it's about Charlie Hatt. In the month of January,' (she didn't give a year), 'I saw him walking into the grounds of a disused manor house.'

'Where was it?' the officer asked.

'It was near the main road in Sevenoaks. Look, the thing that I found strange about it was that he was carrying a spade over his shoulder.' Then the phone went dead.

This information was transferred onto an action sheet and researched.

Since we had put the question of Diana's whereabouts out to the public, we received calls in the MIR from a variety of sources. These phone calls could be from media services, officers or members of the public. In theory, anybody who was part of the team could pick up the calls, even myself. The disused manor house referred to in the call was quickly identified and Charlie Hatt was asked if he could explain the information.

'Charlie,' we asked, 'we know that you were seen near the old manor house with a shovel last January.'

'You bastards,' he replied. 'That is where my dog, Sherry, is buried in the pet cemetery.'

'OK,' the officers replied. 'We'll have to check it out and see.'

The result of this enquiry was brought to my attention. Although I was looking for the body of a female, I could not discount the possibility that a human body might be buried in an animal cemetery. As a result, I ordered for the grave of Sherry to be identified and exhumed in order to confirm that Diana was not also buried there.

Soon after, the work was carried out by members of our uniformed support group. They removed the body of the dog and then dug down another four feet, but found nothing. Charlie had been speaking the truth, his dog was indeed buried there, and only his dog. Sherry was again laid to rest at the conclusion of the search.

I sent DS Driscoll to see Charlie, on my behalf, to offer my sympathy and make an apology for any pain or suffering which may have occurred as a result of our actions. Although I never saw a photograph of Sherry, the sentiment Charlie felt for her was enough to create an imaginary vision of her in my mind's eye and I also carry that picture in my head as if it were a memory! Strange how the mind works.

Goldsmith was invited to attend Sevenoaks police station to be re-interviewed as a witness. Although it was the second time he had been interviewed, it was the first time that I, myself, met him. My team and I found it interesting that he had brought his family solicitor with him. Why would you do that when you come into a police station to be interviewed, unless you have something to hide? A family solicitor is more relevant in cases pertinent to the custody of children – this was the first and only time in my career that a family lawyer accompanied a witness.

I introduced myself and re-introduced DS Driscoll, who had already met Goldsmith. We told him that we wished to review his original witness statements regarding his movements at the time of Diana's disappearance, but he made it very clear that he had no intention of helping us.

'I'm not answering any of your questions,' he said, aggressively. 'I have already told you everything I know.'

'Mr Goldsmith,' I said, 'the last time you were interviewed you had scratch marks on your neck. Will you please explain to me how those scratch marks came about?'

'I'm telling you nothing else,' he replied. 'I've told you everything.'

He was then asked if he was willing to provide his fingerprints and a DNA sample. At which point, he hit the roof.

'You lot are trying to fit me up,' he shouted. 'You just want to use my DNA to blame me if Diana is found dead.'

Thankfully, his solicitor advised him that since he had done nothing wrong, he should provide the DNA sample and fingerprints. Since he had previously had legitimate access to Diana's home, it would be of no surprise to us if his prints and DNA were there.

Reluctantly, he agreed to provide them, but I sensed that he left the police station a very worried man.

> The term DNA has now become a common phrase and is often used in a police investigation where a suspect is arrested after their DNA has linked them with a crime, a victim or a crime scene. It stands for 'Deoxyribonucleic Acid', which is defined as a molecule composed of two polynucleotide chains which coil around each other to form a double helix carrying genetic instructions for the development, functioning, growth and reproduction of all known organisms and many viruses. Although not entirely unique, DNA is attributed to a person by ascertaining the probability of how often that DNA would occur in the population.

Unfortunately, since we still had not found Diana, we had nothing to link Goldsmith's DNA to. A few weeks after the first anniversary of her disappearance, just as the leads on Diana's disappearance were drying up and other major crimes were occurring throughout the force area – all of which needed resources – we finally had a breakthrough.

Every detective's dream came true for us when the Station Officer at Bromley police station called our incident room at FHQ. He informed one of my colleagues that a young lady had come into the police station stating that she had some information which might help the police in relation to 'the missing lady and a car being found at Lakeside Shopping Centre'. Thankfully, the officer was aware of the recent appeals which had been made on the anniversary of Diana's disappearance, so he took her details and relayed her information directly back to our force.

I was engaged on a serious rape investigation, so I deployed two officers to travel to Bromley at once, to meet up with the witness. A few hours later, they relayed her story to me in person.

She was a young, unmarried mother living on a council estate in Bromley with her four children aged 1, 2, 4 and 5 years of age. Over the previous weekend, she had been at a neighbour's house, in the company of her neighbour and the neighbour's boyfriend, Michael Danaher. They were watching the television when the local news came on.

She described Danaher's bizarre reaction when the newsreader covered an article about the anniversary of Diana's disappearance, at which point Danaher got up, barricaded the front door with a settee, and started shouting.

'If Fitzie finds out I was there,' he cried, 'he will kill me.' Danaher carried on in this strange manner until she left the house a short time later.

She decided not to report anything to the police until she had first talked to her friend (Danaher's girlfriend and mother of his child) who she visited the following day to discuss what had happened. This was when Danaher's girlfriend revealed that Danaher had done a job with a guy called Colligan last year, which was organised by a local guy called Michael Fitzpatrick.

The job had involved attending a woman's house and abducting her. When they got her back to the estate, Danaher had to get out of her car because 'Fitzie' wasn't aware that Danaher was the man on the job. Danaher was told to wait until Colligan had dropped the woman off at 'Fitzie's' scrap metal shop. Danaher and Colligan then took her car to Lakeside. Danaher was told that the reason they took the car to Lakeside was to make sure the lady would have difficulty getting her car back.

The witness went on to say that she knew each of the men named – she had been on the same estate as them since they were all kids. Danaher's girlfriend also told the witness that Colligan had visited their house and warned Danaher that he'd better keep his mouth shut, otherwise he'd be getting a beating.

Initial Arrests
An immediate check with the Intelligence Department at Bromley police station, confirmed the identity of each of the three named men. They were all known associates with criminal convictions, and Fitzpatrick

was the owner of a scrap metal business in the area where they all lived. Colligan had a reputation as a 'hard man', suspected of committing high-value burglaries at chemist shops, and supplying the stolen drugs throughout south-east London and Kent.

This was a game-changer for the enquiry. I arranged for some of the officers who had worked on the enquiry to return to my MIR the following day. I would now have to make plans for a coordinated operation to arrest these three individuals. We had already been forced to wait for over a year so, rather than rushing their arrest, it was imperative that our strategy be meticulously thought out. In doing so, we needed to find out everything we could about them. I liaised with colleagues in the MPS in Bromley and prepared an operation for the following week.

A Monday morning strike was scheduled to take place on each of their homes. As the plan developed, however, we were forced to re-orchestrate the operation. The MPS were concerned because their intelligence sources indicated that Fitzpatrick and Colligan had access to firearms, which meant the arrest was now a firearms operation. Undertaking such an operation means that armed officers must be responsible for ensuring 'safe entry to a property'. There can be no risk, whatsoever, that anyone will manage to obtain and deploy a firearm whilst police are present.

This forced us to consider budget constraints. In order to arrest the suspects before 0900 hrs on the Monday morning, MPS would require a firearms team by 0400 hrs. Police duty rotas regard 0600 hrs as the start of the working day, so the timing (0400 hrs) was regarded as the Sunday and classed as a Rest Day Call Out. There is only so much money in the pot – the MPS were not prepared to fund it and nor was I. It is always wise to consider alternative options in such cases, as you may need to fund an alternative line of enquiry later in an investigation. The Monday arrest was subsequently cancelled.

It was decided that the arrest would proceed on the Tuesday. This meant that we had several days to prepare our own investigation teams and to decide which police station in our force area to take the suspects to. A twenty-four-hour delay in an investigation which has already lasted more than twelve months will not have an impact.

The Superintendent whom I had been liaising with at Bromley police station phoned me on the Sunday morning prior to our operation, to inform me that a uniformed Constable, who had attended an incident in a pub, had arrested Danaher the previous evening.

Danaher was a petty crook with a string of previous convictions, so it came as no surprise that he had managed to get himself arrested prior to the dawn raid set to take place on his house that Tuesday.

The officer in the pub had recognised Danaher and knew there was a warrant out for his arrest for Breach of a Probation Order. He was also aware that Danaher would be kept in custody in order to appear before the magistrates' court the following day, and that it was very likely he would be released afterwards.

That was not all. The MPS Superintendent informed me that the plan to arrest Colligan at home would also have to be changed. An incident following a domestic dispute had been reported, in which Colligan had allegedly produced a gun and threatened a neighbour, saying that he would 'blow her head off'.

Additionally — as if we needed any further obstacles — it was now reported that Colligan had young children in the house. The arrest would simply have to be made elsewhere, since it was now clearer than ever that Colligan very likely had a firearm hidden in his house.

All detectives and support staff who deal with major crimes are used to missing rest days, holidays and family events. Both my plan and my Sunday were now ruined. It was back to the drawing board.

The following day, I sent two officers to Bromley Magistrates' Court with the remit to liaise with the court gaoler and make sure that Danaher would be obliged to return to the cell block after the magistrates had dealt with him.

Prisoners are only allowed to keep things like glasses, if they wear them. All other property is listed on the custody record at the police station. In this case, the property would be handed to the escort team who were taking him to the court, so — no matter what the outcome of the case — he would have to come to the cell area to collect his possessions. Unless he is going to be sent to prison, this is the standard procedure.

Our plan might seem fairly cunning on our part. We would arrest him once he had been formally released by the court, just as he was about to collect his property. I grant you, it may seem like a sneaky manoeuvre by us to be nasty, but it was simply the most opportune moment for us to arrest him.

All went to plan. My officers promptly arrested Danaher whilst he collected his property, and took him straight to Dartford police station. We finally had our first suspect in custody. Our only hope was that the other two would not get wind of his arrest, which would have ruined the next part of our plan.

This was where the real work started. We had the statement from the lady who first reported Danaher's strange behaviour, but nothing else. The operation to arrest Fitzpatrick the following morning with an MPS Firearms team was all organised, and a new plan to arrest Colligan was starting to take shape. I tasked colleagues with researching the incident between Colligan and his neighbour. Yet again, we struck lucky.

My officers liaised with the MPS Domestic Violence Officer who had been allocated to investigate the incident. This officer knew Colligan, so she agreed to phone him that day and fix a time and date for him to come into the police station to see her and discuss the complaint against him. The appointment was made for him to see the officer at 1430 hrs the following Thursday, 8 February 1996. My officers would take the opportunity to arrest him then.

It would have been better to get the three suspects arrested at the same time, of course, but this seeming setback worked in our favour in the end, because another breakthrough came in – and much sooner than anyone could have anticipated. This time it was from the interviewing officers who were assigned to interview Danaher.

As expected, Danaher had his solicitor with him when the officers interviewed him. As soon as he discovered that his client had been arrested in the cell block, the solicitor had travelled to Kent from Bromley Magistrates' Court. He first consulted privately with his client and then, during the initial interview, the solicitor advised Danaher that if he had nothing to hide then he should simply tell the truth.

Danaher was having none of it, he continually replied 'no comment' to every question put to him.

In the initial interview, our strategy for Danaher had been to avoid sharing all the known facts our witness had given us and invite him to tell the officers what he knew about the disappearance of Diana Goldsmith. Of course, since Danaher gave a 'no comment' interview, the interview did not last very long.

Further interviews were planned and Danaher was given more time with his solicitor between each interview to consider the advice he was getting. This is standard procedure when interviewing criminal suspects. Police do not know what advice is given by the solicitor.

Danaher gave his fingerprints and a DNA sample. This process was recorded on his custody record by the Custody Sergeant, who was responsible for the ongoing management of prisoner-handling, as well as their general welfare.

Whilst Danaher was being returned to his cell, he turned to one of my officers. 'Do you think I killed her?' he asked.

At that very moment, a tannoy system sounded in the police station, and the officer thought Danaher had said, 'Do you think I've kidnapped her.'

'Yes,' the officer replied, 'and we will prove it.'

Danaher was taken aback, and asked the officer if he could see his solicitor again. The officer took Danaher back to his solicitor and the officer repeated what he had thought Danaher had said.

Danaher insisted that he had said 'killed' not 'kidnapped', and said he now wanted to tell the truth.

With the agreement of his solicitor, Danaher's second interview commenced immediately.

At the time of the abduction, Danaher did not know what the lady's name was, but in this interview he made an initial admission to his involvement.

When this interview was finished, the interviewing officers gave me a summary on the telephone of what Danaher was now saying. He initially told the officers that he did not know the lady who he and his mate, a guy call Ian Colligan, had to take (by force if necessary) to a scrap yard in Bromley, where someone wanted to 'teach her a lesson'.

He described, in detail, Colligan's request to help him out on this job, and said that Colligan insisted no one was to know Danaher was involved. Colligan said he would be paid a couple of hundred pounds but Danaher could not remember the exact amount.

Colligan, he said, had picked him up in a white van and they drove out of London to Sevenoaks. They watched as the lady and her children left the house, after which Colligan produced a set of keys and they walked up to the house to enter the premises through the front door. He described the interior of the ground floor and how they waited. When the lady returned, they tried to stop her from screaming by shouting at her to 'shut up' and Colligan put his hand over her mouth. He bound her wrists with the plastic tags which he had brought with him, taped her mouth, and together they shoved her into the back of her car, ordering her to lie down on the seat. They then drove away from Sevenoaks. Danaher did not go into further detail about what happened in the house, in this interview. He did say that, at some stage, as they travelled back towards Bromley, Colligan stopped the vehicle and went to a nearby telephone kiosk to make a phone call.

Afterwards, as they approached Fitzpatrick's scrap metal shop, Colligan pulled over and ordered Danaher to get out of the car and wait for him to return. Colligan then drove off in the direction of Fitzpatrick's shop. This was the last time Danaher saw Diana.

He went on to describe Colligan returning a short while later and the two of them taking her car to Lakeside Shopping Centre. They parked it in a bay, walked through a nearby department store to a bus station and took a bus back to Bromley, where they parted company. He went back home. When asked about the white van they travelled in to Sevenoaks, he claimed that it was a stolen van on false plates. He did not return to Sevenoaks with Colligan to collect it. The van has never been recovered.

When the interview concluded, at the request of Danaher's solicitor, I travelled over to the police station. We discussed what would happen to Danaher, and the prospect of Danaher turning Queen's Evidence.

Queen's Evidence is defined in law as 'Evidence given on behalf of the prosecution by an accused person who has pleaded guilty and is thus no longer on trial in the proceedings and who then acts as a witness against his accomplices.'*

Danaher agreed to this process and was subsequently charged with the abduction of Diana Goldsmith. He appeared before Dartford Magistrates' Court the following day and was remanded in custody to HMP Canterbury. His story of events was confirmed by both his girlfriend and sister, to whom he had confessed his involvement in the abduction after seeing our media appeal, and out of his fear of Fitzpatrick.

The raid on Fitzpatrick's flat was carried out the day after Danaher's admissions but he was not there. Clearly someone informed him that the police had raided his flat, because a few hours later he walked into the station by himself to complain about his flat being searched.

I received a telephone call in our MIR from an officer at Sevenoaks police station telling me that Fitzpatrick had arrived at the station.

'Have him arrested immediately on suspicion of the abduction of Diana Goldsmith,' I told the officer.

'But I'm a civilian employee,' the officer replied, 'and I'm not allowed to do that.'

'Well, get someone who can arrest him immediately.'

'Yes, sir,' he replied. 'Hold on.'

After a few minutes holding on to the phone, I grew frustrated and hung up. I rang DS Bob Rutherford at Sevenoaks and explained the situation.

'Dennis,' he said, 'leave it with me. He'll be in custody within a couple of minutes.'

Fitzpatrick was indeed taken into custody.

When someone comes into custody, you can only detain them for a maximum of twenty-four hours. Throughout that period, however, their detention must be reviewed regularly in order to make sure that the offence they are in custody for is being dealt with efficiently.

---

* www.oxfordreference.com/display/10.1093/oi/authority.20110803100358411

If you reach the twenty-four-hour mark and you still want to hold a suspect in custody, the judgement as to whether their custody warrants an extra twelve hours is made by an officer of Superintendent rank, who is not involved in the investigation. There are three criteria that must be fulfilled, namely:

1. The offence being investigated must be an indictable offence (liable to be charged with a serious crime that warrants a trial by jury).
2. The detention of that person without charge is necessary to secure, or preserve, evidence relevant to an offence for which he is under arrest, or to obtain evidence by questioning him.
3. The investigation is being conducted diligently and expeditiously.

As we approached the end of Fitzpatrick's thirty-six hours in custody, he was put before Maidstone Magistrates' Court where an Extension of Detention was applied for. The same three criteria as mention above also apply to these proceedings. The magistrate granted an additional period of twenty-four hours' detention.

In the Interim – A Few Dead Bodies

DS Driscoll and myself visited Fitzpatrick's scrap metal shop, where we discovered a small gym in a rear outbuilding. It appeared to have only recently been re-decorated and a new concrete floor had been laid. Based on the time scale provided by Danaher, between the time he watched Colligan drive off with Diana until the moment Colligan returned to pick Danaher up, it is most likely that Diana had been dropped off at the scrap metal shop.

Could this be where Diana lost her life?

Was she buried under that concrete floor?

We examined the floor closely. There appeared to be a shadow in the concrete. To my eye, it seemed slightly different from the rest of the floor and the shape was approximately 5ft long and 18in wide. This indicated to me the possibility that a body had been laid upon it, or perhaps beneath it.

I decided there was sound justification for digging up this concrete floor and authorised the application for a search warrant for the gym area. I also mobilised a team of officers from Kent to join us, requesting that they bring sufficient equipment to dig up a concrete floor. Both the warrant and our digging team duly arrived, together with an MPS cadaver dog and handler.

> Cadaver dogs are also known as human-remains detection dogs. They will, however, also detect other forms of animal decomposition, which means they can locate body parts, tissue, blood and bone.

There was a slight delay with the digging team due to some confusion regarding whether anyone was fully trained or authorised to use the Kango hammer. There were plenty of volunteers, so I simply authorised the lot of them to use it so we could push on with the job at once. There are occasions when the needs of an investigation force us to pursue the case quickly and as the 'custody time-clock' for Fitzpatrick was ticking away, we just had to get on with the job, despite objections from Alex Whear, one of Fitzpatrick's employees.

We drilled several boreholes into the concrete, then stepped aside for the cadaver dog to do its work. Within seconds the dog indicated to its handler that there were, indeed, remains beneath the concrete.

I was delighted. My hunch, it seemed, had been correct. Diana was most probably buried there in that floor. I instructed the team to go ahead and dig the floor out completely.

Did we find Diana there?

Sadly, we did not. What we did recover were several carcasses of animals which had most likely been buried there since Second World War.

A Major Crime Department is often running several complex enquiries simultaneously, which means staff are in high demand. There were many incidents in our force area at this time, and I was running out of available personnel. I still had hundreds of hours of CCTV recordings which needed to be viewed from the Lakeside Shopping Centre (more specifically, the department store) where Colligan and Danaher had been after parking Diana's car there.

I arranged for a ten-screen video-viewer to be set up in our MIR. With no extra staff to do the work, DS Driscoll and I had no choice but to scour the footage ourselves.

Since we knew approximately what time Diana had been abducted, we were able to estimate what time she would have been dropped off. That is, if Danaher's account of events was correct. We added on the time it might take to drive from Bromley to Lakeside, in order to evaluate which time-parameters would be most relevant on the videos. We selected the closest store to the car parking bay Danaher and Colligan had used, which was House of Fraser. The store opened that day at 0930 hrs so that is where we began, well aware that we could be at this all day.

After only twenty minutes of intense observation, however, we both shouted simultaneously.

'Yes!' we yelled. 'Got them!'

In fact, we had spotted them simultaneously on separate screens, from completely different cameras. Colligan was wearing a light-tan leather jacket. Whilst the quality of the footage was adequate, we knew it would need enhancing to obtain a clearer view, but if we could find that jacket in Colligan's possession then it would prove for sure that it was him in the video.

Thursday, 8 February, came around rather quickly. Despite complaints from his solicitor, who had opposed the application for further detention, we still had Fitzpatrick in our custody. Today was the day we were due to arrest Colligan, and hopefully locate that jacket (today was also the day we would finally have the opportunity to search his house) along with any other potential evidence.

A team of officers was ready to enter his house the instant they got word from us that he was in custody. Colligan duly turned up for the interview and the DVO interviewed him regarding the alleged argument with his neighbour. Naturally, he denied ever having threatened her. The interview was concluded and the DVO introduced him to our officers.

Job done. Colligan was at long last in custody and on his way to Kent.

Next, the search of Colligan's home, which was conducted in the presence of his wife, resulted in a light-brown leather jacket being recovered from his wardrobe. Furthermore, a sawn-off shotgun was recovered from the top of his bedroom wardrobe and it was loaded. We also found an interesting letter in his car from an unknown female. In any case, it was certainly someone close to him. (This woman is identified later.)

Every interview conducted at a police station is tape-recorded. After a maximum of forty-five minutes the interview had to be suspended to allow for the tapes to be changed (nowadays, however, most police stations have digital recording systems in place) and for the interviewee to speak with his solicitor.

Colligan made no admissions in front of his solicitor but he made a request at the end of the interview. 'I want to speak to whoever is in charge here,' he said.

I duly made my way to the custody suite, making sure to speak with him in front of the custody officer. It was then that he made a proposal.

'If you release me,' he suggested, 'I'll give you everything you need to know about where Diana is and who killed her.'

'I will be doing nothing of the sort, Mr Colligan,' I replied. 'Helping with the investigation, however, might help you in the long term.' It was at this point that I felt that Colligan's silence could be costly for both himself and our investigation. However, after considering all the evidence we had, the bottom line was that he was the one person who we could prove had last seen Diana alive. In my mind, Goldsmith was the only person we knew who had a motive to get rid of Diana, and Colligan could nail him for us.

Colligan preferred his idea to mine, of course, and with his solicitor present, he maintained his silence for the remainder of our interview.

The following day, both Fitzpatrick and Colligan were charged with the criminal offence of conspiracy to abduct Diana Goldsmith. In addition to this, Colligan was charged with possession of a firearm. They appeared before Maidstone Magistrates' Court. This hearing lasted approximately ten minutes and no application was made for bail. This came as no surprise to me as these were serious charges, and solicitors know that at the first appearance on these charges, without the prosecution serving papers, the court would not consider releasing them. They were both subsequently remanded in custody.

During this time, other important considerations had to be undertaken regarding the safety of our witnesses and Danaher. We sought assistance from the Operational Partnership Team Police Advisers at the Home Office. They arranged for Colligan and Fitzpatrick to be remanded at a different prison from Danaher, which ensured that Danaher would be safe.

The Operational Partnership Team Police Advisers are responsible for providing advice to a wide range of prisons, the National Offender Management Service (NOMS), Law Enforcement Agencies (LEA) and police personnel on policing issues in prisons; in particular, on Category A prisoners, High Security Estate issues, threats to life in prisons and criminal gang issues.

They also link those forces and security sections of the Prison Service which require armed support from the police when transporting dangerous criminals from prison to prison, or from prison to the court or police station.

Keeping Danaher safe and away from Colligan and Fitzpatrick was of top priority.

The question of safety regarding the lady who first came forward to assist the investigation was also of paramount concern. She accepted our offer of witness protection. Later in the investigation, the same level of protection was granted to Danaher's girlfriend and their son.

In most cases, the police will consider witness protection if the witness fears that they, or their friends and family, will be at risk of serious harm if their identity or whereabouts are revealed to the defendant, his/her associates, or the public generally. The threat against them usually aims at silencing the witness in order to prevent them giving evidence in court. It is an extremely costly operation and, in the most serious of cases, is likely to change the witness's way of life forever.

Over the coming weeks and months, my team and I reviewed the enquiry continuously in our efforts to uncover more evidence and, most importantly, to find Diana. We were almost certain she was dead, so, in theory, we were looking for her body. We updated her sister and relied on our FLO, DC Johnson, to speak to Goldsmith and his wife on behalf of Diana's children. It was our hope that having an FLO explain just how keen we were to get to the truth would put more pressure on Goldsmith.

We instructed a Forensic Imagery Analysis company to examine the video footage of Colligan and Danaher at House of Fraser. They used the photographs of the two suspects (which we had taken when they came into custody) to provide us with unequivocal expert evidence of their identification. That same company also examined Colligan's leather jacket and offered the same evidence we had initially noted: a stain on the jacket was identical to that which could be seen on the video footage. So, in the days after the three suspects were charged, things were looking quite good for the enquiry.

Until I took a telephone call from the Crown Prosecution Service.

The Crown Prosecution Service (CPS) prosecutes criminal cases that have been investigated by the police and other investigative organisations in England and Wales. The CPS is independent, and we make our decisions independently of the police and government.

Our duty is to make sure that the right person is prosecuted for the right offence, and to bring offenders to justice wherever possible.

The Crown Prosecution Service*

We initially had CPS permission to charge the three suspects based on Danaher's admission. However, now our case was being formally reviewed by a senior member of the CPS, and in particular the case against Colligan and Fitzpatrick. The CPS decided that we could not use Danaher's evidence until such time as he had pleaded guilty at the Crown Court. Despite my objections to this decision (which I expressed in as

---

* www.cps.gov.uk/

gentlemanly a manner as I could), the abduction charges against both men were 'discontinued' and Fitzpatrick was released from prison immediately. Whilst discontinuing the abduction charge against Colligan, the CPS still agreed with evidence regarding the firearm offence, so Colligan remained in custody. This was infuriating, but police are investigators not prosecutors.

Throughout the entire time that Danaher, Colligan and Fitzpatrick were implicated, no evidence was uncovered which proved any motive to harm Diana. Nothing revealed any personal grudge and the only link back to Diana was via Goldsmith. Our entire team were certain that he not only had the motive but that he was also 'the money' behind Diana's disappearance. In order to investigate, police always look for 'reasonable suspicion' and it was I who made the ultimate decision to take Goldsmith into custody. The timing to interview him under caution seemed right to me.

I spoke with his solicitor and agreed upon a time and date – the following week – for him to surrender himself to custody at one of our police stations. In the meantime, I appointed a civilian financial investigator, Nick Wheeler, from our Fraud Squad, to examine Goldsmith's bank accounts to ascertain if there were any unexplained cash withdrawals which may have been used to pay Colligan.

Financial Investigation is a discipline concerned with exploring the finances that relate to criminal activity. Financial Investigators can benefit an enquiry, whether the crime is profit-motivated or not.

The role of the Financial Investigator has developed substantially in the years since Operation Boxer. Nowadays, a financial investigation may be undertaken to support a wide range of criminal investigations including murder, missing persons, human trafficking, firearms, sex offences, drugs offences, economic crimes such as fraud and asset recovery. Their work is covered by legislation which may allow them access to bank accounts and other financial records.

Our small team of detectives were busy trying to collate all the information to assist with the interview strategy. These were trusted detectives, or, as I prefer to call them, 'God's Own Detectives'. The next thing

I knew, however, I received a telephone call completely out of the blue which made me feel sick to my skin. One of my worst fears was realised.

It was mid-afternoon and I was working in my office at Force Headquarters, when I took a telephone call from DC Johnson, who was still at Orchard House in his role as the FLO. He informed me that Goldsmith had just told him about a telephone call he had received the previous evening, from a male who was offering information about the interview he was to have in exchange for payment, the following day at Maidstone police station. The individual had given Goldsmith details of Goldsmith's own NatWest Bank accounts and claimed that he was in a position to help Goldsmith if he co-operated. He had offered to meet Goldsmith that very evening, at the White Hart Hotel in Sevenoaks. Goldsmith agreed. Goldsmith then gave DC Johnson the telephone number from which the person had called. It was traced back to Maidstone, to a kiosk on a large housing estate directly opposite Police Headquarters.

I was absolutely horrified. One of my respected, trusted team members was corrupt. I most certainly had not seen this coming.

I spoke to Goldsmith personally, giving him approval to meet the individual. I suggested he use his own car so my officers could more easily monitor his movements, identify and, hopefully, arrest the individual in question. I also informed Goldsmith that we needed, as a matter of urgency, to record his telephone calls just in case the individual made contact with him again. Our conversation was terminated with me reassuring him that we would identify the individual involved in this. I instructed DC Johnson to stay at the house and told him I would update him as soon as possible regarding the recording device on Goldsmith's telephone. I instructed DC Johnson not to say a word to any of his colleagues.

The big question now was: *who can this individual possibly be? Is there anyone in my team I can still trust?*

The answer was simple. I had no idea who it was so, naturally, I couldn't trust anyone at this point. It was a truly awful situation. Work colleagues in such stressful, ongoing cases, develop a strong and closely bonded team. We share both our successes and our upsets. We form friendships which last a lifetime. As the SIO, however, it was my job to prioritise the integrity of the police force and uncover the corrupt individual in order to ensure the enquiry stayed on track.

I contacted the head of the force's Technical Services Department. The lovely, gentle giant of a man, Brian Brimmell, arranged the telephone-taping facility for me immediately. I then contacted another SIO, DCI Alan Gimes, telling him I needed his urgent assistance. I took him into my confidence and explained the horrendous situation. He was a trusted colleague, who understood that the integrity of the police must be at the forefront of any successful investigation. I updated DC Johnson, notifying him that DCI Gimes would bring the taping facility to Goldsmith's home within the hour.

I had asked DCI Gimes to go to Goldsmith's home and liaise with DC Johnson and to remain there until Goldsmith left his house for the meeting. My thought process was that if the caller called back before Goldsmith left, then there was a chance the two officers might recognise the voice. Unfortunately, no such call came.

I then had to take the Sergeant from the force surveillance team into my confidence. I explained to him that I personally needed to brief the surveillance team on what I required them to do that evening. I mobilised the force surveillance team and briefed them on what I required that night. Goldsmith knew my officers would be nearby in the hotel but, of course, I did not fully trust him. Without Goldsmith's knowledge, I decided to put the meeting itself under surveillance and subsequently positioned undercover officers in the bar.

There was nothing more I could do now but sit back and wait to see what developed.

Unsurprisingly, the following few hours went very slowly for me. A scheduled telephone call I received from the surveillance team sergeant at 2300 hrs revealed no productive news. He informed me that they had started the surveillance on Goldsmith as he left his house. They followed him directly into Sevenoaks town centre and out the other side to the White Hart Hotel, where two officers had been deployed who witnessed Goldsmith's arrival.

Goldsmith sat alone without ordering a drink. He watched everyone who entered the pub but nobody approached him. After twenty minutes he got up and left without speaking to anyone. The Sergeant of the Mobile Surveillance Team (MST) told me that they had 'taken him back to his house and put him to bed'. In surveillance terms this meant that they would watch his premises to make sure he did not go out again.

The surveillance team would not be stood down until the house was in darkness.

Surveillance was carried out on every telephone kiosk on the estate opposite FHQ. This also proved negative. Needless to say, I did not sleep too well that night and was back in my office at 0700 hrs the following morning. Goldsmith was due to surrender himself at Maidstone police station in just under three hours' time.

I sat alone in my office sipping a hot cup of tea when I was startled by my telephone. It was Goldsmith. He told me what had happened the previous evening, completely unaware that he had been under surveillance or that I already knew what had or had not happened the previous evening. He explained that when he got home, he switched the ringtone on his phone off and went to bed. When he checked the phone that morning there was a message on the device that we had fitted. I told him not to touch it, that an officer would be at his house within the hour to deal with it.

Not long after that call, members of my team began filtering into the MIR. The first officer through the door was DC Johnson. He was the one officer I knew I could trust to send straight back out the door, and over to Orchard House. His remit this time was simple: collect the tape and our recording facility, then return to my office as soon as possible. DC Johnson was told (and fully understood) that no matter who he saw once he stepped out of my office, he was not to stop or talk; no one was to suspect that he was on an errand. No one must know where he was going. It was too dangerous for anyone to get even the slightest whiff of what was happening in the background of this enquiry.

The following hour was the longest hour of my life. I sat alone in my office without wishing to speak to a single soul. All I could do was think over and over, through each member of my team, imagining the ramifications of what might be disclosed.

DC Johnson arrived back. He knocked on the open door, approached my desk and placed the recording equipment before me.

'There you go, guv,' he said. I thanked him and promised to update him later. I knew that he understood how crucial it was that he keep my confidence.

'Thank you, Lenny,' I said. 'Please, shut the door on your way out.'

DC Johnson probably had no idea just how grateful I was for him that morning. He was the epitome of the type of officer I worked with every day – decent, trusted and reliable. There was, however, one bad apple who did not deserve such respect and who did not belong on any team of mine.

My finger hovered over the play button on the recorder. I knew that – in only a matter of seconds – everything was about to change. I pressed play and listened to the message which had been left for Goldsmith.

I recognised the voice at once but I listened again, just to make sure. Yes, I was confident I knew who it was – the very person I had tasked to investigate Goldsmith's finances. That same individual who was currently in an office two floors below me.

I would hope that most people who know me regard me as relatively easy-going but, like anyone, I have my limits. I get angry or upset when provoked, betrayed or pushed beyond the tipping point. The knowledge that this one individual could have potentially ruined an entire investigation and run the risk of tarnishing both the reputation of my department and the integrity of the force infuriated me. More importantly, however, what I found most offensive was that his actions could have prevented us from recovering Diana's body and returning it to her loved ones for a proper funeral. Hard as it was, I remained calm, whilst what I really wanted to do was to go down the stairs and confront him face to face.

The message he had left for Goldsmith started with an apology for not making it to the meeting. The caller said that there seemed to be a lot of police activity when he had arrived in Sevenoaks, so he decided to leave. He stated that he would be back in touch very soon.

My next course of action was to get the two officers who were to interview Goldsmith that morning into my office. I explained to them what had happened and instructed them to go to Maidstone police station at once, without breathing a word to anyone, and liaise with the Custody Sergeant. They were to explain that, when Goldsmith surrendered himself into custody, he was to be released immediately on bail so that he could make a statement about the events of the previous day. Of course, this would delay the interview about Diana's disappearance, but it had to be prioritised.

Goldsmith was now a witness in a corruption investigation.

When Goldsmith attended the police station with his solicitor that morning, he brought with him a bag containing a pair of pyjamas, slippers, toothbrush, etc. Clearly, he expected to be charged and kept in custody in connection with the disappearance of his former common-law wife. Goldsmith and his solicitor were taken to the custody area where a Custody Sergeant formally registered their arrival and detention. The Custody Sergeant had been briefed by my staff about the nature of all these very unusual circumstances. He went through the relevant legal process (including Goldsmith's rights when in custody) and then formally released Goldsmith from custody on police bail with a stipulation to return to the police station on a given date.

Goldsmith and his solicitor were taken to an interview room to await the arrival of the team member dealing with Wheeler, at which point Goldsmith made a witness statement and left the police station, a very nervous but relieved man.

Tempting as it was, I did not venture down the two flights of stairs to confront Nick Wheeler (the financial advisor in question). I went straight to the Head of the CID instead, to inform him of what had transpired. We agreed on a course of action and my colleague, DSU Nic Biddiss, opened an investigation into Wheeler's conduct.

That day, Nick Wheeler was arrested, interviewed and released on bail. He was subsequently suspended from duty. A report was sent to the CPS, and soon after, he was charged with attempting to pervert the course of justice. Once again, he was released on bail.

We still had no firm evidence and so, when Goldsmith was re-interviewed a few weeks later and answered with 'no comment' to every question put to him, he was subsequently released without charge. Speculation on a motive was simply not considered to be enough evidence with which to charge him.

Danaher

Spring 1996. Time moved on and my workload grew heavier. Other investigations came my way, along with several court commitments for other serious crimes.

At last, the day came for Danaher to appear at Maidstone Crown Court. It is usual for the courts to commence at 1030 hrs but we got permission from the presiding Resident Judge to hear Danaher's case at 0900 hrs. His situation about turning Queen's Evidence was presented to the judge but, thankfully, an early morning court hearing did exactly what we had intended it to do, which was to prevent too many members of the public or press getting wind of what was happening.

Danaher pleaded guilty to abducting Diana and was remanded in custody to await sentence. This would take place only after he had completed a formal agreement with the prosecution team to give evidence against all his co-accused as and when they were charged.

Danaher was transferred to police custody where he made a detailed witness statement to us, the details of which would be heard in court soon after.

His statement began with him explaining that he and Colligan had been mates for a long time, and that they saw one another regularly. He confirmed how Colligan had asked if he wanted to earn some cash and Danaher had replied that he did.

Colligan told him that they had to grab a woman from her house and take her to Fitzpatrick's shop, but that Fitzpatrick must not know about him being on the job.

He explained that he knew Fitzpatrick and was aware that Fitzpatrick had no time for him and didn't like him.

He recounted how Colligan had picked him up in a white van and they travelled to Sevenoaks. During the journey, Colligan told him that what they were about to do should have been done at Christmas time, but the woman had not been alone so they had abandoned the plan back then. Danaher didn't ask who else had been there, but assumed it was one of their other mates from the estate.

He said that he did not know the area, but after they pulled up, Colligan produced a set of keys which he said were 'for the lady's house'. They watched the lady and three children leave before walking casually up to the house and going inside.

The house was clean and tidy. They had a good look around before deciding to hide in the closet behind the front door, and to grab her as she entered.

After a while, her car pulled into the driveway. She was alone. Once she was inside the house, she saw them and screamed.

Colligan was the first to grab her. 'Shut up and you won't get hurt,' he shouted at her. He confirmed that she struggled as fiercely as she could, but they held her so tightly that she really could not move. He explained that this was when Colligan tied her wrists with plastic ties and pushed her into a chair.

'Be quiet,' he warned her, but she carried on shouting.

'What on earth are you doing?' she screamed.

'If you don't shut up,' Colligan threatened, 'then I will have to shut you up.'

She shut up.

'You're going for a ride,' Colligan said. 'Somebody wants to have a little chat with you about your behaviour.'

It was at this point in the statement that Danaher explained he actually offered to make her a cup of tea, which she accepted. He made a cup for each of them, after which he washed the cups in the kitchen.

He confirmed that Colligan taped her mouth in preparation to leave the house. Colligan took her car keys out of her handbag and they placed her, lying down, on the back seat of her car. Colligan got in and moved the driver's seat back. Danaher got into the front seat. They left the area and headed off towards Bromley.

Danaher confirmed that he didn't know the area and said that he could not identify the location of a telephone kiosk where Colligan had stopped to make a phone call (mobile phones in those days were available but they were not the must-have accessory they are now).

He confirmed that he didn't know who Colligan rang, and that Colligan made no reference to the phone call when he returned to the car.

They drove to the estate where they lived, and Colligan pulled over once again as they approached Fitzpatrick's shop. Here, Colligan told him to get out of the car and await his return. He confirmed that he hung around on the side of the road until Colligan returned, without the lady now. He recalled that Colligan was only gone for about five to six minutes. He explained that this is when the two of them drove directly to Lakeside Shopping Centre, parked her car before walking through a large shop to the bus station, from where they bused it back to Bromley and parted company.

He confirmed that Colligan paid him a couple of hundred pounds a few days later. Finally, he explained that he did not speak to Colligan about what they had done, other than on a few occasions when Colligan had warned him that he had better keep his mouth shut, and that if he ever said anything he would get a beating.

Frustrating as it was, we still had no evidence against Fitzpatrick. Danaher refused to say a word against him since he was terrified of the man, and was well aware that Fitzpatrick would have hit the roof if he had known Danaher was on the job in the first place. All we had was the policeman's strong hunch that if Danaher got out of the car near Fitzpatrick's scrap yard, then Colligan had been heading there.

The video evidence of Colligan and Danaher in the House of Fraser shop was also good evidence as, at that point in time, Diana was in the hands of someone else (probably Fitzpatrick and Goldsmith).

In addition to this, Danaher's girlfriend made a witness statement, details of which included an account of his behaviour when the first anniversary appeal was broadcast on television, and Danaher's admission to her regarding his involvement in it.

With the knowledge that Danaher was telling the truth, I took the opportunity to look back at all the evidence we had built up since my initial review of the investigation. If Danaher was indeed telling the truth (and we had no reason to believe he was not) then my hypothesis was that Diana was killed in the gym at Fitzpatrick's scrap yard and that Fitzpatrick (and possibly Goldsmith) were present when the killing took place.

If Goldsmith was, in fact, there, then there is little doubt that when Diana saw him (despite her wrists being bound) she would have tried to defend herself, pushing him away and in doing so, scratching him. The scratch marks on Goldsmith's face indicated to us that this may very well have occurred. Perhaps that was why he was reluctant to provide us with a sample of his DNA. If we ever found her body then traces of Goldsmith's DNA were likely to be left under her fingernails.

It was through Danaher's admissions that another avenue of enquiry became available to us. That is, we were able to identify who had been the first-choice individual on 'the abduction team' – the man who Danaher had replaced. We contacted the collator at Bromley police station. It was from his records that we identified a criminal associate of Colligan's by the name of Andy Mills. He lived on the same housing estate in Bromley. He was known to the local police and had several convictions for dishonesty. DS Driscoll and DC Johnson paid him a visit and he too was subsequently arrested on suspicion of conspiracy to abduct

Diana Goldsmith on the Christmas Eve before her actual abduction took place. He admitted that he had been with Colligan on the Christmas Eve but, at the time, he thought they were going to be doing a burglary. When Colligan explained what had, in fact, been about to take place, my guys said that he told them he was genuinely relieved that house guests at Diana's home had prevented Colligan and Mills from carrying out the crime and that, from that point forward, he had refused to get involved.

He also told the officers that he had received abusive telephone calls from Colligan, telling him to keep his mouth shut. He was released on police bail but would eventually make a witness statement, which served as another piece of evidence when he was used as a prosecution witness. Incidentally, he also accepted a police caution for having cannabis plants in his flat.

Summer 1996

I continually reviewed the evidence we had accumulated throughout this investigation. I was now confident that the time was right to ask the CPS to reassess the evidence against Colligan, and after a short period of time, they finally agreed that Colligan should now be charged with the abduction of Diana. I sincerely hoped that, due to the length of time Diana had now been missing, there was also sufficient evidence to charge Colligan with conspiracy to murder. Unfortunately, however, this was not the case.

Colligan was already in custody (for the firearms offence) so he was produced from prison to Sevenoaks police station, officially charged and remanded in custody on both matters. His next significant court date would come up in December.

From a personal point of view, I was away from this investigation until mid-October. I had taken on a new investigation which took me to Pitcairn Island, a British Overseas Territory located in the South Pacific Ocean some 9,000 miles away. The Pitcairn Island investigation was launched after a young girl was sexually assaulted on the island. I travelled there with my colleague, Detective Inspector Peter George. The investigation quickly identified the offender, and the case against him was handed over to the Pitcairn Legal Advisor. Prior to returning to the United Kingdom, it came to our notice that there were indications of historical sexual abuse on young girls. Eventually, evidence to substantiate these issues was forthcoming and I led a second investigation which eventually resulted in several island men being convicted. *

In my absence, the case against our Financial Investigator, Nick Wheeler, was listed for trial on 25 September 1996. On the 24th, however, he drove to Sussex where he took his own life after deliberately (it was later uncovered) crashing his car into an articulated lorry. There had been a strong case again Wheeler. Had he pleaded guilty he would have faced a sentence of approximately four years' imprisonment. Her Majesty's Coroner later recorded a verdict of suicide.

This was the first funeral and second burial in relation to this investigation, and there were more to come. Every time I think of Wheeler, I see the face of a man who, in the name of greed, was prepared to jeopardise a crucial investigation.

On my return from Pitcairn Island on 14 October, I was told that I had been promoted to DSU and transferred from Major Crime to take charge of the Crime Management Department for the force.

Crime Management is a desk job and I was glued to that office ten to twelve hours a day. Of course, if you were operational then you could go out for fresh air, speak to other people and so forth. Thankfully, it was agreed by the Head of the CID that in addition to my new role, I should retain Operation Boxer. This gave me the opportunity to play 'proper detective', as opposed to an administrator. For the previous twenty years (at least, at that stage) I'd been an operational detective, which meant I was constantly on the go.

I still had several officers on my team working on Diana's disappearance and, together, we prepared for Danaher to give his evidence against Colligan in court. DS Driscoll and myself had conferences with the CPS and our Prosecuting counsel, Mr Andrew Patience QC, who was supported by his colleague, Mr John Hillen. The law at that time meant that these criminal proceedings first had to go through the magistrates' court.

---

* Full details of the appeals related to this case are available under *Christian & Ords v. the Queen (Pitcairn Island) Privy Council (Oct 30, 2006)*: www.casemine.com/judgement/uk/5b2897ff2c94e06b9e19ec35

Provided the magistrates were satisfied with the evidence, they would send the case to the Crown Court.

Current procedures have now eliminated this type of court appearance and thus sped the entire process up quite a bit. Nowadays, once you are charged with murder, the case goes before the magistrate, you are remanded and the case is transferred immediately up to the Crown Court. So, if this case had happened today, Danaher would have been up before the Crown Court within a week.

The date of these proceedings against Colligan was set for 4 December. This was when Danaher gave his evidence for the first time. His appearance was good. He presented his version of events clearly and without hesitation.

January 1997. The start of a new year meant that the second anniversary of Diana's disappearance was fast approaching, and I instructed officers working on the investigation to spend time in the place from where our suspects had all originated, on the housing estate in Bromley. I wanted to keep people aware that the search for Diana was ongoing and, moreover, that we would do anything and everything to find her, even if this meant digging up every single back garden in the neighbourhood.

It was during this exercise that we received information about Fitzpatrick's plans for an armed robbery. He was now separated from his wife (who had commenced divorce proceedings) and was back in his flat in Bromley.

I informed colleagues in the MPS Robbery Squad about Fitzpatrick's planned robbery. I recall that conversation with them very cleary. They were too busy to take Fitzpatrick on. Their boss had prioritised identifying the last member of a team of armed robbers, who were operating from a large housing estate in the Bromley area. When I asked them to share some of the names they had identified with me, they did so reluctantly. I recognised several of those names. As far as I was concerned, there was only one man missing from their list.

'The missing name and last member of that team is Fitzpatrick,' I told them.

A week later, I received a telephone call from the robbery squad telling me that the team of robbers had been arrested, including Michael Fitzpatrick. He had held a loaded gun at the head of a young boy who happened to be in a building society in south-east London with his grandad when the robbery took place. Fitzpatrick was now remanded in custody to HMP High Down near the village of Banstead, Surrey.

Fitzpatrick was not a nice man, that much was evident. Any man happy to put a gun to a child's head and threaten the elderly for money was a danger to the public.

During this time, we were monitoring Colligan's communication in prison. It appeared that he was having marital problems. I decided this was the perfect opportunity to approach the wives of both Colligan and Fitzpatrick just in case either one of them might be willing to provide information to assist our investigation. Neither wife, however, no matter how unhappy, was willing to tell us anything about their husband. What did become clear, however, was the degree of concern Colligan's family had about his state of mind and his future.

In all cases, prisons are required to ensure that inmates are safe from self-harming and suicide. We took the decision to liaise with the Operational Partnership Team Police Advisers, who alerted Colligan's prison about his family's concerns. We were then notified by a member of staff in the security section of the prison that Colligan was receiving mail from a female outside his family and this developed into another line of enquiry. We were given access to this correspondence and could see that it was in the same handwriting as the letter we had found in Colligan's car. It was clear that Colligan and the 'pen-pal' female had been in an intimate relationship for some time.

At this point in the investigation, I still believed that someone involved in Diana's abduction could be in possession of her handbag and keys. Colligan may have confided in someone as to what he did with the keys to Diana's house and/or car. We knew that Colligan had had the keys, because he had driven the car to Lakeside and the vehicle had been locked. Because of this, I felt it was safe to consider the possibility that Colligan still had the keys somewhere. I didn't think he would have taken these items to his own home. Were they possibly located at the property of the lady writing to him? It was essential that we identify the female writing to Colligan for this reason.

Diana's handbag was also missing, which caused us a degree of confusion. Finding it would have helped us piece things together. Of course, it was unlikely that someone with bound hands would still carry a handbag, but Colligan or Danaher may very well have picked it up to take it (along with Diana) to the scrap metal shop.

What I was wondering was, when Colligan got to the scrap yard and Diana got out of the car, had he possibly picked up the handbag and put it down? Unlikely. He certainly kept the keys – we knew that because he was the one who drove the car away, so it stands to reason that he still had the handbag in the car when they went to Lakeside. We didn't see them carrying anything like a handbag in the video, however, and nothing was found in the car. Perhaps the handbag was thrown into a bin before the video caught them?

The point is, we needed to identify this lady. Colligan told us that if we got him out then he would tell us exactly what had happened, and he had indicated that the keys and handbag were somewhere safe. If this girl was writing to him in prison (and we knew it had been going on for quite some time, since we found the love letter in his car) her home could be the perfect place to hide Diana's keys and handbag!

It is worth mentioning that, at this point, Colligan was going to ask a judge in chambers to give him bail, because he had already served his sentence for the firearms offence. It was suggested to Colligan that if he was going to apply, he would need someone of good character to stand as surety that he wouldn't disappear. The person nominated for this role was his wife's brother.

Firstly, we needed to eliminate the possibility that the letters were not from Colligan's wife, and so I authorised my officers to speak discreetly ('discreetly' for obvious reasons) with his wife's brother.

As expected, on discovering that his sister was being cuckolded the brother-in-law was not too happy with what he read. Showing him the letters had been a sneaky tactic on our part, to be sure. We were well aware that the brother-in-law would refuse to stand as surety for

Colligan if the letters were from another woman, and the plan worked. As a direct result of that information, he refused to even consider standing as surety.

Secondly, he knew who the lady in question was and he shared this information with us. She had previously lived on the housing estate in Bromley.

We located her to a house in Bicester and continued to monitor communication between her and Colligan. Eventually, we decided to search the lady's house for Diana's keys and/or handbag. With the assistance of the Thames Valley police, we executed a search warrant at the property and discovered that the front bedroom had been converted into a cannabis growing facility. A false wall had been built in front of the bedroom windows and halogen lamps were in full use.

Unbeknownst to us, Colligan was now feeling the pressure in prison; not only had his wife commenced divorce proceedings but his girlfriend had been identified, arrested and her house had been searched. Thames Valley police dealt with her drugs offence. She was eventually charged and later appeared in court. But we still had not found Diana's handbag nor car keys.

Leads and pieces of information often filter through to us in the strangest of ways. On the morning of 5 March 1997, I was listening to the local radio whilst driving to my office at FHQ when the eight o'clock news headlines announced that Metropolitan police officers in Bromley had commenced a search in a garden. They were looking for the body of a millionairess. She had been missing for several months and a local man had been arrested in connection with this. I could not believe my ears. Because of the location of the housing estate where the MPS were digging, I was immediately convinced that it must be Diana they were digging up and not the MPS missing person they thought they were seeking. As soon as the news broadcast finished, I was on the car phone organising my team to meet in ten minutes in my office.

No one in the team had yet heard the news headline back at FHQ. There certainly had been a mix-up. Metropolitan Police were looking for the body of a millionairess who had recently disappeared from

Knightsbridge. An easy mistake to make when you receive titbits of information regarding a woman buried in a garden, I guess!

I tasked my team to get hold of whoever was in charge at the Bromley site and we did our best to explain that the body they were probably looking for was Diana, another multi-millionaire's ex-partner. In a way, the MPS's negative response was understandable because the source of their information had been from HMP High Down, which, let's face it, may not provide the most reliable or accurate pool of informants.

My team were not put off so easily and, after a quick check, they confirmed that Fitzpatrick was still on remand at HMP High Down. A message was sent to the officer in charge of the scene at Bromley, telling him that myself and two members of my team were about to attend the scene, in person.

It did not take us long to get to Bromley, but along the entire route I remained preoccupied and anxious, wondering what kind of reception we were about to receive there. The instant we arrived, however, my concern vanished, because the very first officer I spotted at the site was friend and colleague, Mr Andy Trotter. He had previously been a Kent police officer and was now a Commander for this area of London. (He would go on to become CC of the British Transport Police.)

We spoke to the officer in charge of the dig and quickly established that the suspect they had in custody was a man called Michael Howard, a lifelong friend of Fitzpatrick.

Over the course of that morning, the body of a female was recovered. It had been wrapped in a carpet. The victim had her hands tied together in front of her with plastic tabs. I was satisfied that we had found Diana but, of course, we had to formally identify her. Her keys, handbag and contents were still missing and a ring had been removed from her finger at some time prior to her burial.

Digging for Body Recovery – Sparking the Case Back to Life
The standard procedure followed by police officers and SOCOs in such situations is, firstly, to identify and secure the scene. Since this was an exterior location, it had to be protected from inclement weather by a tent. Video and photographs of the scene were taken, along with photographs of the surrounding area.

We were in the back garden of a mid-terrace house on a large housing estate. The only access to the rear garden was via a shared alleyway with the neighbouring house. The garden was poorly maintained and mostly covered in grass. Six-foot-high panelled fencing bordered both sides and two children's bicycles lay unattended at the bottom of the garden.

As soon as the dig began, initial soil samples were taken and the process was recorded on video from beginning to end. Every step of the dig's progression was photographed. The officers knew exactly where the dig was to take place in this case, because the suspect had pointed it out to them.

In such cases as this, soil samples are usually taken every few inches, but what would turn out to be the tip of a carpet was identified very quickly. Since the body was wrapped in a carpet, any leakage from the body was going to be contained in that carpet, so soil samples weren't necessary – we didn't need to establish how long the body had been buried, nor whether or not it was human.

The police team had been digging for about forty minutes prior to our arrival, and by the time I entered the back garden there were approximately ten police officers and SOCOs gathered around a very large hole in the ground. Although the rolled-up carpet was clearly visible, it took a further hour of digging before officers were able to lift it entirely out of the hole.

I asked for great care to be taken with the victim's hands, just in case there was any foreign DNA found under the victim's fingernails, so the hands were carefully protected with a plastic bag when the carpet containing the body was laid gently beside the ditch.

I could not see the body clearly but I was certain it would turn out to be Diana. I noted, with curiosity, that the corner of the carpet was damaged – it had an unusual slit in it.

The senior officer in charge of the dig was also managing the source of the information who had led us to this major development in our investigation. I made it clear to him that it was highly likely this would not turn out to be the female victim he had believed he was digging for. He was extremely professional and agreed to work together with me, acknowledging that once the post-mortem was complete, our team would take over the investigation as well as the prisoner, who was in their custody.

After consulting with HM Coroner for that area, the body of the female (still wrapped in the carpet and sealed in a standard body bag) was taken to a local mortuary. A leading forensic pathologist in the UK, Dr Richard Shepherd, with whom I had worked before, met us at the mortuary. Dr Shepherd has been involved with the investigation of many high-profile deaths.

Forensic pathologists are specialists who investigate deaths which have 'medico-legal' implications. The term 'medico-legal' refers to the study and application of medicine and scientific methods as evidence in legal cases e.g. cause of death in custody, murder, rape and other complex cases.

After the body was removed from the carpet, the carpet was sealed in plastic for examination. It was now a piece of evidence. The carpet stank, so once we had finished with it forensically (that is, taken all sorts of swabs and fibres off it), we took it to be cleaned, which made it much easier to handle. We needed to ascertain where it had come from, and check it against Fitzpatrick's properties. We found that there was a carpet missing from the lounge in his flat and the measurements fit exactly. This was how we arrived at the assumption of where it came from.

The body was dressed in clothing and boots identical to those Diana had been wearing the last time the children had seen her. The body was very badly decayed, so facial identification was not possible. There was a clear outline on the area around the mouth, indicating that some sort of covering had been over it, but it had either been removed, or rotted away. Skin samples were taken from around the mouth but nothing of evidential value was found. Organ samples were examined but, due to the state of the body, this also lacked evidential value.

It is strange that when I think of Diana, I do not see her face from the mortuary. I can still only remember her as the face from photograph we used on her Missing Person posters. Perhaps one day someone will explain this to me!

As the post-mortem examination continued, I grew more and more conscious of time passing. I had to keep reminding myself that there was a man in custody on suspicion of murder, and it was crucial that this be addressed. I was also concerned that the identity of the female would be leaked to the media.

Knowing already what the identity of the body would be, I prepared a statement in advance. The message was extremely clear.

'We have recovered the body of a female which matches the description of Diana Goldsmith. Mr McGookin is reasonably satisfied that it is her, but her identity is yet to be formally and scientifically confirmed.'

It was crucial, however, that Diana's family be the first to hear the news. Thankfully, my staff were on standby, back at our MIR, and ready to get in touch with her family when the time came. I decided that Diana's sister should be the first to be told, then Hatt, and finally Goldsmith. My decision to inform Goldsmith was two-fold. Firstly, it was only right that Diana's children be told. Secondly, the pressure on Goldsmith might encourage him to tell the truth at last. He was, in the minds of the investigation team, our main suspect. Only time would tell.

The post-mortem examination was completed but due to the decomposition of the body, cause of death was unascertainable. Dr Shepard did find evidence, however, that she had died a violent and unnatural death. In due course, Diana's identification was confirmed by a Forensic Odonatologist. The serial number on breast implants, which she had had in the past, provided additional confirmation of her identification.

The suspect, Michael Howard, was initially interviewed under caution by MPS officers. It was clear, during this interview, that he was willing to tell all, and to support the police investigation all the way. He was subsequently handed over to my team and taken to Kent.

Howard's story began back in January 1995 when his best friend, Micheal Fitzpatrick, rang him to tell him he needed his help because Fitzpatrick had stolen a large stash of cannabis and needed to bury it urgently, until such time as all suspicion of Fitzpatrick being responsible had passed. The men were life-long friends – Fitzpatrick had been best man at Howard's wedding – and Howard had never been in any trouble, so Fitzpatrick suggested Howard's back garden as the perfect place to hide it. Howard agreed, with few questions asked.

(Note: If what he said was true, then this certainly is a salutary lesson for us all, to question even those we trust!)

Fitzpatrick then asked him if he would come around and look after the scrap shop whilst he and his employee, Alex Whear, moved the gear. Howard was happy to comply with the request since his wife was at work and his children were at school. A perfect plan for Fitzpatrick – he could now bury the 'body' without fear of being disturbed whilst he did so.

Yet another burial was taking place – our third burial and second exhumation. Confused yet? Stay tuned.

That afternoon, Fitzpatrick and Whear returned to the shop, and Howard returned home. He made no mention of the burial to his wife or family. It was winter, in any case, so his rear garden was of no interest to the family.

About six weeks later, Fitzpatrick used Howard to look after the shop again, whilst he and Whear, supposedly, removed the drugs.

Spring and summer passed. The grass grew over the garden, and Howard thought no more of the favour he had done for his best friend. He even recalled that his daughter sunbathed on the exact spot where the burial had taken place.

As time passed for Howard and his family, he kept in touch with Fitzpatrick but nothing was ever said about the drugs. Howard genuinely believed that they had been dug up and removed, just as Fitzpatrick had promised him.

It came as no surprise to Howard when Fitzpatrick was arrested for armed robbery – he was well aware of his best friend's dubious background – but then, to his horror, Howard heard rumours about the police threatening to dig up people's gardens around the estate, in their search for a lady who had gone missing several years ago. Then Howard discovered that the lady who had gone missing was Fitzpatrick's wife's stepmother, and the terrible truth hit him all at once.

He felt utterly sick when he realised what an idiot he had been; he had blindly trusted his friend, Fitzpatrick, utter fool that he was. Howard was frantic. It was possible that there had been a body in his garden, not drugs. Worse still, it might very well still be there!

Howard described, in detail, how he arranged to visit Fitzpatrick in HMP High Down. The instant he saw Fitzpatrick he suspected something was amiss because his so-called friend could not make eye contact with him.

Apparently, Fitzpatrick apologised over and over, and yet admitted nothing.

'Sorry, sorry, sorry,' he repeated, whilst continuing to deny everything to his friend, insisting it was merely drugs that had been buried in his garden. Howard left the prison completely confused and in shock. He didn't know what to believe.

According to Howard, his life began to spiral out of control that day. He took to heavy drinking and his relationship with his wife went into serious decline. He started shouting at his children, something he would never have previously done. He failed to go into work and said he felt suicidal.

He described how he was alone at home drinking, when he took a large kitchen knife and went into his garden. He plunged his knife into the earth where Fitzpatrick had dug and, to his horror, saw the tip of a carpet. Howard described how he pushed the knife into the carpet and sliced through it. A ghastly smell had him reeling with nausea, so he pushed the earth and turf back into the hole and retreated into the house. His worst fears had become a reality.

Howard felt his life utterly falling apart after this. He was totally ruined, he was sure of it. His brother asked him several times what had caused such a change in him but he could not share his trauma with anyone. What Howard did not know was that whilst in HMP High Down, Fitzpatrick had put the word around that he was willing to pay someone to dispose of a body. Perhaps he was feeling remorse about how badly he had treated his friend. Perhaps he was merely concerned that his friend might crack under the pressure. In any case, sadly for Fitzpatrick, he chose the wrong people to ask. One of the inmates he approached was, in fact, a police source.

Michael Howard's nightmare started to come to an end in the early morning of 5 March 1997. When police officers arrived at his house at

0700 hrs, he knew immediately why they were there. He took them to his rear garden and pointed to the spot where the body was buried.

Unsurprisingly, Howard was arrested but, after both a full investigation of his version of events and consultation with the CPS, he was released from custody and treated as a prosecution witness.

Off the back of Howard's account, Alex Whear was also interviewed under caution. Whear distanced himself from any involvement in either the death of Diana or the burial of her body. On the day she was buried, he claimed that he'd left Fitzpatrick at the shop and gone off to dismantle a greenhouse for the scrap metal. He also claimed that he was not with Fitzpatrick on the day Fitzpatrick allegedly went to recover the 'drugs'. This was yet another area of frustration for us. We had no direct evidence that Whear had buried the body. Aside from the fact that, on both occasions, he was in the shop when Howard went to take care of the business, Whear could not (or would not) remember where the greenhouse was and the records of scrap metal purchase from that day did not stand up to scrutiny. No further action was taken against him.

Following the recovery of Diana's body, the case against Fitzpatrick and Colligan also took a turn when Colligan's associate, Andy Mills, agreed to be a prosecution witness regarding the events of Christmas Eve 1994. Bit by bit, we were building a stronger and stronger case.

At the end of March that year, Fitzpatrick was brought to Sevenoaks police station and interviewed under caution. He made no comment to the questions put to him and was then charged with Conspiracy to Abduct Diana Goldsmith, Conspiracy to Murder and the Obstruction of HM Coroner regarding the disposal of her body. He was remanded in custody to HMP Belmarsh, where he was graded as a High-Risk Category A prisoner. Let's not forget that he was also still facing charges of armed robbery and possession of a firearm.

The case for the prosecution was served on the defence solicitors, and a date was fixed for the magistrates to hear and consider the prosecution case. If they were satisfied that there was a case to answer, they would formally send the case to the Crown Court for trial. The date of these proceedings was fixed for 20 October 1997.

The most significant event of all was due to take place before that hearing. Diana's funeral was to be held near her sister's home in Trowbridge, Wiltshire.

In the days just prior to the funeral, I received a panicked telephone call from Diana's sister. Both she and the funeral director had received silent phone calls. The undertaker received two silent phone calls in the middle of the night. The number ID was located to the area where Goldsmith lived.

The phone calls to the funeral director turned out to be a faulty facsimile machine in a printing company in Edenbridge, which sent advertising merchandise during the night. The silent phone calls to Diana's sister were never traced. In any case, they ceased straight after they were reported to us.

The funeral, which DS Driscoll, DC Johnson and I attended, went ahead without further problems. This was the fourth burial (albeit a cremation) in this investigation.

At the end of the funeral service, which was only attended by Diana's sister, brother-in-law and ourselves, I was approached by the crematorium superintendent, who asked if we could remain behind for a few minutes. I agreed.

The superintendent came up to me after Diana's family had left.

'Sorry, Mr McGookin,' he said, 'but as we have had silent phone calls to the family and strange goings-on with the funeral director's telephone, I'm a bit worried. I'd be grateful if you could witness the actual cremation and thus confirm that her remains are cremated straight away. That way, no one can claim somebody broke into the crematorium and tampered with the body, or stole any of her DNA or anything.'

I thought it a very strange request but, at the same time, I thought, *What harm would it do to give him the reassurance he needs?*

'That is not a problem,' I agreed. 'We certainly will do. I'll just ask Lenny here to tell the family that we will be a little delayed but will be out in a couple of minutes.'

'Thanks very much,' the superintendent said.

All three of us, myself, DS Driscoll and DC Johnson, had experienced death from a police point of view, but none of us had ever witnessed a cremation from behind the curtain.

We were invited to go through two doors into the back room of the chapel. There were approximately ten coffins lined up, ready to be individually cremated. The cremator stood at the end of the room.

I led the way.

An eerie hush hovered in the space. It was particularly daunting, given the number of coffins around us. The three of us remained completely silent, all we could do was stare ahead, towards the cremator. We were out of our comfort zone, that's for sure, but we did our best to remain respectful and outwardly calm, trying not show how unaccustomed we were to such things.

All of a sudden, from behind the coffins, a massive, unkempt ginger-bearded man, dressed in a bright green boiler suit, jumped out in front of us.

'Boo!' he shouted.

The three of us practically jumped out of our skins. Apparently, this was the gentleman responsible for loading the coffins into the cremator. He had obviously spotted how uncomfortable we were and was either trying to make light of the awful situation or had a very wicked sense of humour.

We regained our composure and, after the crematorium super-intendent formally introduced us, we returned to our former, dignified stance and prepared to witness the cremation.

Identification checks were carried out, which involved checking the nameplate of the coffin. The crematorium worker turned out to be a very nice man. He handled everyone with care from there on in. He loaded Diana's coffin into the cremator. We stayed for several minutes whilst the flames engulfed the coffin and then we left. We were in dire need of fresh air and a change of scene following this task, I tell you!

I remember the faces of so many unfortunate, dead victims but one face I will never forget is the face belonging to that great idiot of a cremator.

It was around this time that we learnt that Goldsmith and his then wife, Sarah, had separated after Sarah discovered Goldsmith was having an affair with the widow of a close friend who had recently died. In addition to this, we were told that Goldsmith had purchased a book called *When Dad Killed Mom* by Julius Lester, and another book about the recovery of ancient bodies in Egypt. In most circumstances this would mean little, but in this case, it made us even more convinced that Goldsmith was indeed behind Diana's murder.

Later, I received a telephone call from Charlie Hatt. He was in hospital in Milton Keynes dying from cancer. This was tragic news. In any case, we still had to secure the evidence he had given us about the keys and did so in the form of a Dying Declaration.

> In the law of evidence, a dying declaration is testimony that would normally be barred as hearsay. In common law, however, such a declaration must be admitted as evidence in criminal law trials because it constitutes the last words of a dying person.

The rationale is that someone who is dying, or believes death to be imminent, has less incentive to fabricate testimony and as such the hearsay statement carries more weight and, therefore, sounder reliability.

The declaration was organised by DS Driscoll with the clerk of the local magistrates' court present. He had arranged for a nurse in the hospital, who happened to be a magistrate, to preside over the process with representatives from the prosecution and defence present.

Hatt died the following day. This was our third funeral and our fifth burial in the investigation.

Colligan

On 14 October 1997, I received a telephone call from HMP Elmley telling me that Ian Colligan had been admitted to Medway Hospital after having slashed his wrists. This may have been a genuine attempted suicide but it could equally have been part of a plan to facilitate his escape from custody. When the Prison Governor was informed of our concerns, his guards at the hospital were doubled until he was treated and subsequently returned to prison.

The committal proceedings began the following week, on 21 October 1997, and continued for several days. The additional charge of the murder of Diana Goldsmith was served on both defendants. Since Fitzpatrick and Colligan were already in custody, they were brought to court with armed escorts provided by the police and organised by the Operational Partnership Team Police Advisers. Barristers representing them asked that three witnesses, Danaher, Mills and Howard, give their evidence to the magistrates. This was agreed.

It was clear when Mills gave his evidence that Collagan was furious with him. As soon as this came to my attention, and with Mills' agreement, I authorised for all calls received on Mills' home telephone to be recorded for the duration of the proceedings.

Sure enough, when he returned to prison that evening, Colligan phoned Mills. Colligan threatened and abused Mills for giving evidence in this call and it was recorded. In court the following morning, an additional charge of 'Interfering with Witness' was served on Colligan. At the end of this process, both men were sent for trial on all charges. They were remanded in custody and sent back to their respective prisons. It is a criminal offence to intimidate witnesses in a manner that is likely to deter them from giving evidence or to influence their giving of evidence.

> Interfering with Witnesses is a serious offence and treated as criminal contempt of court, which has no maximum penalty. These types of offences are dealt with under UK Law by the introduction of The Criminal Justice & Public Order Act 1994 Section 551 (1) (2).

We now had to wait a year for their actual trial. Yet again, I did not expect much else could happen to affect this investigation. How wrong I was!

On the morning of 25 October 1997, I received a telephone call from a lady who identified herself as Ian Colligan's mother. She expressed concern about her son's welfare. She had apparently persuaded him to talk to me and asked if I would visit him in prison. I explained that either I or one of my officers could visit, but only if the CPS gave their consent. The

CPS did give their permission and DS Driscoll and DC Johnson visited Colligan in HMP Elmley. At the end of their meeting, they returned to my office and relayed the details of what had taken place:

The officers' identities were checked upon arrival at the prison, before they were taken through the standard search procedure. They were escorted through the prison to an interview room. Colligan was brought to the interview room and the prison officer informed him of his rights; he was not obliged to speak to the officers and he could leave the interview room at any time. Colligan agreed to see the officers and the interview commenced.

He explained to the officers that he believed the interview room had been bugged and their conversation would be recorded, and that he risked getting himself into more trouble if he made any admissions. He told the officers that he would not answer any questions verbally, insisting instead on writing his answers down on paper and showing them the answers.

He then produced a pack of cigarette papers and a small pencil.

'I'll do a deal,' he wrote, 'if you take me out of the prison.' He showed the cigarette paper to the officers before putting it in his mouth, chewing it a few times and swallowing. Colligan was told that they could not authorise 'a deal' and asked what type of deal he expected.

'I'll give you proof,' he wrote. 'I have hidden some important things.' Again, he put the paper in his mouth and swallowed it.

They asked him what it was that was hidden.

'I can take you to it,' he wrote. Swallowing the paper, once again.

This process continued with him refusing to reveal a thing unless he was taken out of the prison. Once more, the officers advised him that they could not arrange such a thing. The interview was concluded without any promises made.

Whilst it was tempting to get the correct evidence in place and to try and secure a conviction of the instigator and organiser of Diana's murder, I could not ignore the fact that Colligan had taken part in what must have been a terrible death. I could not stop imagining how frightened Diana must have been to have been confronted in her home, gagged, tied up and driven to her death in such a way.

After discussing this with DS Driscoll and DC Johnson, I referred the information to the Operational Partnership Team Police Advisers,

who advised the prison service that Colligan's status should be upgraded. He then became a Category A prisoner and was transferred to HMP Belmarsh.

On the morning of 18 November 1997, I was back in my office when I took a telephone call from HM Coroner's Office in Woolwich informing me that Ian Colligan had taken his own life in his cell at HMP Belmarsh. Death appeared to be self-inflicted; suspension by ligature. Ian Colligan's was the fourth funeral and sixth burial in this investigation.

In view of Colligan's death, the charges against him had to be formally endorsed by a judge at the Crown Court. Before I could give that evidence, I was required to identify Colligan's body. The following year, I gave evidence at Colligan's inquest, explaining the charges he had been facing, to a jury. The inquest jury returned a verdict of suicide.

I will always believe that Colligan took the coward's way out. If he had only told the truth – after all, he had an alibi in Danaher which could have proven he did not kill Diana. In saying nothing, they used the fact that he was the last person to see her alive against him. I looked at his face as he lay peacefully in the morgue, and simply wanted to shout at him, 'Wake up! Tell the truth, you fool.' Still to this day, when I think of his face, I shake my head, wishing I could turn his decision around.

Fitzpatrick's trial was fixed for 29 June 1998 at Maidstone Crown Court. The court building is located on the outskirts of the town centre and overlooks the River Medway. It is a relatively modern building. We were in court number 5. (I will never forget which court number we were in, this was our big day after all.)

All the courtrooms in this building are identical, and designed in such a way that members of the jury sit together, to the side of the presiding judge and opposite the witness box. Members of the public are permitted to sit in the courtroom. They are located beside the main entrance to the courtroom. Members of the press are also permitted into the courtroom. They are located beside the public seating. Barristers and solicitors are in the body of the courtroom. The dock which houses the defendants is located behind the barristers.

All our witnesses were ready for the trial to start on time, and Danaher was brought out of prison in order to give his evidence, but there was an intense air of suspense around the courtroom. It was out of the ordinary for a trial to start late. The prosecution barristers were present but the defence barrister, Mr George Carmen QC, was not. Fitzpatrick wasn't in the dock – he must have been down in his cell. Neither the judge nor the jury had come out. All these things put together meant that I had an opportunity to speak with our barrister, Mr Patience QC. Of course, you cannot interrupt them or speak with them once proceedings begin. It does happen, however. Later in this book, in the Kenneth Noye proceedings, you will read about how I interrupted at one stage of the proceedings. I got quite a rollicking over that at the time, but I was right to have done what I did.

Our barristers were always very relaxed. They were having a talk amongst themselves – most probably talking about horse-racing or sherry-drinking that night and things like that – when I leant over to speak with Mr Patience.

'What's going on here?' I asked. 'Why does there appear to be such a delay?'

Mr Patience had a lovely, laid-back manner. He tilted his head and peered over his glasses.

'A bit of plea bargaining, Mr McGookin,' he whispered. He never called me by my first name, this was just the way the barrister people were, always very polite. 'They are going to offer a deal.'

The moment finally arrived where people began shuffling back into the courtroom. Mr Patience spoke with Mr Carmen. They had a little whisper between them before the courtroom fell silent and the judge entered. Mr Carmen was invited to address the judge and in doing so, asked if he might be permitted to approach the bench.

The term 'approach the bench' is a formal legal phrase since 'the bench' is regarded as the sacred territory of the judge, and an attorney needs to ask permission to speak with the judge there, out of the hearing of the jury and members of the public and press.

This was granted to Mr Carmen, and once he returned to his position in the body of the court, the usher asked the two barristers whether they were ready for the jury to come back in. They nodded yes.

The jury returned but the judge told them that there was a legal issue which still had to be finalised and he ordered them back to their jury-room.

The courtroom was also cleared of members of the public and press, and Mr Carmen formally invited the judge to consider an application for a plea bargain in relation to the prosecution case against Fitzpatrick.

Plea bargains are defined as 'an agreement between the prosecution and the defence by which the accused agrees to plead guilty to a lesser charge in return for an offer by the prosecution'.* It is in fact the barristers who lead these negotiations and then seek agreement of the prosecution barristers, the CPS, the police, and (in some circumstances) the victim or their next of kin is also required. The presiding judge may also have a say on whether a plea is permissible.

The judge adjourned the proceedings for the remainder of the morning and I subsequently met with our counsel and our CPS representative.

Fitzpatrick was offering to plead guilty to four charges:

4. Conspiracy to abduct
5. Conspiracy to murder
6. Perverting the course of justice in respect to the disposal of Diana Goldsmith's body
7. Armed robbery.

In return, he was agreeing to give evidence against Goldsmith. On that basis, he would tell us his side of the story but only if it were agreed that a not guilty verdict to the murder of Diana Goldsmith was acceptable to the prosecution and to the court.

---

* www.oxfordreference.com/display/10.1093/oi/authority.20110803100331478

I was reticent about this because the only deal I wanted to accept was Fitzpatrick's outright admission to introducing Colligan to Goldsmith with the intention of abducting Diana, which therefore would have implied his culpability in taking steps which ultimately led to her death.

At the end of the day, however, the CPS and our barristers were still going to have to decide who it was that had a motive to kill Diana and, with all the facts of our investigation taken into account, everything indicated that Goldsmith was the one person who had motive.

Although Colligan could be said to have had a financial interest in killing her, this would still point the finger at Goldsmith. What would have been ideal, and what we would have preferred in the first place, was to have all the suspects, Goldsmith, Fitzpatrick, Colligan and Danaher, in the dock at the same time. Unfortunately, that was not going to happen; we needed Fitzpatrick's evidence as a witness if we were ever to get the CPS authority to bring Goldsmith to justice. Each party present in the decision-making process agreed that we should accept the plea, knowing he would at least get a lengthy custodial term and we could then go after Goldsmith.

When the court resumed at 1400 hrs, the jury was formally discharged. In their absence, Fitzpatrick pleaded guilty to all the offences, with the exception of murder. His plea of not guilty was accepted by the prosecution and ultimately by the judge. Fitzpatrick was remanded in custody and would be sentenced at a later date.

During these proceedings, I received a message that Goldsmith and his new girlfriend had taken a flight to Barbados with Goldsmith's youngest son and his girlfriend's daughter. We knew how incredibly wealthy he was and wondered if he would now try to use his money to disappear.

Days after the court hearing, in consultation with the CPS and Fitzpatrick's solicitor, DC Johnson and I visited Fitzpatrick in HMP Belmarsh. It was my first visit to this prison. Fitzpatrick was now convicted and awaiting sentence so he had been upgraded once again to High-Risk Category A.

We were not aware that just prior to Colligan's death, Fitzpatrick had successfully applied to the Prison Governor to be downgraded to

Category A status, in fact, but had had to wait until a cell became vacant in that particular section of the prison. He explained to us that he had received his transfer on the morning of Colligan's death and that he had been placed in the cell vacated by Colligan – the very cell where Colligan had taken his own life a few hours before!

In those days, security varied from prison to prison. During this visit I realised that Fitzpatrick was being held in what the prison authorities refer to as a 'prison within the prison'. The security in that facility is the highest in the country. It houses some very dangerous men. Simply checking-in to the prison is an experience in itself. One is forbidden to carry valuables, cases, telephones, writing paper or pens, etc. Everything you have with you is placed in a locker to which you are given the key. Obviously, you have no knowledge of what has been in the locker before you use it.

I carried our key with me. I did not notice the piece of cling film wrapped through the hole in the ring. After identifying ourselves, we went through standard security checks and searches – the fact that I was a senior police officer made no difference to the prison staff. We were escorted to an outside area where a prison minibus awaited us. It carried us around the prison until we reached the 'prison within the prison'. We were greeted by more staff and informed that we would have to go through yet another security check.

This check appeared to be fairly straightforward. We stood on a painted line, facing the other side of the room where a Weimaraner dog and its handler waited patiently for us. We were to walk towards the dog, one by one, as the dog walked towards us.

I must point out here that I am genuinely terrified of dogs. People often say to me, 'This/that is a lovely dog,' and I say, 'I don't like dogs.' My family often suggests it is time for me to get a dog, but I don't want a dog.

It probably goes back to my early days as a young Constable when, one cold winters night, I went to answer a complaint about a dangerous dog on a council estate in Gravesend. I remember it vividly because I got out of my car, wearing my great big Annex coat as well as a jumper, a uniform, a shirt and leather gloves. I went to the front door and could hear this blasted dog barking. I had been told that it was an Alsatian, which made it even worse for me. The lady opened the door.

'Keep that dog away,' I said. She opened the door more fully and this blasted dog came charging at me and jumped straight up on me. I threw my left forearm out to protect myself and screamed at it. The thing bit straight through my thick clothes and into my arm. It wouldn't let go.

She eventually called the thing off me and asked, 'Are you alright?'

'No,' I replied, 'I'm not bloody alright. That bloody dog of yours should be put down.'

I stormed off in agony. I was terrified as I got back into my police car to drove nervously to the station where my Sergeant, Dick Barton, was on duty.

'What are you doing back here?' he asked.

'That dog's bloody bitten me,' I said.

'Well, what did you do to upset the dog in the first place?' he asked.

'Don't speak to me like that, Sarge,' I said. 'I want that dog put down.'

The thing was that he was a former police dog handler, and soon after he returned to the dog section in his capacity as a Sergeant, so he had absolutely no sympathy with me whatsoever.

'Go up to the hospital and have a tetanus injection,' was all he said.

I did so but I will never forget that dog and, to this day, I am terrified of most dogs, especially Alsatians. When I pass one or am near one, I know they sense my fear and I imagine they have no compassion for me. It is an irrational notion, of course, but I believe they almost revel in the barely discernible tremble they register on my own face which further feeds my unease in their presence.

So, here I was in the jail, confronted with my greatest fear. DC Johnson went first with no problem. As I walked past the dog, however, it jumped upon me without so much as a growl or a bark (they are trained not to do so), signalling to the security officers that something upon my person was afoot.

'Sir, we are terribly sorry,' they said, 'but you will have to go back and walk across the room again please.'

DC Johnson fell into a fit of giggles upon seeing how extremely uncomfortable I was and, needless to say, the dog jumped up on me again. It was a very unnerving experience.

I was not too impressed by all this, and to make matters worse for me, DC Johnson, who had found it so uproarious the first time the dog had jumped up, was now in absolute fits of laughter. When you are the big boss and you see your DC lying on the floor, giggling like an idiot...I tell you, I was furious.

Eventually we established that the prison key and cling film were the culprits. The last person with that locker key must have secreted drugs into the hole of the key, wrapped it in cling film and handed it over to whoever it was they were visiting. I had reaped the very uncomfortable consequences of a remnant, just the slightest sniff, of some drug left on the key.

'I'm warning you, Lenny,' I smiled. 'Not a word of this to anyone.'

'Of course not, boss,' he replied, still chortling. 'I won't breathe a word of it.'

Back at our office, however, the story did leak out, and haunted me for the rest of my career and beyond.

Fitzpatrick

Eventually, we got to interview Fitzpatrick, but this interview was taking place in the High Security Wing of HMP Belmarsh so we were not permitted to having any writing material with us. This did not concern me as I would be making arrangements for Fitzpatrick to be transferred to our custody where he would make a full written statement. In any case, the initial interview did not last long so we had a clear recollection of the conversation. We made a detailed record of it once we returned to the office to put pen to paper.

Fitzpatrick told us straight off the bat that it was Goldsmith who had planned everything. The interview began with me asking Fitzpatrick to go back in time, to the first time he met Goldsmith. He told us that he had met Goldsmith's daughter from his first marriage, on a flight to Greece. They fell in love, and he was subsequently introduced to Goldsmith, along with the rest of the family. They married soon after and had a daughter. It was at this time that Goldsmith set Fitzpatrick up in his business as a scrap metal dealer.

He told us that Goldsmith had grown to utterly despise Diana, especially after they separated, which was when Diana moved into the house in Sevenoaks. He disapproved of her heavy drinking and his rancour only grew after the stream of endless grief she put him through in her determination to prevent him from seeing his children.

Fitzpatrick told us that in Colligan's presence Goldsmith had said, 'It's time she was taught a lesson.' This was not the first time this exact phrase had come up in our interviews – Danaher had also said it verbatim.

This is why we came to the conclusion that Goldsmith had indeed wanted Diana dead, and since Fitzpatrick was the only person he really trusted, it came as no surprise that he had told Fitzpatrick so outright.

Fitzpatrick then went on to say, 'He asked me if I knew anyone who could get rid of her, and I told him I knew someone, but they would want to be well paid. Goldsmith told me to, "Get it sorted."'

Fitzpatrick told us he asked Colligan to do it and Colligan agreed.

I challenged Fitzpatrick, asking him to explain exactly what Colligan was expected to do with Diana. He replied that he was to abduct her and give her a beating, in order to teach her a lesson. He then told us that this was originally planned to take place on Christmas Eve, since Goldsmith would be on holiday with the kids and therefore have the perfect alibi.

He then told us that Colligan and another guy called Andy Mills were paid to do it, but when it came to the job, Diana was not alone and so they abandoned the plan. Goldsmith was furious when Fitzpatrick rang him that night. When Goldsmith returned home from his holiday, he visited Fitzpatrick in the shop and told him to 'get it sorted'. Fitzpatrick then spoke to Colligan, who said it would be done.

'The day came when I knew they were going to do it,' Fitzpatrick said, 'and Colligan rang me to say they had got her and he was bringing her to the shop.'

Fitzpatrick rang Goldsmith, who said he was on his way over.

'Colligan arrived first,' Fitzpatrick told us. 'I had removed a panel of fencing at the side of my shop so Colligan could bring Diana straight into the out-building I used as a gym. When he arrived with Diana she had her hands tied to the front, and tape over her mouth. Colligan left immediately in Diana's car, saying that he was going to get rid of it. Diana went for Goldsmith as soon as he arrived at the gym, she went absolutely wild and grabbed him around the neck, despite her hands being bound.'

(As well as getting a more detailed description of events than we had before, this interview provided further evidence which fit our theory as to how Goldsmith had suffered the scratch marks on his neck.)

Both Fitzpatrick and Goldsmith held her down whilst she struggled. Then Goldsmith produced a plastic bag. Fitzpatrick was unable to recall whether Goldsmith had brought the bag with him, or if it was already in the gym, but Goldsmith most certainly put the bag over Diana's head and tied the ends in a knot. Fitzpatrick used the expression 'to calm her down' in his effort to minimise Goldsmith's reasoning as to why he did this.

Finally, Fitzpatrick went on to describe how Diana was killed.

They dropped Diana to the floor and held her there until she went quiet. According to Fitzpatrick, Goldsmith looked like a wild man in those moments. He kept swearing under his breath, calling her a 'fucking bitch'. After a few minutes, they realised she was still not moving. Fitzpatrick claimed that was the moment that he ripped the bag off her head and tore the tape from off her mouth, but she was dead.

He told us that Goldsmith lost it and stormed off muttering, 'Just fucking get rid of her.'

Fitzpatrick admitted to going home and lifting his lounge carpet up. He returned to the gym, wrapped Diana in the carpet from his flat, then moved the body to his mother's outdoor shed for a few days. It was after this that Fitzpatrick came up with the idea of burying her in his friend's garden.

It was at this point that our visit had to be terminated as we had used up our permitted time. As mentioned before, we had had no writing material with us for this first interview in the prison, so we arranged to get Fitzpatrick back into police custody in order to formally take his evidence down on paper. It is required that the suspect has an opportunity to read his statement to check it is recorded accurately and to sign it.

The process of getting a prisoner of this status out of a high security prison is not straightforward. With the assistance of the Operational Partnership Team Police Advisers, however, we were able to make the necessary arrangements.

Over the following week, the Prison Service delivered Fitzpatrick to Maidstone police station and his interview commenced. His solicitor was invited to attend the interview but he declined. His reasoning was simple: Fitzpatrick was on Legal Aid, which does not cover the costs of someone who is now turned witness.

I appointed DC Johnson to conduct the witness interview and take the statement from Fitzpatrick. My reasoning was that he had already heard what Fitzpatrick had told us in prison, and it was paramount we get all the finer details regarding Fitzpatrick's involvement accurately recorded.

This more detailed witness statement was taken over three days, whilst Fitzpatrick remained in our custody. It reached 103 pages. The vast majority of Fitzpatrick's evidence was consistent with what he had already told us in prison (and included information we already had from other sources) but he did alter some rather critical sections. It may seem that there is repetition in this account, but the facts became clearer as we put the final pieces of this complex jigsaw puzzle together and so the repetition is necessary.

Fitzpatrick's Written Statement

Fitzpatrick confirmed to the interviewing officer how he first met Goldsmith's daughter en route to a holiday destination when she was working as an air stewardess. They eventually fell in love, got married (despite Goldsmith's reservations about him) and had a daughter. Goldsmith knew Fitzpatrick had a criminal record but accepted him for what he was. Fitzpatrick was aware that Goldsmith was not married to Diana and that she had simply changed her name to Goldsmith by deed poll for the children's sake.

Despite them having children together, the relationship between Goldsmith and Diana was unstable and they eventually broke up in 1991. As we already knew there was a bitter dispute over the care and control of their son, though not the girls, and it ended up with the High Court giving custody of the child to Diana. Goldsmith provided Diana with the house in Sevenoaks and allowed her to keep the car but he never accepted the fact that he did not have control of his children (especially his youngest son).

The children were well cared for but the relationship between Goldsmith and Diana remained strained. Diana was abusive towards Goldsmith, particularly when she was drinking. Furthermore, the fact that she allowed her boyfriend (Charlie Hatt) to stay overnight in what Goldsmith still regarded as his property irritated him no end.

Fitzpatrick confirmed how during the summer of 1994, Goldsmith came to see him and ordered him to break into Diana's house, whilst she was away on holiday, with the objective to retrieve keys which

Goldsmith knew Charlie Hatt had dropped through the letterbox. It was that very night that Fitzpatrick visited the house, forced a window open, gained entry and got the keys, which had been left on the mat beneath the letterbox. He took them to a key-cutter close to his scrap metal premises, where he had a replica set of keys cut. DC Johnson subsequently interviewed the owner of that shop, during which his witness statement stated that he recalled making a copy of said keys, to the extent that he was able to provide copies of the uncut type of keys which he had made.

Fitzpatrick then returned the original keys back through Diana's letterbox and the replicas were delivered to Goldsmith.

A burglary was never reported to the police at the time, but as soon as this information came to light, the window through which Fitzpatrick said he gained entry was examined. Indeed, there was evidence of a previous forced entry so his story was corroborated.

Fitzpatrick then went on to explain how over that summer, Goldsmith told him he had had enough of Diana's behaviour and asked him outright whether he knew anyone who could 'get rid of Diana'.

Fitzpatrick asked Goldsmith exactly what he meant by this.

'Kidnap her,' Goldsmith replied, 'murder her and get rid of the body so I can have my children back.'

'I think Colligan would be prepared to do that,' Fitzpatrick replied. 'I'll come back to you, but he will want to be well paid for it. £20K at least.'

(Our investigations showed that Goldsmith withdrew between £1,000 and £3,000 cash from his account, on a weekly basis, over a long period of time. This proved that he did have the ability to hold £20,000 in cash.)

'Get it sorted,' Goldsmith had said. 'And by the way, if he's your guy, I'm low on Prozac. That woman has given me such a bloody headache – I need some more.' (Fitzpatrick stated that he had supplied Goldsmith with stolen Prozac pills in the past. They had allegedly helped him with the depression Diana had caused and that's when he had originally introduced Goldsmith to Colligan, as his supplier of Prozac.) 'Get it done over Christmas because I'll be with the kids in my villa, which means Diana will be on her own.'

Fitzpatrick confirmed that when Colligan agreed to abduct Diana for Goldsmith, Goldsmith agreed to pay him £20,000 and Fitzpatrick arranged for Colligan to meet with Goldsmith again. Fitzpatrick claimed he was not involved in what was to happen and was not present when money was handed over to Colligan.

Fitzpatrick said he became aware that the job was to be done on Christmas Eve, when Goldsmith would be abroad, and that he gave Colligan the keys to the house. He knew that Colligan had recruited a guy called Mills to help him but Colligan phoned him on the actual night and told him that the job had to be postponed, on account of some unexpected house guests at Diana's place. When Fitzpatrick called Goldsmith and told him what had happened, Goldsmith was not happy.

'You owe me big time,' Goldsmith had said, when he visited Fitzpatrick at his shop after his holiday at the villa. 'Get it sorted.'

Fitzpatrick then spoke to Colligan, who assured him the job would indeed get done.

It was at this point in his witness statement that Fitzpatrick changed the story he had relayed to us in prison. This adjustment in his story was not good news for us.

Fitzpatrick had originally told us that he knew the job was to be done early one morning and that, on that day, he got a phone call from Colligan telling him the job was done. Fitzpatrick then rang Goldsmith to inform him that the job was done. Goldsmith didn't ask any questions, he simply hung up.

Now, however, in Fitzpatrick's new rendition of the story, he jumped forward two days to when he was working in the scrap metal shop. He was now telling us that Colligan had pulled up in a white van and came into the shop in an utter panic, and told Fitzpatrick that he had the woman's body in the back of the van and wanted Fitzpatrick to get rid of it.

Fitzpatrick said he was annoyed by this but told Colligan to put the body in the gym. Colligan moved the body and left. Fitzpatrick then returned to the original version of the story about how he wrapped the body in the carpet and disposed of it in his friend's garden.

At the end of the interview, Fitzpatrick read and signed his statement. He agreed to give evidence if Goldsmith was charged with either her killing or conspiracy to kill her.

I was not in the least bit happy after reading this new statement. Fitzpatrick was firmly placing the blame for Diana's death on Colligan (who was, of course, now dead). He did re-state that this course of action was on Goldsmith's orders, but this time he made no mention of Danaher. He appeared to be giving Goldsmith an avenue to escape going to prison for life.

My thoughts once more turned to Goldsmith. Where exactly in Barbados was Goldsmith, during the time that Fitzpatrick was making his new witness statement? We knew he was staying in a villa he had rented at the Almond Beach Village. From an investigation point of view, though, we needed to know his exact movements and whether he made any plans to travel elsewhere. We liaised with his credit card company who informed us, within minutes, of all transactions he had made. We subsequently monitored his proposed flight back to England.

Whilst we were doing this, the news we had waited for arrived: the CPS had given us approval to charge Goldsmith with the murder and conspiracy to murder Diana.

Goldsmith's Trial
Goldsmith and his party were due to return to Gatwick Airport at 0900 hrs on the morning of 10 July 1998. Unbeknownst to him when he boarded the flight in Barbados, he would be met at the other end by DS Driscoll and DC Johnson.

This was also a special date for our enquiry team because Danaher was now the longest serving remand prisoner in the country. He had been held in custody for over two and a half years but was yet to give evidence against Goldsmith. Whilst in custody, his legal team decided that he should be sentenced sooner rather than later and a judge at Maidstone Crown Court agreed.

He had previously pleaded guilty and was now, finally, sentenced to five years imprisonment. He was subsequently transported to yet another prison for his own safety.

Meanwhile, at Gatwick Airport, my officers boarded the recently landed plane with the assistance of several uniformed officers from Kent and Sussex. All other passengers were prevented from leaving the aircraft, including the President of Antigua and his entourage. Goldsmith was arrested. He tried to resist arrest but was swiftly removed from the aeroplane in handcuffs. Goldsmith's son and luggage were left with his girlfriend.

Goldsmith was transported to Tonbridge police station, and later that day he was interviewed in the presence of his solicitor. He declined to answer any questions but was charged with the murder of Diana Goldsmith. He appeared before Maidstone Magistrates' Court and was remanded in custody, despite an application for bail. He sacked his solicitor immediately.

His new legal team made a further application for bail to a Judge in Chambers at Maidstone Crown Court but that was also refused.

Despite further applications for bail at the High Court in London, Goldsmith remained in custody for over six months. In January 1999, however, following some smart tactics by his legal team, a judge sitting alone at the High Court was persuaded to grant him conditional bail. He was required to deposit £1 million worth of shares to the court and was forced to obtain three sureties of several hundred thousand pounds each.

Goldsmith's trial was due to start on 29 April 1999 at Maidstone Crown Court. Danaher was produced from HMP Dartmoor in Devon and, yet again, he gave his evidence. Since he had never met Goldsmith, there was no real challenge to his evidence. Then he started the long journey back to Devon.

The prosecution's next witness was Fitzpatrick. He came into the courtroom handcuffed and escorted by three burly prison officers. The handcuffs were removed but one prison officer stood by the witness box as his evidence began.

He was smartly dressed and started off quite well, appearing calm as he took the oath, swearing on the Bible, 'To tell the truth, the whole truth and nothing but the truth.'

When asked if he had pleaded guilty to a charge of conspiracy to murder Diana Goldsmith, he simply replied, 'Yes.'

He described his relationship with his father-in-law Goldsmith in detail.

It was then that Fitzpatrick recalled the information about supplying Goldsmith with Prozac and introducing him to Colligan, who had access to Prozac. When Goldsmith asked Colligan if he knew anyone who would get rid of Diana, Fitzpatrick replied that he had told Goldsmith he did indeed know someone: Colligan. This is the point at which the fee of £20,000 was put to Colligan. He replied that this was the amount he believed the fee had been but he insisted that he was never involved in the actual transaction.

As we know, Fitzpatrick had admitted to talking to Goldsmith about burgling Diana's house, taking the keys to get them copied, giving them to Colligan just before Christmas and knowing that Colligan had planned to get her on Christmas Eve.

Fitzpatrick was then asked about the events of the day Diana disappeared from her house. He said he had nothing more to do with the abduction but that Colligan did phone him to tell him that he had got her. He admitted that he rang Goldsmith to pass this information on.

The prosecution put to him that Danaher had told the court that he and Colligan took Diana to his shop, with Danaher getting out of the car en route, leaving Colligan to take Diana to the shop.

Fitzpatrick disagreed, claiming he did not see Diana until Colligan brought her to his shop and that she was already dead.

On hearing this, and with the agreement of the prosecution, the defence barrister, Mr Timothy Langdale QC, made an application to recall Danaher in order to clarify the evidence regarding Diana being taken to Bromley. This application was allowed and the problem was passed on to me and my officers. It was up to us to find out where Danaher was and, given that he would now be located somewhere between Maidstone and Dartmoor, the case was adjourned until the following day.

Danaher eventually returned to HMP Dartmoor only to be told he was going back to Maidstone the following morning. I don't think he was happy about this – to say the very least.

The following morning, we were all back in the Crown Court building when a tannoy announcement requested the officer in the case of Goldsmith to please visit the cell area. I knew exactly what that was for. Danaher had arrived back and was irate. I sent my Office Manager and colleague PC Bob Kelly to go and placate him.

As the trial resumed, I sensed Fitzpatrick starting to squirm in the witness box. He was still being questioned by the prosecution, and seemed very uneasy.

I noticed some members of the jury turning to one another, with perplexed looks on their faces, whispering amongst themselves from time to time (something jury members don't usually do) as if to say, 'Hmmn, that's strange,' or 'I don't believe that.' They were clearly questioning his overall credibility.

The prosecution case continued, and Fitzpatrick related his version of events in detail, regarding the disposal of the body in his best friend's back garden. He had passed the point where he had changed his part of his story (from what he said in prison to what he said in his statement) and was suddenly confident again. It was clear that he was now telling the court something which he knew to be true.

The prosecution case finished, it was now the defence barrister's turn.

Mr Langdale QC looked directly at Fitzpatrick and slowly rose to his feet. He started his cross-examination of Fitzpatrick by accusing him of being dishonest and lying to the court. It was put to him that Danaher had already given an account of what happened when Diana was abducted, and that he was now back in the court building simply to clarify the exact details.

Fitzpatrick interrupted the barrister at once. 'I have never heard Danaher's evidence,' he shouted, in an extremely aggressive manner.

Mr Lyondale QC looked directly at Fitzpatrick. 'You have heard Mr Danaher's evidence in the magistrates' court,' he said quietly, before adding, 'and you must be lying now because it was, in fact, you who killed Diana.'

Fitzpatrick began cursing. 'I've been fucking-well set up for something someone else has done. It ain't fucking me.'

'Mr Fitzpatrick,' the judge said, 'control your language in my court.'

Fitzpatrick calmed down a little but he could not entirely regain his composure. Eventually, he pointed at Goldsmith sitting in the dock.

'Get him to tell you the truth,' he shouted. Again, he was warned by the judge but it did no good. He failed to offer any further clear or useful evidence. In any case, it was too late; his credibility in that courtroom had all but diminished.

We knew deep down that his very first version, the rendition we had heard in prison, was the real sequence of events, but those were not the events presented before the court today. Fitzpatrick's demeanour undermined everything he had formerly said, even the truthful parts of his story.

Mr Langdale QC remained professional and calmly sat down. The judge asked the prosecution if they wished to put any further questions to the witness.

Mr Patience QC stood up and replied, 'No more questions to ask, Your Honour.'

Fitzpatrick's time as a prosecution witness had finally come to an end; any goodwill offered to him had gone. He was handcuffed in the witness box before being taken out of the courtroom by the prison officers and returned to prison.

The atmosphere in that courtroom was electric. The jury looked startled, baffled. The courtroom fell silent. The judge asked if Mr Patience QC wished to call any more evidence. No, he said, he did not. That was the case for the prosecution.

Since the prosecution evidence had been completed, Mr Langdale QC seized his opportunity to tell the judge that he had a legal submission. The jury were excluded from the courtroom whilst Mr Langdale QC made a 'no case to answer' submission to the judge. The QC was able to undermine everything Fitzpatrick had said, he weakened the case against Goldsmith and, as such, that there was no case for Goldsmith to answer.

No Case to Answer to a criminal offence is dealt with under the Criminal Procedures Rules and were tested in a famous case recorded as R v Galbraith 73 as follows:

(a) where the judge comes to the conclusion that the prosecution evidence, taken at its highest, is such that a jury properly directed could not properly convict upon it, it is his duty, upon a submission being made, to stop the case.

There is a second limb to this ruling, (b) which deals with some evidence, but it is so poor that it would be unsafe to leave it to the jury.

Much to my disappointment, the judge ruled that the case was 'not safe' and therefore, the trial should not continue. The trial judge, Mr Justice Newman, allowed the application, recalled the jury and instructed them to find Mr Goldsmith not guilty, stating that it was 'unsafe' to continue the trial.

'The prosecution,' he said, 'must accept that the jury is entitled to reject the explanations which Michael Fitzpatrick has tended in the witness box and thus conclude that Michael Fitzpatrick did, or may have, murdered her.' He went on to refer to Goldsmith directly, saying, 'Despite ordering him to be acquitted, by behaving the way he did, he brought suspicion upon himself.'

The jury appeared stunned and the police team were devastated. They sat silently in the court, shaking their heads in disbelief. We all did. Disappointment weighed heavily on every brow, as weary eyes followed Goldsmith walk free from the court that day.

Once outside the court, I was asked for my views on the ruling.

'The prosecution,' I said, my heart sinking, 'maintain that no one other than Mr Goldsmith had a motive and, whilst we are hugely disappointed, we have to respect the judgement of the court.'

Post-Verdict – More Dead Bodies

Fitzpatrick was subsequently sentenced to ten years' imprisonment for the armed robbery offence and a further seven years for conspiracy to murder Diana Goldsmith. This sentence would be served consecutively, and amount to a total of seventeen years' imprisonment. He appealed against this sentence on the basis that he had not been given credit for his pleas of guilty and for giving evidence on behalf of the prosecution. His total sentence was reduced to fourteen years' imprisonment.

His wife divorced him and, once he was eventually released from prison, he returned to his life of crime, carrying out a series of armed robberies in Sussex. On 10 February 2011, armed police officers challenged him whilst he was in the process of committing another robbery. He produced a handgun from his waist-band and was shot by the police as he discharged his gun. He died soon after, bringing the burial count in this enquiry to seven and funeral count to five.

As mentioned earlier, Danaher was sentenced to five years' imprisonment but was given credit for:

- Pleading guilty to the charge of Abducting Diana Goldsmith
- Giving evidence on behalf of the prosecution.

Having served over half his sentence on remand, he was released from prison on parole in 1999. He moved to Hampshire, where he believed that all he had to do was to mention my name when he got into trouble with the police. He often suggested the police get in contact with me, assuming I would arrange for his immediate release. Sadly for him, he was mistaken about that. I took several such telephone calls in the years after his release and my reply to every one of them was simple.

'If you have evidence to charge him,' I said, 'then you must charge him.' Which they did on several occasions.

Goldsmith returned to live in his mansion in Sevenoaks. His wife, Sarah, divorced him. He died of natural causes in 2018. Here lies our eighth burial and sixth (and final) funeral in this tale.

Some believe that Goldsmith now stands before the greatest judge. Others, myself included, believe he got away with murder.

I did not see Derek Goldsmith after he had died, but I will never forget the smug look he had on his face as he stood in the dock at the Crown Court, knowing full well he was about to walk away, scot-free, from a life sentence for the murder. There we have the all-too-common unrepentant face and brutal nature of crime.

So where did I go next in my career? My old colleague, Nic Biddiss, retired as Head of the MCD and our CC appointed me to that position. Upon doing so, he told me that I was, personally, to take over the 'M25 Road Rage' case involving Kenneth Noye. I had met Noye many years before, after he was arrested for killing a policeman. Here we go again.

5

ROAD RAGE ON THE M25

The story about my dealings with the now notorious English criminal Kenneth James Noye relates to two killings, eleven years apart, of two men. It is subsequently split into two parts. Much has been written and broadcast about both these deaths, but the depth with which I will take you behind the scenes of these major criminal investigations is not commonly known or broadcast. These stories are entirely factual.

In both cases, there are victims left behind amidst the many family members and friends who still grieve the loss of their loved ones. I will always bear this in mind, however, I will still include several humorous and serendipitous incidents which took us by surprise along the way.

Part One

In Memory of DC John Fordham

By January 1985, I was a DS at Dartford police station. I had moved house from Tunbridge Wells to the village of Hartley, which is adjacent to the A20/M20 motorway and lies close to the village of West Kingsdown and the world-famous Brands Hatch Racing Circuit. I was the on-call detective for the subdivision on the weekend of 25 January. Things were pretty quiet on the Friday, and remained so, well into Saturday. I left work at around 1830 hrs but, within about half an hour after arriving home, I received a telephone call from the police station informing me that a Metropolitan police officer had been stabbed at a large, detached house called Hollywood Cottage in School Lane, West Kingsdown.

The scene was a ten-minute drive from my home. By the time I arrived, the location was swarming with scores of MPS and Kent Police vehicles with their blue lights flashing, police dogs and handlers, uniformed officers and plainclothes officers, a helicopter overhead and an ambulance leaving the scene. It appeared to be total chaos, so I didn't even try to access the scene. I drove my car to the nearby Swanley police station and rang the force Control Room (FCR) to ensure that our Divisional Commander, the on-call Senior Detective for the force and duty Assistant CC (who oversee all police activity in the county) were aware of what was happening. I also suggested the FCR inform the MPS that the incident was to be controlled from Dartford police station with a briefing facility at Swanley police station.

I soon received a message from the FCR informing me that an unknown male had left the scene of the incident and two other people, a man and a woman, had been arrested, and police staff at Swanley police station awaited their arrival. I telephoned my general office over at Dartford police station to prevent any of my officers going off duty but there were only two officers there – DC Barry McAllister and Temporary DC Paul Gladstone. I instructed them to come over to the Swanley area in an unmarked police car and head towards West Kingsdown to commence searching for an unknown male, travelling on foot. This resulted in an excellent piece of policing.

My officers travelled along the A20 road from Swanley towards Brands Hatch and the village of West Kingsdown. They saw several MPS marked vehicles in the area and spotted a middle-aged man on the opposite side of the road, trying to hitch a ride as traffic passed. They turned their car around, and as they approached him, he started thumbing a lift once again. They pulled alongside him and asked him where was he going.

'Dartford,' he replied.

They told him they were headed that way themselves and suggested he get in the back of the car. Once he was in the car with the child-lock on, they identified themselves and instructed him to put his hands on the top of the front seat, which he did. He was quickly handcuffed and told that he was under arrest in connection with an event which involved a stabbing. He identified himself as Brian Reader and denied any knowledge of the incident. They informed our FCR, who confirmed this was the man who was believed to have fled the scene of the stabbing.

Reader was taken to Swanley police station and later that evening he was transferred to Dartford police station, where he was interviewed by officers from the MPS. The following day he was taken into the custody of the MPS and moved to a London police station.

Although my DI, David Clapperton, was not on duty that weekend, I knew he would want to know about something as serious as an on-duty police officer from another force being stabbed in our area, so I phoned him.

I still only had limited details about the incident, but as MPS officers started turning up at Swanley police station, I learnt that the officer who had been stabbed had been carrying out surveillance in the grounds of Hollywood Cottage and that his name was John Fordham. I was also told that the man and woman who had been arrested were Kenneth Noye and his wife, Brenda Noye. Brenda Noye was detained at Swanley police station. Kenneth Noye was initially taken to Swanley police station but, because his wife was there, the Custody Sergeant decided to keep the pair separated. Noye was subsequently taken to Dartford police station.

I had previously heard of Kenneth Noye but I'd never had any dealings with the man. He was believed to have been involved with the criminal fraternity in London, but had not come to the attention of local officers.

Over the following hour, as officers gathered at Swanley police station, I discovered that a police surveillance operation at Noye's home address had been going on for several weeks. He was linked to a major robbery at Heathrow Airport, where millions of pounds' worth of gold bullion had been stolen. I also learned that Noye was believed to be involved in the smelting down and disposal of the gold and that Noye's dogs had been running loose and barking around the garden of Noye's property. They had then attacked someone who turned out to be the victim, DC John Fordham. I later found out that Noye had armed himself with a knife before leaving his house to go in search of whoever was disturbing the dogs. This was when he stabbed the officer.

I waited in the CID general office at Swanley for updates, aware that senior officers were keen to be kept well informed. It had just gone 2030 hrs when the phone rang. I picked up and identified myself to the caller.

'Hello,' said a female voice on the end of the line. 'I am calling from Queen Mary's Hospital. I regret to tell you that John Fordham has died from his injuries.'

'Oh, my goodness,' I said. I thanked the lady for the information and told her that I would deal with the appropriate authorities immediately.

By now, the canteen area of the police station was full of MPS uniformed and plainclothes officers. An Inspector was in the process of organising his staff and I quietly introduced myself before informing him of the dreadful news that their fellow officer had died. The poor man looked totally shocked. His eyes glazed over.

'Would you like me to inform your officers?' I asked.

Given the nature of the news it came as no surprise to me that he was left speechless. He simply nodded. 'Yes, please,' he said. 'That might be the best idea.'

'Ladies and gentlemen,' I announced, 'may I please have your attention.' It was almost eerie how quiet the room fell. None of these officers knew me but they all looked over. 'It is with deep regrets,' I said, 'that I have to inform you that your colleague has died.'

The suspended lull only lasted a few seconds before a mix of distressed crying and cursing rippled across the room. It was evident in that moment just how many of these people had worked alongside the late officer, and knew him well. There was little I could do aside from leave them with their grief.

I headed over to nearby Dartford police station where the two main suspects, Reader and Noye, were detained. I met my Divisional Commander Chief Superintendent, Brian Kendall, in the back-parking area of the police station. I had worked closely with Mr Kendall over several years when he was a Detective Superintendent (DSU); we had a terrific professional rapport. He was the senior officer who had recommended me for promotion to Sergeant. Later in my service, he recommended me for promotion, once again, to Inspector.

'Hello Dennis,' he said, 'what the bloody hell is going on here?'

I updated him on all I could. 'The officer died, sir,' I told him.

We walked through the police station together. My office upstairs had filled up with senior officers: the Head of the CID for the force, Detective Chief Superintendent (DCS) Duncan Gibbons, DSU David Tully and several other officers, whom I rightly assumed were senior MPS detectives. My colleague, DI David Clapperton, and our Divisional DCI, Peter Humphries, arrived soon after, followed by the arrival of our Assistant CC, Mr Anthony Coe.

One of the Kent senior officers decided to hold a meeting (from which myself and DI Clapperton were excluded) in a private office next door. After about fifteen minutes I was summoned into the meeting and told to accompany an MPS Commander to the cells, to speak with the arrested man, Kenneth Noye.

I did not know this MPS Commander and he never introduced himself to me, but what was about to take place was the most uncomfortable prisoner visit I have made throughout my entire career.

I unlocked the cell door and allowed the Commander to step into the cell in front of me. Noye was sitting on the bed of his cell, sporting a black eye. As soon as he saw the MPS Commander he stood up, coolly addressing the senior officer by his first name. The two men shook hands.

'I didn't know the guy was a policeman,' Noye told the Commander (referring, of course, to the late DC Fordham). Their conversation only lasted a few minutes. I was shocked that they knew each other and wondered about the handshake! It ended with MPS Commander informing Noye that he would be going back to the MPS to be dealt with.

The Commander continued to ignore me completely as we exited Noye's cell and walked away, down the corridor.

Well, at least I'll never see either Noye or the MPS Commander again in my life, I thought.

How wrong can you be!

I returned to my office whilst the meeting of senior officers was breaking up. The majority of the MPD and Kent senior detectives left the station. DI Clapperton and I remained behind for a brief update from DCI Humphries. It turned out that our ACC agreed that the investigation into the death of DC Fordham should be dealt with by the MPS, as the police operation was being linked to the theft of gold in the 1983 Brink's-Mat gold bullion robbery at Heathrow Airport. The crime scene, however, would be searched and forensically examined by joint Kent Police and MPS teams.

Much has been written and reported in books, newspapers and throughout the media regarding the events of that night. For me, however, that night was about a brave, undercover police officer who lost his life doing his job, and the unbearable journey through grief which his family, friends and colleagues were about to embark on.

Kenneth Noye, Brenda Noye and Brian Reader were all charged with the murder of DC John Fordham and remanded in custody. The case against Brenda Noye was subsequently dropped by the Crown Prosecution Service, based on her claim that she was inside her house at the time of the incident, away from her husband and from Reader. Only Noye and Reader stood trial for DC Fordham's murder. (The charges of conspiracy to handle stolen bullion and conspiracy to fraudulently evade VAT against both men were dealt with separately, after their murder trial.)

The murder trial opened in November 1985 at the Old Bailey, London. The trial judge ordered that the jury of seven men and five women be given twenty-four-hour witness protection. Noye admitted killing the officer but claimed that he was acting in self-defence because the officer was wearing a ski-mask and a camouflage jacket at the time, and Noye believed he was being attacked. Reader was seen by an officer approaching the scene kicking DC Fordham, before fleeing. Every aspect of the prosecution case was challenged by the defence on the basis that Noye acted in self-defence.

In his summing up, the trial judge explained to the jury that Reader could only be found guilty if the charge of murder was proven against Noye, and if Reader had assisted or participated in the assault on the officer.

The jury retired, returning twelve hours later with a verdict of not guilty on both men. Despite being acquitted, both men remained in custody to await their trial for the conspiracy to handle stolen bullion and to fraudulently evade VAT.

This trial commenced in May the following year. Both defendants were joined in the dock by five other defendants charged with the same offences. The trial judge told the jury that, given the nature of the complex conspiracy, this case was likely to last several months.

'You need to be fair, decisive and courageous,' he said, 'when the time comes for you to retire and consider all of the evidence presented before you.'

Eventually, on 24 July 1986, the jury returned their verdicts. Noye, Reader and one other defendant were found guilty on both charges.

'I hope you all die of cancer,' Noye shouted at the jury, thus showing his true colours. The other defendants were acquitted of all charges. Noye was sentenced to a total of fourteen years' imprisonment and Reader sentenced to eight years' imprisonment.

After sentencing, Noye was served with a one-million-pound writ for VAT evasion and a High Court writ from the Inland Revenue claiming almost £1 million in back tax. In a civil action brought by the loss adjusters of Brink's Matt insurers, £3 million was recovered from Noye, including the property at Hollywood Cottage, whilst he was in prison.

Noye was released from prison in the late summer of 1994 after serving eight years. He went to live with his family in the town of Sevenoaks.

In respect to DC John Fordham, a police memorial stone was laid on a small green at the top of School Lane at the junction with the A20 in the village of West Kingsdown.

Part Two

Britain's First Road Rage Murder

19 May 1996

What driver can honestly say that someone else's driving has never frustrated them on the road? We have all experienced it, that's for sure, but few people are so overwhelmingly triggered by their frustration that they act upon the urge to get physically violent.

Road rage was a hot topic in the nineties. It was common for the press to cover stories of people driving aggressively and shouting abuse out their windows. At this stage, however, to my knowledge no lives had been lost as a result of such behaviour.

I had reached the rank of DCI by 1996 and was working as an SIO in the Major Crime Department. Just after lunchtime on Sunday, 19 May 1996, I was paged with a request to contact the Force Control Room (FCR) as a matter of urgency, following a stabbing on the M25 motorway at the junction with the M20 motorway.

I was the duty on-call SIO for the force. The duty on-call senior detective, who had an overview of all aspects of crime across the county, was my colleague DSU John Grace, who lived in East Kent.

It was our force policy that only the senior detective on duty had the authority to call out an SIO. John had been alerted to the incident and requested that I attend the scene, since I was only twenty minutes away and it was at a location I knew well.

I requested for the FCR to inform the SOCOs and for a S/SOCO to meet me at the scene. A S/SOCO's role is to liaise with the SIO and agree a forensic strategy for a particular incident. They deploy and supervise SOCOs, ensure that there are no cross-contamination issues, coordinate forensic samples taken from scenes and prioritise submissions to forensic laboratories.

Traffic was heavily congested on the approach to the scene. A quick manoeuvre on the hard shoulder, with headlights blazing, allowed me to reach the slip road and park my car safely. It should be noted that in today's modern smart motorways, where hard shoulders are fast becoming a thing of the past, it is unlikely I would have managed to get through. The incident was on a large roundabout above the M20 motorway where it joins the A20. It has four approach slip roads and four exit slip roads to and from the roundabout and is often described as one of the busiest roundabouts in Europe.

I parked my car on the edge of the roundabout and when I got out, I walked towards a uniformed Sergeant from my force. He told me that the victim had been stabbed and the situation did not look good.

I began assessing the situation as soon as I arrived. An ambulance had its blue lights flashing as it pulled away from the scene. Numerous marked police vehicles from both Kent and the MPS were parked at angles around the roundabout. A large milk-tanker was parked on the opposite side. A dark-coloured SUV sat unattended, by a set of traffic lights. A small red Bedford Rascal van parked behind it had damage to the rear offside but there was no other evidence of a collision. The scene was best described as chaotic, with traffic trying to pass the abandoned vehicles and several television news vans with satellite dishes on board manoeuvring their way to the nearside lane of the roundabout.

The weather conditions on this May afternoon were dry and cloudy, with a gentle chilly wind. At the top of the slip road and upon the roundabout, however, the wind was significantly stronger and colder. There was no rain, which was at least one godsend.

I instructed uniformed officers to seal off the roundabout completely so an actual 'crime scene' could be properly established and preserved. This should have been done much sooner. Whilst officers carried out this order, news reporters and photographers began coming out of the woodwork! Several times we asked them to leave so we could do our jobs, but in their determination to nab the story, they refused to budge.

The reporters were keen to report a road rage murder, but what a story this would turn out to be. Little did I know just how big it would get.

You would imagine that someone being stabbed at such a busy location was enough to make a headline, but the added fact that the victim was a good-looking, young chap who had been trying to protect his fiancée proved to be of much more interest to the press. Even so, no one imagined – least of all the press – who the perpetrator would ultimately turn out to be.

Large-scale numbers of motorcyclists were on their way to the nearby Brands Hatch motor racing circuit that day, which lies on the nearby A20 road where a world series motorcycle event was taking place. This was wretched timing, and did not help our situation at all – time moved as slowly as the traffic. The roundabout closure caused endless problems and tailbacks, not only on all surrounding roads within Kent but on all roads leading in and out of London. To make matters worse, a tailback in the nearby Dartford Tunnel had begun affecting traffic in Essex. This situation led to police switchboards being inundated with calls. So many, in fact, that I started receiving requests from my own FCR to push on as fast as possible so that I could reopen the roundabout at the earliest opportunity.

I soon received the tragic news – the young man who had been stabbed at the scene had died in the nearby Dartford West Hill Hospital, and his parents and fiancée were at the hospital with uniformed officers. This was no longer a road traffic incident, it was now a murder investigation.

My colleague, John Grace, had arrived at the scene by this time, and I briefed him as best I could. We agreed that I should remain at the scene to deal with the media whilst he went to Dartford police station to organise an MIR and arrange to call out extra staff, who would certainly be required.

Detective officers from the Major Crime Department and local divisional detectives were called out to take witness statements (at both the scene and the police station) from members of the public who had witnessed the incident and from family members at the hospital. The SOCOs under the command of the S/SOCO Mr Alan Gilbert dealt with the scene.

I was under even more pressure now, not simply to reopen the roundabout, but to give the media a statement. Nonetheless, my main priority was to keep the scene secure in order to collect any physical evidence which might identify the murderer.

Following a serious crime incident, it is usual for an SIO to identify which crime scenes need to be protected and guarded, for them to be forensically examined. Scenes will not be released until such an examination process is completed. This can take hours but, depending on the size and location, it can even take several days, or even longer. In this situation, we had a busy and complex roundabout, which fed many major roads. Trying to set parameters for the forensic examination in this case was proving to be extremely challenging, to say the least.

Whilst examining the area in which the Rascal Van had been abandoned, I noticed numerous patches of red staining. It was obviously blood. The immediate question which sprang to mind was whether this was solely the victim's blood, or whether there was some offender's blood there too. It was because of this that, after consulting with the S/SOCO, we decided to prioritise the vicinity of the van. The trouble being, of course, that some article (such as the weapon) might have been lying elsewhere on the roundabout, or at one of several exit roads leading off the roundabout.

I stared at the M20 motorway, where it runs underneath the roundabout. The cars and lorries approaching the slip roads to the roundabout now stood completely stationary in the nearside lanes on either side of the motorway. The queues of traffic trailed back for miles. The state of the M25 motorway was the same in both directions. I thought of the hundreds, perhaps thousands, of drivers whose travel plans were being disrupted. My concern for them, however, was nothing compared to the poor parents and fiancée of the young man who had been attacked and died.

As soon as the majority of our work at the crime scenes had been completed, I spoke to the S/SOCO who told me that arrangements had been made to lift the Rascal van and take it to Dartford police station for further examination. This left only one task: to sweep the entire roundabout.

Several hours had passed since the incident had occurred. I prepared and delivered a brief statement to the gathered array of media representatives who had been waiting all this time for it. The instant they received my statement they vanished, even faster than they had arrived (which was pretty quick!). I abandoned the idea of brushing the entire roundabout because the wind was stronger by now and it was obvious that a mere walk-through would be sufficient. Nothing of evidential value was found, the SOCOs' work was finally complete. Much to the relief of those poor affected drivers in London, Essex and Kent, I authorised the reopening of the roundabout.

The deceased's fiancée, Danielle Cable, had been driving the red van when the incident occurred so she became our key witness. The red van was owned by the young man, identified by Danielle and his family as Stephen Cameron. He was only 21 years of age. They were a fine-looking couple, young and in love.

Danielle told us that she and Stephen had left his parents' house in nearby Swanley, just a few minutes' drive from the M25 junction. She had suggested that she drive because Stephen had been drinking the night before. They had planned to go through the Dartford Tunnel to East London to buy some bagels. Bagels, in those days, were not as popular or well-known as they are today in the UK, hence the special trip. This ended up causing a great degree of confusion for the less experienced officers on the enquiry, who thought the couple was going to East London to buy 'bangles'.

Danielle explained that she had hesitated as she approached the roundabout and that she entered the roundabout just as a Land Rover Discovery (LRD) was approaching that junction. It was her hesitancy which forced the driver to pull out past her which, in turn, made him miss his exit to the A20 towards London.

Unaware of the impact this had had on the driver of the LRD, she drove on slowly before preparing to stop at the next set of traffic lights just as they were turning red. Unbeknownst to either her or Stephen, the LRD driver had had to brake hard on the roundabout. Instead of taking a common-sense approach, however, and driving back around the roundabout, he pulled up sharply in front of the red Rascal van and jumped out of his vehicle to remonstrate with the driver.

Stephen saw the driver getting out of his vehicle and alighted from the passenger's side of his own van to protect his fiancée from the advancing LRD driver. Stephen was a fit lad who enjoyed kick-boxing so, when the other driver confronted him, Stephen was well-prepared to protect his fiancée.

Witnesses gave various accounts of what they saw as they passed by in their vehicles. The two men exchanged blows. The driver of the LRD was seen on the ground where, it was suggested by some, Stephen landed several blows on his assailant. Stephen stepped back as his assailant moved back towards the LRD. Stephen had obviously got the better of him. Stephen assumed the assailant was returning to his vehicle to drive away, and so he turned back to face Danielle, but the assailant had opened his rear passenger door and retrieved a knife. He then came back to attack Stephen with it.

Both men were now on the near side of their vehicles, where the fight resumed in full view of Danielle and the passing motorists. After receiving two stab wounds Stephen fell to his knees, and Danielle left the van and ran towards him whilst screaming for help. The driver of the LRD casually returned to his car and drove off at speed.

Passing motorists, an ambulance crew and a police patrol all stopped to help Stephen and to comfort Danielle in her shock. Danielle phoned

Stephen's dad, Ken Cameron, who called out to his wife, Stephen's mum, Toni. Within a few minutes they were out of their house driving straight to the nearby M25/M20 roundabout. Later, Ken told us that he knew Stephen was dying the moment he saw him being treated by paramedics at the scene.

According to another witness, Alan Decabral, the incident occurred directly alongside the slip road approach to the roundabout from the London direction of the A20. Decabral was the driver of a blue Rolls-Royce. He pulled up at the traffic lights and witnessed the fight between the two men. He saw the older of the two men approach the younger man from the red Rascal van and saw the glint of the blade in the afternoon sun. He watched the hand of the older man thrust forward in a stabbing motion towards the younger man. He then witnessed the older man turning away as the younger man fell to his knees, holding his chest. The older man got into the LRD and drove off at speed towards the Dartford Tunnel.

Decabral allegedly noted down part of the registration number of the Discovery LRD on a cigarette packet. He did not telephone 999 for some ten minutes but when he did, he described the incident and shared the registration number of the LRD as L964, which he had, in fact, not taken down correctly. He described the LRD as blue or green. As far as he was concerned, he had already reported the number plate and so, unfortunately, he tossed the packet away before police officers had the chance to seize it. Decabral went on to describe the older man as white, in his late 30s or early 40s with grey hair, wearing a black jacket, blue shirt and jeans.

Later, I sat down with John Grace in the MIR at Dartford police station where we discussed the events of the afternoon and established our priorities for the investigation. We debriefed officers who had taken witness statements and arranged for our HOLMES MIR staff to set up a MIR at Dartford police station. I phoned key members of staff at their homes and those who were available made their way up to the police station. Officers were used to being forced to leave the comfort of their home, cancel rest days or holidays and work long days, weeks and months in an investigation – this was accepted as a necessary part of the job.

One of the officers I phoned was PC Bob Kelly, who carried out significant research on potential suspects and identified key areas of the investigation. Many years after the incident, I had a wonderful conversation with Bob. He recalled the night I phoned him all too well. His daughter, Yvonne, had answered the phone. I identified myself and asked if her dad was at home.

'Yes, just a minute,' she replied, before covering the mouthpiece and calling out to her dad.

'Who is it?' he apparently asked her.

To which she replied, 'It's somebody called Dennis McGookin. I think he's trying to sell you something.'

Bob says he burst into laughter at this. 'That's actually my boss,' he told her.

Back in the MIR, John insisted that we do a post-mortem examination on Stephen Cameron at once. I would have agreed, if we had someone in custody on suspicion of the offence, but we had no suspect, we had no clue as to who the offender could be. It wasn't as if someone had driven into the police station and said, 'I got involved in a road rage incident. This guy attacked me and I stabbed him, but it was in self-defence.' If that had been the case, then a post-mortem would have been done within hours. I doubted we would have a suspect any time soon, however, so there was no rush to do it straight away, especially not on a Sunday night. John disagreed because, in those days, a post-mortem took place as soon as you had a murder. In any case, with the agreement of HM Coroner, the post-mortem was carried out later that evening by forensic pathologist Dr Mike Heath. The cause of death was recorded as two stab wounds to the chest.

Meanwhile, the Police National Computer (PNC) was conducting a search on LRD vehicles in England, and later that evening an MPS motorcyclist delivered 17,000 records from the PNC at Hendon to the MIR.

I informed John that, although I was the SIO, I was not in a position to lead the remainder of the investigation. I had a long-standing murder trial starting the following morning, to which I would be committed for at least two weeks. John liaised with the Head of the CID and it was agreed that he would take on the role of the SIO. So it was, that I left the investigation that night. I felt I had done my bit and assumed that would be the last I'd see of it. How wrong I was!

The following day, John made an appeal for witnesses to come forward in order to put a name to the photofit of the suspect, provided by a witness who had been at the scene. Initial details of the LRD were also released. Unfortunately, the information which started flowing into the MIR was not actioned quickly enough. Over the following days, the Head of CID was concerned that this was going to be a protracted investigation, so John returned to his position in Crime Management and the Head of MCD, Nic Biddiss, who had just returned from leave, took over the case.

New lines of enquiry developed. Of the 17,000 'L' registered LRDs identified in England by the PNC, 850 matched the criteria which witnesses at the scene had provided. Twenty-nine scene-witnesses offered varying descriptions of the incident itself, the offender and the vehicle – which was now described as green, blue or grey. Apart from the lost cigarette box, none of the witnesses had recorded the full index number of the LRD. The enquiry team were still satisfied, however, that five of the seven numbers/letters of the vehicle's plate had been identified.

The blood found at the scene was identified as belonging to Stephen but there was no physical evidence to identify the offender at this stage.

Hundreds of calls were made to the MIR identifying ninety-three different people as the potential offender. Unfortunately, a great deal of those calls were deemed malicious; naming people out of revenge for minor misdemeanours or altercations. In any case, every suggested name was identified, traced and interviewed before being satisfactorily eliminated from the investigation – bar one. That one was Kenneth James Noye. His very own actions after the murder had aroused suspicion. Although Noye was not, as yet, publicly named as a suspect, initial enquiries to trace him were unsuccessful. A variety of official sources, including a thorough PNC check, provided the investigation team with intelligence that:

- The photofit resembled Noye
- An LRD had been seen on the driveway of his house in Sevenoaks
- Crucially, an MPS officer had had reason to speak to Noye the previous January about an unrelated matter, at which time Noye had been driving an LRD Registration number L794JTF
- A PNC check, however, named the keeper of the vehicle as Anthony Francis of Bexley, London.

When officers attended Noye's house there was a blue LRD with the registration number J283DYP on his driveway. Enquiries revealed that a man by the name of Mr Grittens had paid £12,500 cash to purchase the vehicle from a London dealership at 0900 hrs on Monday, 20 May 1996, the day after the murder. Noye's family denied any knowledge of ownership (yes, despite it sitting on his drive) and the vehicle was seized. Mr Grittens was never identified and no one ever claimed ownership of the vehicle.

Officers attended the Bexley address but the property was vacant. Neighbours told the police that they specifically remembered an LRD had previously been at the house because it often blocked the road, but they could not identify the driver and nor did they know anyone by the name of Anthony Francis.

The previous owner of the vehicle L794JTF was Terence Hole, a known associate of Noye. When his property was searched, numerous parts of stolen LRDs were recovered. He denied any knowledge of Kenneth Noye and was charged with, and convicted for, handling stolen property in relation to the numerous stolen LRDs. There was still no sign of Noye, however, and Anthony Francis could not be identified.

Somehow newspapers got wind of the hunt for Noye and numerous publications started suggesting that Noye was wanted by the police. In reality, the only way information can be relayed to the press is through the loose lips of officers in-the-know, whether purposely or not. This caused enormous problems for the SIO. Identification of a likely suspect sooner rather than later was vital to the investigation, of course. If the offender did in fact turn out to be Noye, then any exposure of his identity in the press would undermine the possibility of a fair trial. Unfortunately, newspapers take no notice of such crucial concerns, and before we knew it, a Sunday paper had published the story, including a photograph of Noye.

Further intelligence suggested Noye had skipped the country. It was at this stage of the investigation that several of his associates were being interviewed. One such man was Jonathan Palmer. Palmer, nicknamed 'Goldfinger', was a well-known criminal involved in mortgage and time-share frauds. He had previously been acquitted of handling some of the gold stolen in the Brink's-Mat robbery. Palmer was allegedly worth in excess of £300 million. He owned a complex network of 122 companies, many of which were offshore (on the Isle of Man, Madeira and the British Virgin Islands), along with sixty offshore bank accounts.

Palmer owned his own helicopter and Learjet. The investigation later proved that he had flown Noye out of the country the day after Stephen Cameron's murder. Unfortunately, Palmer's employees, his helicopter pilot and Learjet pilots, refused to speak to the investigation officers at that time. Palmer was never charged with assisting an offender to flee from justice.

Sadly for Palmer, his story did not end well. He was shot dead at his home in Essex in June 2015. His killer has never been identified. It has been rumoured that his death was one of many linked with the disappearance of the Brink's-Mat gold.

When the one-year anniversary of Stephen's death came around, new appeals for information were made; one newspaper even offered a reward, but all failed to reveal any useful information. It was such a tragedy for Stephen's family and fiancée and it was also frustrating for the officers and members of police staff who had spent so much time trying to track down his killer.

Even if Kenneth Noye had walked into a Kent police station, the enquiry team would not have had sufficient evidence to charge him with the murder of Stephen Cameron. Everyone involved in the investigation tried kidding themselves that there was enough hard evidence to charge him, but the team still needed more — a lot more, in fact.

There were many reported sightings of Noye, in England and all over the world. All these sightings were evaluated and investigated over the following year, but as the second anniversary of Stephen's death neared, the enquiry team still didn't know the whereabouts of their main suspect.

There were no leads for quite some time but, by late spring of 1998, a possible sighting of Noye was reported to the MIR. The report came from a senior police officer in Gibraltar on the southern coast of Spain and was, initially, treated as yet one more 'possible' sighting. The officer, however, was so concerned by the lack of interest being paid to his information that he called ACC Mike Bowron at Kent Police Headquarters. Mike (who later went on to become Commissioner of the City of London Police and later the Chief Officer of the States of Jersey Police) instructed that the matter be actioned immediately.

It was only after the SIO spoke directly with the source of the information that two officers were appointed to travel to the southern coast of Spain. It was not regarded as a formal investigation, only an intelligence gathering exercise, so no official communication with the Spanish authorities was required. The two officers checked local bars, cafes and restaurants at different hours of the day and night over several days, without a great deal of success. And then their luck changed.

Late one afternoon, they were driving along the coast road when they were overtaken by a Shogun car. Looking across at the car one of the officers positively identified the driver as Noye. They followed the Shogun to a driveway off the main road, which coincided with the original information they had received. Having details of the vehicle Noye was using greatly assisted them in monitoring his movements. Official confirmation of this man's identification was vital but still not an easy task, and the officers had to return home in order to progress the investigation.

Meanwhile, I had been promoted to DSU and took charge of Crime Management for the force. Ironically enough, I inherited this position from my colleague, John Grace. If you recall, John and I had already worked on this investigation the very day the murder occurred. My office was located beside the office of the DCS, so people often hovered outside my office door whilst waiting to see the DCS. Two of those waiting turned out to be two of my colleagues from my days as an SIO with the MCD. I was very pleased to see them. I went to my door and asked them what they were doing there.

'I'm afraid we can't disclose anything,' one of them told me. 'We are waiting to go in there,' indicating to the DCS office. 'Our boss, Nic Biddiss, is in there.'

'You rascals,' I said, with a quizzical look, 'have you found Noye?'

They sniggered and hushed me, so I invited them into my office. Though they entered reluctantly, they soon revealed that they had located Noye in Spain. The officers went into details about how they had crept up to a villa in an effort to spot the suspect.

I was horrified. 'Do you realise that's exactly what got poor John Fordham killed?' I asked.

Despite my concern for their safety, they reassured me that no one had been home at the time and I congratulated them on their work. They begged me to let them return to the corridor, which I did with a large grin on my face.

Much has been said in books, magazines and the media about Kenneth Noye being wanted for the murder of Stephen Cameron and how Danielle identified him in a restaurant in Spain. Although this was factually accurate, the full details of how it came to pass have never been explained to the public. I have the greatest respect for the police officers involved in this part of the long investigation and deep respect for Danielle, who agreed to the possibility of having to face her fiancé's killer in that restaurant in Spain.

After the two Kent police officers had identified Noye in Spain, the information was passed back to the SIO, and Nic Biddiss went to see Danielle to inform her, in person, of the development in the investigation. He asked Danielle if she would be willing to travel to Spain, accompanied by a female officer who would be her chaperone throughout, and try to identify Kenneth Noye as the man who had killed her fiancé. Obviously, Danielle would have been very worried about this, but Nic gave her all the necessary assurances that she would be treated sensitively and that her own safety would not be in jeopardy.

Danielle agreed that she would do it, for Stephen's sake.

The female officer and Danielle travelled to Spain, accompanied by a Police Identification Officer (PIO), who was to be responsible for conducting any identification that took place. On arrival, the Inspector liaised with the original two officers who were tasked to find the suspect again! On the evening of 27 August 1998, the officers located Noye's vehicle at a restaurant called Il Forno.

One of the officers who had identified Noye informed the Identification Officer that the restaurant was very busy and that Noye was sitting at a specific table with several other people. In order to keep the integrity of the identification process, Danielle was not to know this information (that way, there could be was no suggestion down the line that officers had influenced or led the identification toward Noye in any way). Neither Danielle nor the PIO were given any details about his appearance. The PIO – and I stress that he did not know Noye – instructed Danielle to walk through the restaurant, go to the other side and then return. During that time, she was to look closely to see if she identified anyone who she believed was similar in appearance to the person who stabbed Stephen.

Danielle did exactly as she was told. There is little doubt that this must have been the most daunting and difficult walk of her life – it was a very challenging and extremely courageous thing for her to follow through with. It says a lot, not just for the strength of Danielle's character, but also the depth of her feelings for Stephen, with whom she had planned to spend her life. Like all involved in this case, Danielle wanted to find some kind of closure – and justice.

The PIO and the chaperone, who had been waiting outside, took her to their vehicle. Danielle was visibly concerned, and understandably so. After all, she had just seen the person who had killed her fiancé. She informed them that she did recognise a man in the restaurant and described in detail where he was sitting, exactly what he looked like and what he was wearing. It was indeed the same person who had been identified by the original officers. The team seemed to have their man.

The details of this identification were relayed back to DSU Nic Biddiss, and the following day he applied for, and was granted, a

European Arrest Warrant for the arrest of Kenneth Noye for the murder of Stephen Cameron.

One day later, another senior officer flew to Spain with warrant in hand. He hooked up with the two Kent detectives, who were now liaising with the Spanish police. A female officer and the Identification Officer accompanied Danielle back to the UK, where she was met by yet another officer who took a full witness statement from her.

Later that night, officers called forward a team of armed Spanish police officers when Noye (in the company of a Spanish lady) was located. He was arrested at once. He initially claimed that his name was Alan Edward Green and produced a fake British passport under that name. His true identification was, however, confirmed the following morning using fingerprint identification

Within twenty-four hours, DSU Nic Biddiss called a press conference outside Dartford police station to announce Noye's arrest and to give a statement regarding Noye's extradition back to the UK, where he would face trial for Stephen's murder. After the press conference, Nic drove to Force Headquarters to inform the DCS that he had achieved what he had set out to do and, now that he had arrested Noye, he immediately handed in his notice to retire from the Police Service.

Over the following week, I was summoned to see the CC, David Phillips (later to become Sir David Phillips), who took great pleasure in telling me that I was to take over command of the Major Crime Department and, more specifically, insisted that I was not to appoint another SIO to take over the Kenneth Noye investigation but to take on the role myself with immediate effect.

In the days and weeks that followed, I liaised with Nic regularly. Nic had built up an excellent relationship with Toni and Ken. He wished to inform them personally about his retirement from the Police Service now that he had arrested Stephen's killer. We visited Stephen Cameron's parents together at their home in Swanley, because we felt this was the best way to tell them that I was taking over the investigation. I assured them that I would maintain a close relationship with them throughout.

In addition to my role with Stephen's parents, it is only right that I acknowledge the role of two of our detectives, DC Charlie Bennett and DC Bryan Harffey, who had been appointed as the FLOs. I would like to take this opportunity to say how very proud I am of the work and support they gave to the entire Cameron family over a period of several difficult years.

It would later become common knowledge in the media that the key witness, Danielle, was under police protection. Going forward, even the officers whom Danielle had formed a bond with could not remain in her life. Once Danielle went into protection she had to be cut off from her family, from Stephen's family and from friends, because it would only take one small breach somewhere along the line to put her in danger. With police protection, a chink in the armour can come from anywhere, including someone's mum and dad. Even a police officer could become sensitive and be careless, so it is important that no one whatsoever knows the witness's whereabouts. Everything needs to be taken into account

This type of protection was by no means a common occurrence in everyday policing, so ours called on the expertise of colleagues in the MPS who had a dedicated unit for this purpose. Even as the SIO, I had no knowledge of Danielle's whereabouts, although myself and the witness protection team did have one very brief meeting (ten minutes only) at a services area, in order to reassure her. That's how tight security is with witness protection. The next time I saw her was at the Old Bailey.

Danielle remains under the scheme to this day. On the day Kenneth Noye murdered Stephen, he took away not only her fiancé, but her life, her family and her friends.

A witness under protection does tend to start a new life. Once the offender is in custody, we remain constantly aware that they likely have many associates and family who might wish to eliminate someone. The only way a witness can come out of protection is if that person demands to come out of it, in which case, they go through a stringent process. They are obliged to sign documents agreeing to undertake this action, against the recommendations from MPS, and they must include assurances that this choice is entirely theirs.

Back at the MIR we continued the extradition work with the same team of officers who had been working on the investigation. As part of this process, I liaised with the then Head of the Crown Prosecution

Service for Kent, Miss Elizabeth Howe OBE. Thankfully, after many years of prosecuting criminals in the county, Miss Howe and I knew each other well. We were told that the prosecution would be led by Mr David Calvert-Smith QC (who would later become Sir David Calvert-Smith). I had the pleasure of being introduced to Mr Calvert-Smith by my CC, at a Senior Officers Mess dinner. It was inspiring to hear how enthusiastic he was at the prospect of reading the prosecution file and conducting the trial. Much to my disappointment (though not his) Mr Calvert-Smith was later appointed as the Director of Public Prosecutions, which meant he could no longer take our case on. On his personal recommendation, a wonderful man, Mr Julian Bevan QC, was appointed as our Leading counsel together with Mr Mark Ellison as his junior. (Mr Ellison was Treasury counsel at this time and has since been made a QC.)

As the extradition process progressed, Miss Howe arranged a conference with our counsel in Mr Bevan's chambers at The Temple in Central London. I was still getting my head around everything that had happened in the interim months and years since that sad day on 19 May 1996. I had my Deputy SIO, DI Terry Gabriel, who was also the Case Officer, and two other members of our team with me.

The conference began fairly informally, as it was clear that counsel and Miss Howe were well known to one another. I introduced myself and our team. Mr Bevan asked me to outline the police investigation and, in particular, the key areas of evidence which would be used to convict Mr Noye. I vividly recall standing up and speaking for at least fifteen minutes before inviting my colleagues to add anything they thought was relevant. Comments were exchanged and as the conference was being wrapped up, Mr Bevan rose to his feet. He turned away from the conference table and spoke in his charming, educated accent.

'Time for a drink I think,' he said.

I was just getting to my feet as I said, 'Thank you, Mr Bevan, that would be very nice.' Quick as a flash Mr Bevan turned around to face me. 'The invitation was for Elizabeth, not you, Mr McGookin,' he said. 'You need to go and find more evidence.'

My team and I remained in the conference room whilst everyone else left. There was a sense of sadness and self-pity amongst us but there are times in this life when the truth hurts! I announced a team meeting for all officers, including scene of crime representatives and all our civilian support team, for 0900 hrs the following morning. We did not go for a drink – there was, after all, too much to think about, too much to do. What Mr Bevan had said was absolutely spot-on – it was all very well knowing Noye's location at long last, and although there certainly was an incredible amount of circumstantial evidence, it was now up to us to prove that the reason he had left the country in such a hurry was to escape justice after he had killed Stephen.

The following morning we assembled in the briefing room, where I started the meeting with an update from the conference we had had with counsel the previous day. I opened by listing both the evidence we did have and the evidence we did not have. Although Danielle's identification was our key piece of positive evidence, I made it clear that it was highly likely this identification would be challenged. Such evidence alone is often insufficient to take such a case to trial. The trouble was that we had little else to go on beyond that.

Crucially, there was no physical evidence, i.e. no forensic evidence, to put Noye at the scene. The best we could hope for was that each of the eyewitnesses attend an identification parade. Noye, however, had to be willing to stand on such a parade and since there was a chance he would refuse, we needed to prepare a video identification, with or without his agreement.

We also needed to re-examine and discuss the LRD enquiries even more thoroughly. Although we had evidence that Noye had an LRD registration number L794JTF in the January before Stephen's murder, we could not confirm (beyond all reasonable doubt) that it was the same LRD with Noye in it, at the scene on the day. We had evidence that a known associate of Noye, Terence Hole, had stolen LRDs in his possession but this actually hindered our line of enquiry and it became confusing for the entire investigation team.

Here are the important details which we had to collate and get our heads around:

- The vehicle we assumed was being driven by Noye, was an LRD Registration Number L794JTF. Registered keeper, Anthony Francis, with a previous keeper being Mr Hole
- A different LRD – which had been rung with the stolen body from another LRD (M667OKN) – had been in Hole's possession when his property was searched
- The car body of the LRD (L794JTF) was placed on another stolen LRD (M566MKR)
- A different LRD altogether (L102VKV) now bore the registration number L974JTE but this was not the one used on the M25 incident (we knew this because it had been stolen after the date of the incident).

You can see how complicated and confusing this was, because of all the different ways the evidence could be interpreted

We did receive anonymous information that an LRD had been crushed at a breakers yard in Dartford soon after the incident, and whilst the owner of those premises was a known associate of Noye, we still could not turn the information into evidence, despite the premises being searched and an AA membership card in the name of Kenneth Noye being found there.

Fortunately, a witness came forward to support the anonymous information and make a statement saying that she had seen an L-registered LRD being driven into that scrap yard the day after Stephen died.

Whilst it was deeply suspicious that Noye could not be traced after the incident, this didn't serve as evidence that he had committed the crime. The one lead that we did have related to the previous owner of the LRD which Noye had in January 1996.

In short, we had a problem. I told the team that, with immediate effect, the famous words of Winston Churchill would be our only way forward from here on in: 'The longer you can look back, the farther you can look forward.'*

I outlined my decision: the first 200 actions raised at the start of the investigation and immediately after Kenneth Noye was mentioned as

---

* www.oxfordreference.com/display/10.1093/
   acref/9780191843730.001.0001/q-oro-ed5-00002969

a possible suspect were to be raised again and reinvestigated. To some this may have appeared as a waste of valuable time but I knew from my early research on the case that there had been 'witnesses' who'd been threatened by members of the criminal fraternity and told not to help this police investigation.

These various enquiries, as well as the disclosure process, were still ongoing on 2 November 1998. The paperwork for the extradition of Kenneth Noye from Spain to the UK was completed and submitted to the CPS which was, in turn, forwarded to the Spanish authorities. The Spanish authorities checked this paperwork before serving a copy on Kenneth Noye and his Spanish lawyer. His first date for the extradition hearing was fixed for 16 November, which was good for us since it gave us a bit of breathing space.

> Disclosure in criminal cases is the process where the crown makes available any documents or exhibits upon which they rely and also anything that could undermine the crown's case or support the defence case. Nowadays the defence are expected to submit a defence statement outlining their defence before the trial begins.

I was well aware what a long shot it was to research the 200 actions again. I was certain, however, that it was the only possible way forward. I felt there simply must have been some angle or piece of information amongst all that material that we had missed. Thankfully, my hunch paid off.

I often refer to my teams as 'God's Own Detectives' because they have the special skills to pin down evidence others would find too difficult to spot. When I train teams of detectives, I try to invigorate them with passion, I tell them how valued and special they are. One of Jonathan Palmer's employees, who previously hadn't been allowed to speak with us, had now left both the 'Palmer Empire' and the West Country where he had been living. Our team tracked him down to the other side of the world and an experienced detective spoke to him on the telephone. This employee told our detective that he knew Noye through Noye's friendship with Palmer. He then informed my officer that he had flown

Noye and Palmer out of the country, by helicopter, on 20 May 1996. Noye had been sporting a black eye and carried only hand luggage. The pilot described the route, explaining how they flew across the English Channel to land at a golf course in Caen in Normandy, France. The pilot still had his flight log and diary, so all this 'evidence' had been recorded.

The detective asked if the employee would consider returning to the UK with this evidence but the pilot declined. The force offered to cover his expenses, of course, but he still declined. That was when the detective asked me to speak personally with the pilot, which I did.

The gentleman remained adamant, however, that he had no wish to return to the UK so I told the pilot that my officers would travel out to him for the interview, and he agreed to this course of action. What I didn't tell him was just how difficult it would be to get the necessary authorities to agree to this. As a result of this 'possible breakthrough' I had to liaise with the Crown Prosecution Service. Thankfully, my colleague Elizabeth Howe dealt with the matter personally, and the necessary legal authority was granted.

The next hurdle, however, was to obtain the necessary authority from the force. I referred the matter to my Head of CID. He, in turn, referred it to the Assistant CC (Crime) and he referred it to the CC David Phillips. If this process was part of a child's party it would probably be called 'pass the parcel'. That's what it felt like. All three of us were then summoned to the CC's office and, once again, I presented the quagmire I was facing.

The CC is a very intelligent man and has always had great respect for those officers at the forefront of fighting crime. There was a general air of reticence because the entire enquiry was being discussed and the evidence against Noye was at the forefront of the discussions. Not everyone believed we were likely to collect enough evidence to get him back and get him convicted. At the end of the meeting the CC promised to consider the matter. I deliberately paused to let the Head of CID and the Assistant Chief Constable leave the office before me, to allow myself a little, private moment with the Chief. After they had left his office, I turned back to the Chief, nodded and thanked him for his time. The Chief did not reply, he simply nodded back to me, smiling and (if I'm not mistaken) he even winked as if to say, 'We know you are going to get this evidence.'

This was good enough for me. Operation go ahead!

Within ten days, my officers had already travelled abroad, interviewed the pilot, recorded the necessary evidence and returned home safely. Even their families did not know where they had been, let alone the rest of our team members. In instances like this, where an officer's whereabouts cannot be disclosed, even to those closest to him or her, a full strategic plan must be in place to ensure that, in the case of an emergency, the family is able to reach me personally so that I can, in turn, contact the pertinent officer. Thankfully, there were no such emergencies, I was not contacted, and a very important piece of evidence was elicited.

Around three to four weeks later, I received a telephone call in my office from the Chief Constable's Staff Officer, discreetly telling me that the Chief had some 'clear time' in his diary and was paying an impromptu visit to my office for an update on major crime investigations in the force area. He had a great habit of just dropping into the Major Crime Department, which he often referred to as 'The Front Window of the Policing Shop'.

When the Chief arrived within minutes, I feigned surprise. He appeared to be in a good positive frame of mind, it was a real pleasure to talk to him over a cup of tea, since he had a genuine interest and passion for major crime investigations. After a while, however, I sensed that he had had enough, at which point (and almost as an afterthought) he asked about the 'Kenneth Noye' case.

I pulled a copy of a statement out of my desk drawer.

'Perhaps you would like to read this, Sir?' I said, handing him the statement.

Out came his glasses. As he read the document, I could tell his interest was piqued. His glasses were back in his pocket within a few minutes and a wry smile appeared on his face.

He stood up to leave and as he turned, he asked, 'Did I actually authorise the financing of this trip?'

I did not reply, I simply smiled and we have never mentioned it since.

Intelligence sources knew from before that Palmer was the owner of a Learjet and said jet had flown from a location in Russia to France on 21 May 1996. It subsequently travelled to the Canary Islands.

This had been one of many priority actions for the original investigation team, but at the time they were met with a blanket of silence. Now it was a priority action for the current team to follow through on all pilots involved in transporting Noye.

Members of the team had already gathered evidence from Palmer's helicopter pilot. Other members of the team now turned to the pilots of the Learjet. The captain of that jet still refused to speak to our officers but we established that the co-pilot had left the Palmer empire and was now employed by a UK registered airline. He was initially reluctant to speak with our team members, but he swiftly changed his mind when I implied that I might be forced to refer the matter to the Head of Security for the airline he was currently employed with. He made a full statement to my officers about the Learjet journey involving Palmer and Noye.

Job done. We'd secured yet another piece of the jigsaw puzzle.

Whenever new evidence appeared, the team served it on the CPS who, in turn, updated our prosecuting barristers. The role of the Police Service is to carry out the investigation and to secure evidence, whilst the barrister's role is to present the evidence at trial. In all police investigations (and other investigative agencies) there is a duty to ensure that the evidence obtained is used in the correct manner. The legislation which covers this requirement is the Criminal Procedure and Investigation Act 1996. In layman's terms, the Act basically stipulates that the police and prosecution must disclose to the defence any evidence which might assist the defence or undermine the prosecution case.

In a large-scale investigation, it is recognised as good practice to appoint the prosecution team (i.e. police/CPS lawyer and barrister) at an early stage so they can check every part of the investigation. In so doing, they ensure that the disclosure rules are followed with 100 per cent accuracy. In this case, Mr Ellison took on this role on behalf of the CPS.

On 16 November 1998, Noye made his first appearance at a Spanish court in Madrid. He was asked if he would voluntarily return to the UK but he declined, and was further remanded in custody. His full extradition hearing was set for 1 February 1999 at the high security Audiencia Nacional Court in Madrid. Once again, this offered us more time to secure further evidence, and once again, we were fortunate.

Due to the publicity of both the arrest and the extradition hearing, a female contacted the MIR to inform us that she recognised Noye as being a guest she had checked in at a hotel in Dartford where she was a receptionist. She did not know him as Kenneth Noye because he went by the name Anthony Francis. She made a witness statement to this effect and she agreed to attend an identification parade if required. Excellent news; we finally had a link to the LRD.

There are times, however, when identification evidence is undermined in court, so it was only right that we considered other ways to prove that Kenneth Noye and Anthony Francis were one and the same person. We needed something extra.

At which point I took a real long shot.

I tasked a member of the team to check whether the MPS still had all the case files for the Brink's-Mat robbery. Although that robbery had been in 1983, the trials of the various individuals involved took place as late as 1988 and I was intrigued to know if Kenneth Noye, who was charged in relation to that robbery, was ever known as Anthony Francis during that investigation.

My hunch paid off. A very helpful Chief Superintendent in the MPS knew straight off the bat where the files were because he had just authorised their destruction from the MPS storage facility. Thankfully, he was able to block that instruction and we were invited to search through the papers.

Two officers were dispatched to carry out this enquiry. The instant they saw the volume of paperwork involved, they phoned to tell me it would take our entire team several weeks to sift through all the documents.

The MPS agreed to give us possession of the files. We stored them in two unused cells at Sevenoaks police station (that custody centre had closed down) and managed to fill both rooms from floor to ceiling. Now the hard work began.

A search of these documents revealed that Noye had used numerous aliases during that investigation. One name he did not admit to using was Anthony Francis. Undeterred, the team carried on searching. They eventually found a signed Abbey National Building Society Mortgage Agreement form, in the name of Anthony Francis. Of course, this did not prove that Noye was Francis, but I authorised that the form be submitted to our Fingerprint Department.

The form was duly submitted to the department and we were elated when they told us that Noye's fingerprints had indeed been identified on the Anthony Francis application form. We now had another piece of evidence that Noye was Francis. We are always cautious, however. Determined to strengthen the evidence, I decided it was imperative to eliminate everyone else in the country who shared the name Anthony Francis. I set the age parameters five years either side of Noye's date of birth and, using public records, my team identified sixty-nine white males who fitted these criteria. Enquiries would trace these people across the UK and to Australia, New Zealand, Canada, USA and Spain. 'God's Own Detectives' came up trumps – each and every person by the name of Anthony Francis was traced and eliminated from the enquiry.

Things seemed to be slotting nicely into place but we never rested on our laurels. We arrived at one of the last actions in the list of 200 and a further stroke of good fortune befell us. A car cleaner had phoned the MIR after the murder to inform us that he regularly cleaned cars belonging to Mr and Mrs Kenneth Noye. The car cleaner had mentioned that, whilst cleaning Mr Noye's car, he found a flick-knife in the glove compartment. This information had never been properly actioned, but written off at the time as insignificant and, consequently, no statement was obtained. Uncovering this enormous oversight immediately changed things for us. Despite the passage of time the individual was located and a witness statement obtained. Yet another piece of the jigsaw puzzle was in place.

Another surprising piece of evidence which came to our attention related to a mobile phone number linked to Noye. Nowadays, smart-phones reveal extensive information about individuals, but in those days we had little experience dealing with mobile phone records. The number dated back to January 1996, when the MPS officer first spoke with Noye. We now had the skills to establish both the general area in which the phone was being used, and who the recipient of the call was, although we could not prove the identity of who was physically using the phone. Still, we were determined to explore every avenue of investigation and again, good old detective-work (plus a little luck) won through when we obtained details of calls made the day Stephen was murdered.

At 1405 hrs, a few minutes after the incident on the roundabout (which is often referred to as the 'Swanley Interchange'), the person who was in possession of that phone called a certain Peter Horton. Horton owned 20 Bridgen Road, Bexley. This call was registered on the Swanley mobile telephone beacon.

At 1411 hrs, 1414 hrs and 1419 hrs the user of that telephone called Terence Hole from this mobile. Hole was the previous owner of L794JTF. All these calls were registered on the Swanley Beacon.

To summarise and interpret into evidence, we now had:

- A mobile phone at the relevant time in the vicinity of the murder
- Said mobile phone is being used to contact a person at an address linked to L794JTF
- Said mobile phone is used to contact the previous keeper of L794JTF
- Within minutes of these calls both recipients are contacted a second time.

The extradition hearing gained a mass of press attention. Elizabeth Howe (CPS) and I, together with another colleague, were all in attendance in Spain. Noye appeared in the dock behind a bullet-proof glass screen from where he denied committing the murder. He challenged the identification process and claimed that he was unlikely to get a fair hearing in a UK court. Personally, I assume this was because he had already been branded as a killer, after the DC John Fordham incident. The judge explained to Noye that the purpose of the court was not to try him for the murder offence (since that was a matter for the UK court), but rather, to check that all the paperwork was correct according to Spanish law. Noye was further remanded in custody pending the final decision of the court.

We returned to Kent the following day, and I am convinced that virtually every other passenger on the British Airways aeroplane was a journalist. Thankfully, when we landed, we were the first off the plane and, because we had a car waiting for us, we managed to avoid the swarming media.

Over the following week, the CPS informed us that the judges in Spain had granted our extradition request. Noye launched an appeal against their decision at once, of course, no doubt hoping to avoid facing the consequences of his actions. All his appeal managed to do, however, was give us more time to find further evidence and help us fully prepare our case.

Noye's appeal was listed for 25 March 1999. There was no reason for us to be there (and the CPS agreed) unless the Spanish authorities requested our presence specifically; they didn't. The Spanish judges dismissed his final appeal, so Noye would soon be returning to the UK.

My priority now was to manage arrangements for Noye's transportation back to the UK. Things did not go as smoothly as I had hoped.

Intelligence sources identified plans for an assassination of Noye, since word had spread that he had made a deal with the police and turned informant. In a similar vein, there was further intelligence suggesting that once he knew when and how he would be returning to the UK, he would plan an escape. I personally thought both scenarios unlikely. For one, I knew there would never be a deal between police and Noye, and two, no one knew at that stage (including myself!) how or when Noye was to be returned to the UK. Nonetheless, I could not ignore such intelligence and was forced to manage the potential issues.

In addition to this, I received a report from the MPS in relation to our witness, Danielle, whose family was being threatened. Her father had been confronted in a public house and ordered outside by two men who he described as being south-east London thugs. Once outside, he was taken to the rear of their car. I can only imagine what went through his mind at the time. Truly, he must have thought he was being taken somewhere to be killed. He must have felt some relief when the boot of the car was opened and a bag full of £50 and £20 notes was revealed. He was told that all he needed to do was stop his girl from giving evidence and the money would be his.

This wasn't the only issue Danielle's family had to deal with. Her two younger brothers were stopped on their way to school and threatened with violence if their sister gave evidence. Both these matters fell within the jurisdiction of the MPS but, due to links we had with the family, they requested that my team deal with them. I agreed and appointed another DCI to deal with the matter. Despite best efforts, however, the offenders were never positively identified, but thankfully there were no more threats after this.

In view of these matters regarding witness intimidation, and knowing that the instant Noye was formally charged at a Kent police station, the case papers served on him would reveal our witnesses' names, we had to exercise extreme caution. We could not rule out the possibility that if their addresses were ever identified, they might be the subject of threats or possibly something worse. I was forced to find some way to arrange a simple but efficient plan to protect them. The witnesses did not all live in our force area, however, which complicated things somewhat, and meant I required the cooperation of other police forces. Each of the witnesses was contacted and all agreed to my plan.

They were to be given a code-word which they were permitted to share with others in their immediate household. If anyone approached them or their property, they could dial 999 and pass the code-word to the police. Each local force where the witness lived signed up to this operation and their emergency call-handlers were briefed. In the case of such a call being made, the police would immediately respond with a priority deployment by uniformed officers, along with an armed police response as backup.

Noye's trial was still a long way off but this tactic was successful, and thank heavens it was. We had one incident where two cohabiting witnesses had bricks thrown through their window. It had occurred in an area of London covered by the MPS. The offenders were not identified but the MPS decided to rehouse the victims at once – which was organised and paid for by the MPS.

❖

We now turned our minds to arranging Noye's safe and secure return to the UK. I consulted with the Head of Security at British Airways for advice since an aeroplane was the cheapest and most efficient means of bringing him back. Under the circumstances (and based on the intelligence we continued to receive) it was imperative I remain completely open and honest. In response to this, British Airways security informed me that no commercial airline would allow Noye to travel upon their aircrafts. We considered travelling by car and ferry, but this was neither a realistic nor practical solution.

I discussed this problem with our Deputy Chief Constable (DCC), Mr Robert (Bob) Ayling (later to become T/Chief Constable Robert Ayling QPM), who gave me permission to contact both the Home Office and the Ministry of Defence for assistance. I was duly invited to visit the Home Office, where I expected to have a nice cup of afternoon tea and a chat regarding my visit. Instead, a senior civil servant constantly challenged me to justify every detail of my request for the military to fly Noye back to the UK. By the end of this meeting, I had received the permission I sought, but it was not quite what I had expected and I was never offered that cup of tea.

I was told that the most efficient method to transport Noye was in an RAF passenger jet from RAF Northolt, which is located close to Heathrow International Airport. Using this facility meant that we were not restricted to specific flight times. This airport is not open to the public nor the media, which meant that we could land on any airstrip of my choosing. I was given the name and contact details of an RAF Officer at RAF Northolt who dealt with my request.

I briefed my deputy SIO DI, Terry Gabriel, back in the MIR and we visited RAF Northolt the following day to meet the officer from 32 Squadron, Royal Air Force, who co-ordinates all flights in and out of that airport. This officer was unbelievably helpful. We agreed on the time and date for the flight out to Spain. He asked me my opinion on where we should land in the UK. I asked if Manston Airport would be suitable and within one minute, he produced a plan of Manston Airport.

His manner was surprisingly jovial for someone in such a position and yet somehow, the way he expressed himself showed that the gravity of our task was not at all lost on him. I was in awe of such an admirable human being. I knew for certain we were in good hands.

'Where exactly on the runway would you like the plane to stop,' he asked. He was, of course, talking within one foot of the precise position on the runway. Quite an extraordinary detail when you consider the exacting minutiae demanded of such a calculation. We agreed on the exact spot.

As an added precaution, the RAF officer and I both agreed that the aircraft's crew should at no time be made aware in advance of the landing at Manston Airport. He recommended that we prepare a sealed envelope with instructions to divert the aeroplane to Manston as it crossed the English Channel and not before. He was to communicate an order to open the envelope at the appropriate moment.

The officer then gave us a tour of RAF Northolt, which included the Royal Lounge and the aircraft which was to be used. He made the arrangements for the aircraft to land at a military airbase along with refuelling of the aircraft in Spain, whilst I liaised with the British Embassy in Madrid to make the necessary arrangements with the Spanish prison authorities at their end, regarding the delivery of our 'cargo' to the aircraft.

I summoned six of my officers, along with DI Gabriel, to my office to ensure they all held current passports, because they had previously volunteered to take part in the extradition when it took place. They were told that DI Gabriel would be placed in charge of this operation and that, from the following day, they needed to dress in smart clothes with collar and tie until further notice. They were to inform their families that if they did not call home at exactly 1700 hrs each day whilst they were at work, then the family should not expect them home until late that night. This was all part of my security plan; even my own staff were not to know the date they were going to collect Noye.

I received permission from DCC Ayling for a firearms team, to escort the prisoner from the aircraft to Dartford police station, where he would be detained. A firearms officer was appointed to organise the collection of the prisoner. This officer went to great lengths to ensure everything went to plan, including liaising with the manager of Manston Airport to shut the airport to all air-traffic on the afternoon in question, and only have a minimum number of airport staff that day. The airport itself would only receive notice of these demands within hours before the operation was to take place. They assured us that this would not be a problem.

I had selected an extremely isolated area on the runway as the spot where the aircraft would stop. A bullet-proof vehicle was to park feet away from this position.

Everything was in place.

In the meantime, DCC Ayling re-designated Dartford police station as a holding centre for prisoners. This police station had stopped taking prisoners and people arrested would be taken to the custody suite for the area to Gravesend police station.

In years gone by, following the arrest of a prisoner by a police officer, the offender would be taken to a police station and locked in a cell. In those circumstances a uniformed sergeant would authorise the detention and record the prisoner's details and any property the prisoner had on a detention sheet. There was little to no framework to care for the prisoner, but following the introduction of legislation under the Police and Criminal Evidence Act 1984, along with a set of Codes of Practice, everything changed.

The term 'cell block' was replaced by the title 'custody suite' and a specific post of Custody Sergeant was made responsible for the running of the suite and the general welfare and care of each prisoner.

With the correct authority in place, we were now legally able to hold Noye at Dartford police station, far away from other prisoners. I required this facility instead of taking the prisoner to a custody suite at a larger police station because it was my intention to install CCTV around the cell area. CCTV at that time was not used a great deal in police stations, although all custody suites were eventually fitted with professional monitoring and recording equipment.

I liaised with my colleague, Chief Inspector Chris Collins, who was responsible for Dartford police station and took personal responsibility for carrying out the plans we had put in place.

We knew we might require identification evidence from our scene witnesses and that CCTV images would be of great use if Noye declined an identification parade. Once this equipment was fitted, I visited the cell area at Dartford police station, along with my firearms advisor, DI Gabriel, and some other officers. Chief Inspector Collins also joined us because I needed to ensure that once the prisoner arrived, everyone involved was aware of their exact role.

This was probably as close as I would ever get to being a film director! I explained precisely what I wanted in shot and for how long I needed each 'character' to pause on their 'mark'. Here was the plan: the officer bringing the prisoner into the cell area would be directed to pause at the cell gate. Another officer would deliberately fumble with the gate key for an exact number of seconds, which would cause the 'character' of Noye to pause on a very specific mark in the middle of the cell. We needed to ensure we caught excellent footage of him from several different angles, without him suspecting a thing.

Everyone was 'cast' in those roles accordingly. Chief Inspector Chris Collins was in charge of unlocking the gate, so he would be the one controlling the timing of Noye's standstill within the scene's required time-frame as he deliberately fumbled with the gate key. The officer who was holding Noye was the force self-defence instructor, so he was the best man for this 'role'.

Our 'rehearsal' (which, of course, I referred to as a practice session) went well but I demanded that everyone do a second walk-through in order to make sure it worked properly. It was at this point that police humour raised its head. One of my cheeky officers had placed a chair beside me with the label DIRECTOR ONLY upon it.

When we did the 'real thing', in fact, Noye was smiling and joking as he looked around, but when his eye caught the camera and he realised that we had captured his photograph, his expression turned to one of fury. Two images of Noye, taken within seconds of each other, showing just how quickly this guy's character could turn. Two images of the same face, one smiling, smug as could be and one in a hate-filled rage. More faces than I will ever need in this chock-full, scrapbook brain of mine.

With the third anniversary of Stephen's tragic death only a few days away, I took the opportunity, along with DI Gabriel and an FLO, to visit Ken and Toni Cameron at their home in Swanley. I wanted to let them know that Noye was due back in the country very soon and that I would phone them once he was safely in custody.

I remember this visit all too well because the subject of the death of DC John Fordham, some fourteen years earlier, came up. I mentioned my involvement in the police response to that incident, including taking the phone call from Queen Mary's Hospital informing us that the officer had died from his injuries. I was shocked and amazed when Toni Cameron told me it had been she, in fact, who had made the phone call and that she was part of the team who had tried to save John's life.

Neither one of us could truly believe that it was me who had taken that initial call. I sensed a welling up of emotion within her and certainly in me as well. The fact that the same two people had come together, all these years later, in the context of yet another tragic event involving the very same offender. What a coincidence and what an awful experience for a parent to have to endure.

Back in my office, journalists from every national newspaper began calling me. Sunday papers and television news teams all over the nation wanted to know when Noye was due to return and at which airport he would be arriving. They had somehow sourced my direct-dial number. They spoke to me as if I were their best friend. I was well aware that they were coming straight to me instead of the Media Services Department because that department had pressed me, time and time again, on a need-to-know basis, for more detailed information, assuring me that they would not disclose the information to anyone unless I gave explicit permission for them to do so. I still refused to tell them, however, so there was little doubt in my mind that they passed the buck and told journalists (and the like) to simply 'ring McGookin direct'.

I fully accept that it is vital to maintain a successful working relationship between the Police Service and the media. It is via the media that the police communicate with the public, and so it is often the media who are crucial components to solving a crime, helping bring offenders to justice and keeping communities safe. The media also gives the public an insight into what the police are doing and why. Media Services departments in the Police Service play a vital role in reaching these goals. On this occasion however, secrecy was paramount in my investigation; it was imperative that no one know when and where Noye was returning to the country. His formal identification and safety were prioritised over bowing to the media's needs.

I can't express to you the hassle from the press which I was constantly having to deal with. 'When's he coming back?' they'd ask. 'What airport will he be coming into?'

I was irritated by the continual interruptions and eventually arrived at the conclusion that something had to be done about it. I suspected that a degree of misinformation might stop them from pestering me so, when I took the next call, I decided to tell the journalist that Noye was coming into Gatwick in the middle of the next week.

Within no time, another journalist phoned me. 'We hear it's Gatwick next week,' they said.

'No, it's Manchester, in fact,' I replied.

Every time I took a call, I changed the airport location. Eventually, one of the journalists whom I trusted (I had worked with him at our Detective Training School), Chester Stern, rang me. He was then the Chief Crime Correspondent for the *Mail On Sunday* newspaper.

'If you're able and willing,' I told Chester, 'to stop all the other bleeding journalists from pestering me then I will give you my word that I will give you the first piece of information when we do eventually get Noye back.'

'I'll do my best, Dennis,' he replied, 'but I can't confirm that they won't be trying to find out when Noye is coming back into the country, for themselves.'

The general feeling in the MIR was that I was planning to bring Noye back on the anniversary of Stephen's death. Even the civilian staff around Headquarters, including the Chief Officer's secretaries, were asking whether it was indeed planned for the anniversary. All of them had it wrong, however.

The anniversary came and went.

The following day, on the anniversary of Stephen's death, I told my secretary, Julie, I would be out of the office for an hour on a personal matter. That's when I drove over to Gillingham Football Club and purchased tickets for myself, my family and some friends to watch Gillingham versus Manchester City in the League One playoff final at Wembley Stadium the following week.

Back in my office that afternoon I checked my plans and headed home early. Tomorrow was another day, and what a day it might turn out to be.

Thursday, 20 May 1999, I arrived in my office just after 0800 hrs. In order to make sure that the officers flying to Spain were at the ready, I kept the morning routine exactly the same as I had when I first briefed them about flying out to collect Noye. They mustered in the MIR daily and, together with DI Gabriel, came over to my office for that day's briefing. They'd been warned that they needed to be prepared to leave on any given day and at any given moment – this included needing to know if they required use of the toilet before convening in my office! They also had to be in possession of their police warrant cards, their passports and their mobile phones (which I would take off them on the big day).

Only I knew the date, of course, but one telltale sign that something might be happening was the unmarked police personnel carrier with a civilian driver in the car park below my office window. The team came in. The door was shut and I notified them that they were on their way.

Mobile phones were locked in my desk and, after a quick briefing, they departed, safe in the knowledge that, at the very least, DI Gabriel knew where they were going.

I was later told that the conversation was good-humoured on the journey and that their first assumption was that they were on their way to Gatwick Airport. As they passed the M23 junction on the M25 motorway, however, they assumed it was Heathrow Airport they were headed for. Apparently, there was much consternation once they passed the M4 junction to Heathrow Airport, suggesting they were going to Luton Airport.

All wrong of course.

The game was over once the signs for RAF Northolt appeared, and their final suspicions were confirmed as soon as the personnel carrier drove through the gates of the RAF base.

At long last, things were moving. I would have preferred to have been with the team on board the aircraft or at Manston Airport, or, at the very least, at Dartford police station, but I heeded the advice received several years earlier from my colleague ACC Keith Biddle:

'You do not need to do everything,' he had said, 'simply let your staff do their jobs.'

All that remained for me was a long, painstaking wait.

Later that morning, my colleague at RAF Northolt rang to confirm that the flight had left. He kept me updated throughout the day to confirm that all was going as planned in Spain and that the aircraft's diversion had been implemented. I kept in contact with my firearms advisor, who confirmed that there was a complete firearm containment in place at the airport.

The flight arrived on schedule and came to a stop on the exact spot we had agreed upon. Noye was removed from the aircraft and placed, hand-cuffed, in the armour-plated vehicle. Then the armed escort moved off.

We had planned two separate routes to Dartford, just in case there was any kind of emergency. I phoned Chief Inspector Chris Collins, who confirmed everything was at-the-ready at the police station and there was no sign of any media.

The 59-mile journey from Manston to Dartford normally takes an hour but, in this case, they had completed the journey and our prisoner was safely inside the police station in forty minutes. At which point, I was updated again; the video exercise had been completed satisfactorily, although the moment he had looked up and seen the cameras, Noye's attitude had changed from good humour to anger.

❖

Once the custody record and detention procedures were completed, the case papers were served. I was told that the first thing he did was to look at the name of the prosecution witnesses. Later that evening, Noye was formally charged with the murder of Stephen Cameron.

I made two phone calls that afternoon. The first (and by far the most important) was to Ken and Toni Cameron, who received the news and wept. They were overjoyed that we had finally brought the man we believed had killed their son into custody back in Kent.

As promised, the second call was to the journalist, Chester Stern. He was in London with a large group of noisy colleagues at the time; a meeting or gathering of some kind was wrapping up and refreshments had just arrived, apparently. After initial greetings, I informed him that Noye was safely back in the UK and was to be formally charged with Stephen's murder that very evening.

'No way,' he responded. 'If that were true then we would have known about it.'

'I assure you, Chester,' I said, 'despite what you think, Noye is back in custody in Kent.'

He shouted out to the gathering for everyone to be quiet, before shouting, 'Noye is back!'

I heard moans and groans of disbelief in the background.

'This is Dennis McGookin on the phone,' he shouted, 'and he has confirmed it.' I heard him add, 'Our editors won't be at all happy with you lot who are covering this case,' he said, 'letting a massive story like this go by unnoticed.'

I said farewell to Chester and put the phone down with the biggest smile on my face since as long as I could remember. We had done it.

I instructed DI Gabriel to inform anyone else who needed to know the good news, including the former SIOs who had worked on the case and the MPS Witness Protection Unit looking after Danielle.

The following morning, an armed containment circled Dartford Magistrates' Court where a large gathering of journalists, TV crews and freelance photographers were in attendance, all determined not to miss this opportunity, as Noye was produced and remanded in custody to HMP Belmarsh.

Reports were published throughout media channels that the police were monitoring Noye, along with any of his visitors, in prison. This was simply untrue. He was now the responsibility of the Prison Service. the Operational Partnership Team Police Advisers were to update either myself or DI Gabriel if there were any issues about Noye's safety inside the prison, but nothing materialised.

Noye's solicitor, Mr Henry Milner, informed us that his client would be willing to stand on an identification parade. From a security point of view, we needed to seek the assistance of the Operational Partnership Team Police Advisers and MPS before arranging to move Noye from the prison to a secure Identification Suite at a London police station. We were advised that Kilburn police station Identification Suite was at our disposal for this purpose. DI Gabriel looked after all aspects of this process and he advised me that the move was planned for Tuesday, 6 July 1999. I kept Ken and Toni Cameron updated with what was happening.

Thirteen witnesses attended the identification parade, during which we drew some good and some not so good results. Though several witnesses identified Noye as the person who had stabbed Stephen, not all thirteen did. Still, this was more than enough evidence for us to proceed and certainly more substantial evidence than we had had before that day. Another few pieces of the jigsaw were now in place!

Noye's trial was fixed for 30 March 2000 at the Old Bailey in London. There was still plenty to do before that date in order to ensure all aspects of the trial ran smoothly.

Firstly, we had conferences with our legal team, who were now satisfied with the value of the evidence we had obtained since our original conference. We had to keep in touch with our witnesses, except Danielle who was still in the Witness Protection Program. (We liaised with the unit in the MPS which was looking after her.) The disclosure work on all unused material gathered during the investigation was vast. This was a full-time job for two of our officers and for our counsel, Mr Ellison. I also had to address the issue of court security, witness protection and jury protection with Mr Bevan. He agreed that these were matters would need to be brought before the trial judge prior to the date of the trial. Furthermore, there were concerns regarding intelligence from the Police Service in general, as well as from other investigative agencies. These needed to be dealt with separately, and prior to the trial.

This process is called Public Interest Immunity (PII) and relates to the disclosure or non-disclosure of sensitive information.

The Crown Prosecution Service (CPS) has issued guidelines that should be followed when these matters arise. They state that:

Where sensitive material is identified as meeting the disclosure test, and the prosecutor is satisfied that disclosure would create a real risk of serious prejudice to an important public interest, the options are to:

- disclose the material in a way that does not compromise the public interest in issue;
- obtain a court order to withhold the material;
- abandon the case; or
- disclose the material because the overall public interest in pursuing the prosecution is greater than in abandoning it.

The House of Lords endorsed this advice in the case of R v H and C [2004] UKHL 3.

The judge selected to hear this trial was Lord Justice Latham. He dealt with all these preliminary matters in what is commonly referred to as a 'Judge in Chambers application'.

The term 'Judge in Chambers' is a simple term used to identify a situation where a Judge will make a decision on an application before him/her in private, with the press and public excluded from such hearings.

I was present in court with Mr Bevan and Mr Ellison. It was suggested to the judge by the other advocates, however, that I should not be present when other agencies made their applications. I was not permitted to even know how many other investigative agencies were making applications, nor what their subject matter was. I still do not know it now. Hence, despite being a senior police officer and the SIO on this high-profile case, I had to leave the courtroom.

Suffice to say that Noye appeared to have his fingers in many pies.

Mr Bevan began to deal with our applications once I was recalled to the courtroom. I had to politely interrupt his opening address and remind him that counsel from the other agencies should not be permitted to hear our application.

The judge addressed Mr Bevan, asking, 'Is there a problem, Mr Bevan?'

Although Mr Bevan was annoyed by my interruption, he said to the judge, 'Mr McGookin, the Senior Investigative Officer in this case, has brought to my attention that my learnèd colleagues should no longer remain in the courtroom.'

The judge addressed those in the courtroom, saying, 'The officer is correct. Those of you not involved in the prosecution case, please leave the courtroom now.'

Upon which, several advocates threw me unhealthy stares, which I acknowledged with a wry smile as they left the courtroom.

Our hearing resumed, and I was called to give evidence about the intelligence we had gathered regarding the threat to Noye's life and the suggestions he might attempt to escape custody, which we had received from a different intelligence source.

The subject of 'jury nobbling' was also raised by Mr Bevan. The term 'jury nobbling' refers to the actual or attempted influence of one or more jury members through intimidation or inducement. The Criminal Justice and Public Order Act 1994 introduced a specific offence of intimidating or threatening witnesses or jurors.

The judge granted each of our applications and further ordered that an armed police officer be present in the court complex (but not the courtroom) throughout the trial. Protection of the jury was also ordered. The Lord Justice's clerk made the necessary arrangement with the MPS for the court protection and the witness protection.

❖

As the trial date approached, we made arrangements with Ken and Toni Cameron for our FLOs to transport them to and from the court each day. This was to ensure that they were looked after throughout what was likely to be a traumatic hearing for them. On top of this, it was inevitable that there would be a media frenzy. There was little doubt that the press (true to form) would be desperate to interview Stephen's parents. The clerk of the court was extremely helpful and arranged for the FLO to drive through the rear entrance to the court complex each day, in order to avoid being hindered by the media.

The safety of our witnesses was also important. We agreed with Mr Ellison specifically which witnesses would be required on any given day.

Danielle was required on Day 1, so her Witness Protection Officers had to liaise with the clerk of the court in order to arrange her entrance and exit to and from both the court complex and the courtroom.

Two of my team visited one of our key witnesses, Alan Decabral, to notify him of the day he would be required to give his evidence. I felt it was important that he, in particular, be collected from his home and driven to the court, to ensure he arrived safely. Unfortunately, what I did not tell my officers was that he should do his best to dress smartly and not bring his mobile phone into the courtroom (!).

The day of the trial finally arrived on Thursday, 30 March 2000. I caught the early train to London with several members of my team, so we arrived at the Old Bailey in plenty of time. Armed uniformed officers had already stationed themselves both outside and inside the building. Whilst awaiting our turn in the queue to go through the court security, the sound of police sirens could be heard in the distance, at which point I joked, 'I think Mr Noye must be on his way.'

My colleagues smiled at my observation.

The sound drew closer and closer, until a prison van's armed cavalcade swung into the Old Bailey road, with one marked firearms response vehicle (ARV) in front of the prison van and another behind the prison van, with two police motorcycle outriders in the rear. The first ARV pulled in just past the side entrance to the court across the road, and the officer leapt from the vehicle with firearms in full sight. As they took up their positions, the prison van veered in through the heavy gates to the cell area of the court complex, followed by the second ARV.

Noye had finally been delivered to face the trial he had done his utmost to avoid for so many years.

We were soon joined by Miss Elizabeth Howe, and then by Mr Bevan and Mr Ellison. I told them everything was going to plan so far and that Noye was in the cells. Mr Bevan and Mr Ellison disappeared into the barristers' robing room, which would be shared by every other barrister working in the courts that day (the robing room is an out of bounds area for police officers).

Not much time passed before Mr Bevan came and found me outside Court No.2. He took me aside and told me that Noye's barrister, Mr Stephen Batten QC, had spoken to his client and that he had admitted to the killing of Stephen Cameron but claimed self-defence. He was prepared to plead guilty to manslaughter on this basis.

I told him in no uncertain terms that we would not accept such a plea. Mr Bevan reminded me that he was not asking my opinion. He asked me to go and speak to the members of the victim's family, in order to pass on this information and ask what their views were. I was certain that deep down Noye knew there was a strong case against him, he was merely trying to claim any grounds he could, in order to be found not guilty of murder, but ultimately Mr Bevan was right: it was the family's view which was important, not mine.

I left Mr Bevan and went to find the family. I told them that Noye admitted killing Stephen but wanted to claim self-defence. I also told them that I did not want to accept this and they didn't argue. We then sat down and had a cup of tea. I said no more.

I returned to find Mr Bevan talking to Elizabeth Howe. I told him that the family agreed with me but, before I could say more, Mr Bevan said, 'Good. So, we are all in agreement then.'

As far as we were all concerned, this trial was for murder and nothing else.

The trial began. The first task was to show the jury candidates into the courtroom and begin the jury selection process. The court needed twelve members of the jury and, eventually, eight women and four men were sworn in as our jury.

Four members of my team, who were not engaged on a specific task at this point in time, accompanied me into the courtroom. Their specific task was to observe Noye's reaction to the jury members, one by one, as they each took their place in the jury box. Other officers observed the public gallery, which was full. As each jury member was selected, Noye did not take his eyes off the jury box. He sat hunched over in the dock of the court, dressed all in grey, wearing dowdy trousers, a wrinkled, blue shirt and a long cardigan. He looked particularly untidy. He appeared to have lost weight and the expression on his face was showing his age and the pressure he was under. His hair had grown long, it had also greyed considerably. Bearing in mind that he was only 52 years old, he seemed to me to be trying his hardest to look like a down-beaten, old man.

The judge explained to the jury that they would receive round-the-clock protection which would, no doubt, affect their private lives, but that this protection was absolutely necessary. He warned them that this upcoming process must not be seen, in any way, to prejudice the case against Noye, and that they should not talk about the case to anyone outside the jury room. Finally, he reminded them that they must only judge this case on the evidence they heard in the courtroom and nothing else. The judge then invited Mr Bevan to open the case for the prosecution.

After introducing himself and Mr Ellison to the jury, and identifying his colleague who represented the defendant, Mr Bevan began his opening address. He referred to the case as being like a 'jigsaw puzzle' in which various witnesses saw the initial scene by the traffic lights. He went on to describe how the vehicle driven by Stephen Cameron's fiancé stopped on the roundabout and a Land Rover Discovery (LRD) car pulled up in front of it. The driver of the LRD alighted from the vehicle – that man was the defendant Kenneth Noye, 'Which he now admits,' he said. Others watched as the two men started to argue. Further witnesses who drove past saw slightly different stages of the fight.

Mr Bevan went on to explain that what we did know for certain was that Stephen was unarmed and that the defendant went back to his car, retrieved a knife, came back to Stephen and stabbed him in the chest. Mr Bevan told the court that a witness who had stopped his Rolls-Royce at the traffic lights on the slip road onto the roundabout saw Noye smile as he stabbed Stephen. After this, Noye returned to his car and drove off. Mr Bevan told the court that Noye now admits that he did indeed stab Stephen, but insists that the killing was an act of self-defence.

The first witness called was Danielle. She initially came into the court-room with her face covered. She wore a long, black wig and her face was coloured with make-up which gave her a heavily tanned complexion. I did not recognise her. She took the oath and began to weep as she gave her evidence. She described the events of the day and, in particular, the fight.

As the courtroom listened in silence, she described how the man came back from his car holding the knife out, then went for Stephen. She said it all happened so fast. When Stephen turned towards her, blood was pouring out of his chest. He collapsed beside his red van. Danielle said she jumped out of the van at once, screaming at passing cars and crying for help.

Representing Noye, Mr Batten cross-examined Danielle. He sug-gested that Stephen was kicking Noye on the ground during the fight, but Danielle's recollection was that the older man did not go down on the ground. Mr Batten challenged Danielle, insisting that she was not giving a true account of the incident because she was finding it difficult to accept that any of it was Stephen's fault, but Danielle remained stead-fast and told the court that she did not believe it was Stephen's fault in any way, shape or form.

At the conclusion of giving her evidence, Danielle covered her face and was assisted out of the courtroom. I was satisfied at the end of the first day of the trial with how the hearing was proceeding so far. I liked Mr Bevan's opening speech and was pleased that Danielle gave her evi-dence so clearly. I only hoped that she could now begin to try her best to rebuild a life for herself.

Day two of the trial saw our witness, Alan Decabral, in attendance. Court normally begins at 1000 hrs but today there was a delay which, in fact, turned out to be helpful because Mr Decabral had still not arrived. I received a message that they would arrive at the court within thirty minutes. I updated Mr Bevan. The court started just after 1100 hrs.

Mr Bevan called for Mr Decabral. When the door opened, I noticed that the jury were smirking, even Noye had a smile on his face. I turned to look at Mr Decabral as he entered the courtroom and my heart sank.

Mr Decabral was a very large man, some 20 stone, not necessarily a bad thing, of course, but the point was that it is usual in a courtroom to wear a suit and tie, or at least a smart shirt and jacket. Not Mr Decabral. He had chosen to wear a pair of baggy tracksuit bottoms, a bright coloured rugby shirt and slip-on sandals which revealed his bare feet. His long grey hair was pulled back into a ponytail and he was completely unshaven. Mr Bevan turned around to give me a questionable look and I, in turn, looked at my two officers who had brought him to court, shaking my head at them in utter disbelief.

Decabral was an intelligent man but our research on him had been interesting. Despite his unkept appearance, he had received a public-school education at a well-known school. As the old saying goes, 'Don't judge a book by its cover.' Whilst he did not have any previous convictions, he had been the subject of intelligence-gathering operations which had been undertaken by a variety of investigative agencies, including Regional Crime Squads (who are now known as the National Crime Agency). All these operations were based on rumours about a shady history involving drugs and firearms smuggling into the UK through his business, and the importation of antique radiators. There was absolutely nothing to claim any link with Noye and, even if he was a criminal himself, we had no reason to disbelieve what he told us he saw on the roundabout that day.

Decabral took the affirmation and stood upright in the witness box. Mr Bevan was just about to ask him his full name when a mobile phone rang out in courtroom. The Lord Justice looked around the courtroom to ascertain whose phone was ringing, at which point Decabral reached down into his pocket and produced his phone. Another dirty look came at me from Mr Bevan and I shook my head at my officers once again.

Decabral did not simply switch the phone off but, much to the amazement of everyone in the court, he answered it in his distinctively loud but educated voice. The jury began laughing. Noye was laughing too. I could not even look at Mr Bevan, Mr Ellison or Elizabeth Howe.

'I can't talk now,' Decabral told his caller, 'I'm in court. Call me back later,' he added, before casually placing the phone back into his pocket.

The judge turned to the witness and said, very simply, 'Mr Decabral, please do not bring your business into my court.'

Decabral apologised to the judge and started to give his evidence.

Decabral went on to prove himself as a surprisingly valuable witness. He described, in great detail, all he had seen from his car, including: the flash of the blade in the sun before the older man stabbed the younger man in the chest; the scornful smile on Noye's face immediately after the stabbing; how he drove off at speed and almost crashed into his car. His evidence ended up going very well.

I looked over at Noye. There was no smile on his face now. He seemed decidedly worried in, fact.

When Mr Batten's turn came to cross-examine Mr Decabral, he accused our witness of making up stories and giving an inaccurate account of what really happened. Mr Decabral was certainly nobody's fool. He responded like a cricketer hitting a six to every single question bowled at him. Each and every time, he painted a very clear picture of all he had seen that day.

Mr Batten continued to call Mr Decabral's memory of the incident into question but he could not bowl him out over anything.

Eventually, Mr Decabral had finally had enough of Mr Batten's line of questioning.

'If you don't believe me,' he said calmly, staring straight at Mr Batten, 'then why don't you just play the telephone recording of my 999 call to the police?'

A winning shot in any cricket match!

'That will not be necessary,' Mr Batten said.

'Well,' he said, 'it will prove I'm telling the truth.' Mr Decabral clearly took the attitude that there was still another ball to bowl, as the over was not finished.

The judge was forced to interrupt. 'What is your view, Mr Bevan?' he asked. 'Should the 999 recording be played?'

'It is my view,' Mr Bevan replied, 'that the witness's integrity is being so forcefully challenged that the recording should indeed be played.'

The judge agreed and the hearing was adjourned so that a sound system could be brought into the court.

Mr Decabral stood in the witness box and silently listened whilst the recording was played. Noye sat staring down at his knees. It was clear to me that the jury were impressed by Mr Decabral's detailed account of the events which had unfolded before his very eyes, on the actual day of the attack. I could tell it was making quite an impression on them.

At the end of the recording Mr Batten stood up. 'I have no further questions,' he said.

This was a good day for the prosecution but I was still unimpressed by my officers. I spoke to them privately outside the courtroom.

'Why on earth,' I asked, 'did you allow the witness to dress like that in a court of law.'

'Mr Decabral had not wanted to come to court at all,' they explained. 'By the time we got him going we were running late. We wouldn't have made it to court if we had waited for him to change.'

'And what about the mobile phone?' I asked. 'How could you overlook that?'

They threw their hands up and simply said, 'We didn't know about it.'

It took some time after these proceedings before we were eventually able to laugh about Mr Decabral 'bringing his business into court'. The national press were captivated by Decabral's evidence. The following day, a court artist's sketch of Decabral in the witness box appeared in every newspaper in the country. A framed mental image I still hold clearly to this day.

Over the following days, all the scene witnesses in attendance at court gave their evidence. The car cleaner gave his evidence about the knife in one of the cars belonging to the Noye family. The hotel worker recounted Noye's visits to the hotel in Dartford under the name of Anthony Francis. The testimony about an LRD being crushed at a scrap yard a few days after the incident was heard. Our evidence regarding the mobile phone calls made immediately after the incident in the Swanley area was presented. Further evidence was read to the jury in respect to Noye leaving the country in a helicopter, flying to Caen in France and then onwards to Spain in a Learjet.

The next evidence to be called was medical. The ambulance crew who passed the incident and stopped to give first aid, which continued until Stephen reached hospital, described their tenacious attempts to keep

Stephen alive. The doctor concluded his evidence by telling the court how he had sadly pronounced Stephen dead at West Hill Hospital, Dartford.

The next witnessed called was Dr Heath, the forensic pathologist who carried out the post-mortem examination on Stephen's body in the early evening of Sunday, 19 May 1996, in the mortuary at West Hill Hospital, Dartford. He described Stephen's body and then went on to focus on the details of the two stab wounds to Stephen's chest. According to him, the fatal stab wound was 18cm long.

A second forensic pathologist, Dr Jerreat, gave evidence about his examination of the body, on behalf of HM Coroner. He disagreed with Dr Heath's evidence regarding the length of the fatal wound, stating that he believed it was closer to 16cm.

A third forensic pathologist, Dr Djurovic, who had examined the reports of both pathologists and the original post-mortem photographs, sided with Dr Jerreat's view.

Mr Batten, however, did not make a major issue out of the length of the fatal wound and, thankfully, the matter was left to the jury to make up their own minds.

As far as I was concerned, such details were all just part of the 'court-room drama'. Even when we went to the court of appeal, we never gleaned any sense out of the legal arguments over the length of the wound. It was all to do with the question of whether the knife had been pushed in forcefully or not – 1cm? 2cm? – it was all so ridiculous. What a waste of public money. The fact is, a man had died violently at the hand of another man and there was no question who had perpetrated this horrendous crime.

This concluded the case for the prosecution, and overall I was satisfied that we had done the best we could for Stephen, Danielle and his family. We now had to wait to see if Noye would choose to give evidence to the court.

In criminal proceeds like this case, it is up to the prosecution to present all relevant evidence to prove their case. The defence do not have to prove their innocence. In a criminal trial, an accused person can choose whether they wish to give evidence or not.

If Noye had pleaded guilty to manslaughter, however (and if this choice had been acceptable to the prosecution and the trial judge), he would need to offer some form of evidence to prove that it was self-defence.

On the Friday morning, 7 April 1999, I was told that Noye was indeed going to give evidence. He could have made a statement from the dock, covering what he intended to say without being cross-examined by the prosecution, but if he wanted to try to persuade the jury that he acted in self-defence, then he would be obliged to stand up to cross-examination.

The trial restarted. Noye walked towards the witness box without looking at the jury. He was still wearing the same old, grey cardigan. An eerie silence fell over the courtroom as he started to give his account of events of that Sunday afternoon almost four years earlier.

Noye blamed Stephen for starting the fight, claiming that Stephen had threatened to kill him. He claimed that Stephen had kicked him to the ground and continued to punch him whilst telling him over and over that he was going to kill him. Noye claimed that he thought he had only stabbed Stephen once, but accepted that it may have been twice. He agreed that he carried a knife for self-protection, but claimed that he only retrieved the knife from his car as a means to threaten Stephen.

Noye then revealed to the court that he had previously killed a man in self-defence. I could see from the look of shock and horror on the faces of the jury, they could not believe what they were hearing: he was actually admitting to killing someone else before this event!

He proceeded to tell the court that the man he had formerly killed turned out to be an undercover police officer and that he had killed him in his garden because he thought the officer was an intruder.

Noye had been charged with the murder of the officer, DC John Fordham, but was acquitted in this very court building back in 1985, on the grounds of self-defence. Noye's Evidence In Chief (EIC) finished. It was now the prosecution's turn to cross-examine him.

EIC is the term used in legal proceedings in England and Wales when a person is called to give evidence first, by the advocate representing the party calling that witness.

Mr Bevan got straight to the point. He challenged Noye with the facts as he saw them – it was clear from what had previously occurred with DC Fordham that Noye knew all too well how lethal a knife could be. This time Noye claimed that he did not know exactly where on a body someone needed to be stabbed in order to die. Most people know that any stab wound to the chest is likely to prove fatal but Noye simply ignored this obvious and widely known fact.

The evidence of Noye being Anthony Francis followed, which Noye admitted was him. He claimed that this was part of his plan to stay safe and to avoid being recognised by members of other crime groups who may have thought that, if he still had missing gold from the Brink's-Mat robbery, they may have tried to kidnap him.

The events of 19 May 1996 were then put to him. Why was he carrying a knife? Why did he stop in front of the red van? Why did he go back for the knife? What had he planned to do with it? Why did he stab Stephen?

Mr Bevan asked him if he had, in fact, lied to the Spanish court during his extradition hearing about not being at the scene of the incident and, therefore, not being in any way responsible for stabbing Stephen – he had since been returned to England and was suddenly claiming self-defence.

'Yes,' Noye replied, admitting he had lied. I could only hope that the fact that he was willing to lie to a court to avoid facing charges would not be lost on the jury.

That concluded Noye's cross-examination. The following day, Noye's wife appeared for the defence. Brenda Noye, who had previously been arrested for the murder of DC Fordham and conspiracy to handle stolen gold (but had these charges dropped) claimed that her husband was not a violent man. She said that after the incident on the roundabout had taken place, she had agreed with him: he needed to disappear because he believed that he was unlikely to get a fair trial in England. She admitted visiting him in Spain, on several occasions, whilst he was on the run.

An associate of Noye's son gave evidence against Stephen, stating that he had seen Stephen lose his temper on two separate occasions. This evidence, however, was totally discredited when he admitted to his own criminal record. He also shared the fact that Noye's family had paid his hotel bill the previous night, and that whilst he was there, he was with Noye's son and they had discussed both the case and his evidence.

The following day, prosecution counsel and defence counsel gave their closing speeches.

Mr Bevan summoned up the prosecution case on the basis that, even if Stephen was winning the fight, there was no justification for Noye to turn away from the fight, go to his car, retrieve a knife, return to the unarmed victim and stab him – not once, but twice in the chest – and that, under the circumstances, the use of such force was way beyond any kind of response which could ever be considered reasonable.

Mr Batten addressed the jury on the issues of a fair trial. He asked the jury to ignore all publicity they may have been exposed to regarding the case, as well as the fact that his client fled the country because he knew he would not get a fair trial. Regarding the incident itself, he maintained that Stephen was kicking his client and that Stephen had in fact put his extensive martial arts training into practice. His client merely acted in self-defence.

Lord Justice Latham then summed up the case and stated that the jury had four options to consider:

1. Guilty of Murder
2. Not Guilty of Murder but Guilty of Manslaughter
3. Not Guilty of Murder but Guilty of Manslaughter by reason of provocation
4. Not Guilty.

The judge explained the rationale behind the four choices, clarifying that a person was entitled to 'defend' themselves and to use such force as was reasonable in the circumstances. Such a person had to have an honest belief that they were under attack. However, if it was 'retaliation' then the use of a knife was unlawful. He explained further that, in this case, if the defendant used the knife instinctively, whilst not 'intending' to cause the victim serious harm, but 'risked' causing the victim some harm then, in this case, the verdict could be construed as manslaughter.

The jury retired on the morning of Thursday, 13 April 2000. It was a long wait and by no means did it end there. The jury could not reach a verdict and so they were sent to a hotel for the night, under armed police protection. The following morning, we were back in court and the judge called the jury into the courtroom. He advised them that he would accept a majority verdict and sent them back to deliberate until at least midday.

> In the first instance, a jury are given enough time to return a unanimous verdict. However, if they are unable to do so, they are permitted to return a majority verdict.
>
> Under 'normal' circumstances (i.e. with a full jury) a 'majority verdict' means that the judge is content to receive a verdict if ten or more of the twelve jurors are in agreement.
>
> Please note: If you have a jury of twelve, then you can accept the verdict of ten to two majority verdict. There are occasions where a member of the jury, for whatever reason, has to leave the jury during the trial. What happens in such cases is that the judge allows the trial to continue with eleven jurors, and in that case, the 'ten to two majority' is out the window, and the judge is then allowed to accept a ten to one majority.

After lunch, we heard that the jury had returned. My team and I attended court hoping and praying for the guilty verdict.

The jury filed in and Noye was ordered to stand up. The foreman of the jury was first asked to stand and then asked whether they had reached a verdict. The foreman said they had reached a majority verdict of guilty by 11-1.

Noye was visibly shocked.

Ken Cameron jumped up with his arms stretching to the sky. 'Yes!' he shouted.

What happened next was nothing short of astounding.

The instant the verdict was delivered and Ken reached up his arm to the sky, a bright ray of sunshine drenched the courtroom through the large, glass dome in the ceiling. This was a truly astonishing sight and the timing couldn't have been more perfect. Incredibly, this has occurred twice in my career. It honestly makes me believe that there is more to this life than we know.

Lord Justice Latham addressed Noye.

'The jury,' he said, 'have found you guilty of murder. There is only one verdict I can impose and that is one of life imprisonment. Take him down.' At that stage the judge gave no tariff, but a letter was later written with a suggested term.

> The tariff is the minimum period a life sentence prisoner must serve to meet the requirements of retribution and deterrence before being considered for release. After this minimum period has been served release will only take place where the prisoner is judged no longer a risk of harm to the public.
>
> Hilary Benn, Parliamentary Under-Secretary of State for Prisons and Probation*

The prison officers who had sat in the dock with Noye led him down the step to the cells. Lord Justice Lathan thanked both sets of counsel before standing up, bowing and leaving the courtroom. Because of all the time they had spent investigating the matter, my entire team had stayed to hear the verdict, of course. Each and every one of them was smiling, some even had tears in their eyes. We had championed justice for Stephen and all those who loved and missed him, at long last.

There were jubilant scenes outside the courtroom. Ken, Toni, all the Cameron family and my team hugged. We were surrounded by journalists, court staff and eventually joined by Mr Bevan, Mr Ellison and Elizabeth Howe. Toni placed a kiss on Mr Bevan's cheek. We finally had something to smile about after four long years. What a wonderful feeling of relief.

I made sure to send a message to the MPS Witness Protection Team so Danielle could be told the verdict before hearing it from any other source. I also sent a message to the Chief Constable, who sent his congratulations to the entire team.

---

* web.archive.org/web/20110605010309/http://www.parliament.
the-stationery-office.co.uk/pa/cm200102/cmhansrd/vo020708/
text/20708w27.htm

I had prepared packages for the media with our force Media Liaison Department in anticipation of this result, containing a formal statement acknowledging the verdict, thanking everyone who had been involved in the investigation, thanking Stephen's family, including his fiancée, Danielle, and all the witnesses. It contained an official police photograph of Kenneth Noye as well.

I had also prepared an alternative media package, in case the verdict had gone against the prosecution, but that was safely locked away in my briefcase and would never see the light of day.

Most people will have seen the scenes on television and in newspapers, when a newsworthy trial concludes successfully outside a court building. I was aware that we would be facing such a situation in only a few minutes. As things started to calm down, I took Ken and Toni back in to the witness waiting-room and told them what to expect outside the court building. I asked them to wait in the room until I had spoken to my team and to Elizabeth Howe.

Elizabeth and I had previously discussed what our joint Police/CPS response to the alternative verdicts would be. Elizabeth had arranged a large conference room in the nearby Crown Prosecution Service Headquarters, where a formal press conference was due to commence within the hour. I prepared my team for a potentially overwhelming media scrum and instructed them to lead Ken and Toni safely out of the court building. Once Ken, Toni and their family were ready to go, I followed my team as they walked slowly along the first-floor corridor and down the large staircase into the foyer of the court building. I paused one last time to check that Ken and Toni were truly prepared for what lay ahead, before we exited the building to face an enormous cheer and thousands of camera snaps. What a marvellous experience.

Although a large scrum encircled us, we were given enough breathing space to get through, thanks to the professionalism of our team and the City of London Police.

Questions came in from all directions as I gave my formal reply on the verdict. I believe the media 'grabbed' the following quote from me: 'Kenneth Noye ran, but he could not hide,' I said.

Ken Cameron told the press how 'overjoyed and relieved' they were, before going on to say, 'The day Stephen died we felt we had died. It is only our family and friends who have kept us going.'

'Our lovely son is dead,' Toni Cameron added, 'and our lives will never be the same again. Our thoughts are with our son's fiancée, whose courage in flying to Spain in August 1998, in order to identify Noye as the killer, was fantastic. She is trying to get on with her life but until today, she hasn't been able to. She has been an inspiration to us.'

Eventually, we managed to go back inside the court building, but the journalists and news broadcasters continued to hover for most of the afternoon. Our FLOs accompanied Ken and Toni home, I went to the press conference at CPS headquarters and the rest of my team went out to celebrate.

Elizabeth Howe and I offered our comments on behalf of Kent Police and the CPS at the press conference and, after questions, we were able to join my team, along with Mr Bevan and Mr Ellison, for a celebratory drink at long last!

Mr Bevan and I laughed when I reminded him of our very first conference – the time I thought he had invited me for a drink. Ultimately, we had uncovered the very evidence he needed.

The afternoon stretched into the evening – it was just as well that everyone had been given the next day off work.

The force received letters of congratulations from people of all walks of life in the weeks following the verdict. Letters from members of the public across the country, from members of the military abroad and from police officers from across the UK of varying ranks right up to Chief Constables. There was one, however, which really stood out for me. This letter was from one of the late DC John Fordham's colleagues. It was the words he used in closing his letter which touched my heart the most:

If the number of popping champagne corks in the Met outnumbered those in Kent last night, it is only because the Met is larger than Kent – the fact remains that you did something we couldn't.

As was convention at the time, Lord Justice Latham wrote a report for both the Lord Chief Justice and the Home Secretary, recommending a tariff of sixteen years. In 2002, the then Home Secretary, David Blunkett, duly set the tariff before Noye would be able to apply for parole at sixteen years, as recommended.

❖

As life started to return to normal, many other serious crimes needed to be investigated, but I knew Noye wouldn't wait long to appeal against his conviction, so we needed to be prepared for any appeal with immediate effect.

On 5 October 2000, I was sitting on a promotion board, interviewing officers who were applying for promotion to the rank of Inspector. The boards were held at a local hotel on the outskirts of Maidstone. My colleague and I had finished our first interview and were about to have a coffee when I received a message informing me that a man had been murdered at a retail park on the outskirts of the town of Ashford, a mere fifteen minutes away. I was first and foremost a detective, which meant I was more interested in crime than paperwork, so, despite feeling sorry for the officers awaiting their interview – men and women who had no doubt studied hard for their potential promotion – I responded to the call and informed the FCR that I would attend the scene at once.

I was at the scene in Ashford soon after, and liaised with one of my SIOs, DCI Bob Nelson. He had everything under control but he had an inkling that of all the detectives on the force, I would take a special interest in this particular victim because the victim was Alan Decabral, our star witness at the Kenneth Noye trial.

He had been sitting in the front passenger's seat of his son's car with the nearside window down, whilst his son had gone into a motor accessories shop. His son returned a few minutes later to find his father had fallen asleep. It only took a moment before he realised that something was not right. Whilst he was gone, in fact, a hitman had shot Mr Decabral in the side of the head.

One of our key witnesses, and one who had been so crucial to the prosecution's case, had been brutally murdered in cold blood.

DCI Bob Nelson led the hunt for Decabral's murderer, and although he had no doubt that the culprit was a professional hitman, there were no witnesses to the killing, no forensic evidence nor any CCTV footage which was of any assistance to the investigation.

Decabral had been suspected of drugs and gun smuggling for some time, and although he had extensive criminal contacts, he had never been convicted. His estranged wife told the enquiry team that he had been a drug dealer who owed money to others but no evidence was found to support her claim. Noye was questioned by the enquiry team but denied having any knowledge of it.

The case remains unsolved.

The big question now was exactly how this witness's death would assist Noye's legal team once he inevitably lodged his appeal against his conviction of murder.

In the early summer of 2001, the CPS informed me that Noye had launched his appeal and it was set to be heard on 10 October of that year. His appeal would set out to discredit Alan Decabral's evidence on the basis that Decabral was a man of bad character. It was his estranged wife who was to provide proof of his bad character, in a letter written to Noye whilst he was in prison, telling him that her husband was, essentially, a liar and all-round evil person. Proving Decabral had a disposition towards misconduct and thereby discrediting his reputation (and therefore his evidence) when he had been such a crucial witness to us could certainly strengthen Noye's appeal, especially given that he was no longer alive to speak for himself.

On 19 October 2001, I was in attendance at the Court of Appeal with a few members of our team. Once again, Mr Bevan was our QC and Mr Ellison was also in attendance. Noye's legal team was led by Mr Michael Mansfield QC.

Considering I had seen Mr Batten QC in the court building that very morning, I was surprised that he was not representing Noye. The reasons for this would become pretty clear soon enough.

The appeal was to be heard by Lord Wolfe CJ. It was not solely based upon Decabral's questionable character, but the fact that these questions regarding his character had not been previously disclosed to the defence. This meant that Mr Batten had not been given any opportunity to cross-examine Decabral on it and, therefore, had no opportunity to undermine Decabral's account of what he stated he had seen.

It turned out that the reason Mr Batten was in the courthouse was because he was giving evidence in this very appeal. I later found out that this was most irregular. When he entered the witness box, Lord Wolfe addressed him.

'This is a very unusual sight, to see counsel in the witness box.' Mr Batten made no reply.

It was a real telling-off to those involved in the defence team. Mr Batten shared his view, but by the end of this hearing the appeal was nonetheless dismissed.

Lord Wolfe declared, 'There was absolutely no justification for the appellant to take out a knife, whether it was a flick-knife or a knife that required two hands to open it, and use it in this fracas.'

I suppose it is inevitable that someone like Noye, with money and narcissistic personality traits, will continually challenge his incarceration. He also applied through his legal team to the Criminal Cases Review Commission to review his case, but they found no grounds to refer the case back to the Court of Appeal.

> The Criminal Cases Review Commission (CCRC) is the independent organisation set up to investigate suspected miscarriages of justice from magistrates' courts, the Crown Courts in England, Wales and Northern Ireland and the Court Martial and Service Civilian Court. Their principal role is to investigate cases where people believe they have been wrongly convicted of a criminal offence or wrongly sentenced.

Noye would make application against the Criminal Case Review Commission not to refer his conviction in 2007 to the Court of Appeal. Two senior judges considered the application and granted a full hearing but his case was refused. He later made an application to have his minimum term of imprisonment reduced but this was rejected.

The date was then set for the hearing into the CCRC refusal to refer the case to the Court of Appeal. The hearing on 13 October 2010 was short and the decision was made that the CCRC should refer the case back to the Court of Appeal.

The next appeal by Noye on the CCRC's report to the Court of Appeal was based on two grounds:

- New evidence that is capable of significantly undermining the credibility of an expert prosecution witness Doctor Heath (the forensic pathologist) and the evidence he gave at trial
- New evidence that there was bruising to Mr Cameron's knuckles.

Noye was represented by Miss Montgomery QC at this appeal, which was heard on 22 March 2011. Mr Ellison QC represented the Crown. The issue with Dr Heath's evidence at the original trial was that a number of complaints had severely damaged his reputation, since he gave that evidence. A Home Office Tribunal was convened to examine his professional conduct and performance, and it called into question whether he was fit to remain on the Home Office Register of Forensic Pathologists. On hearing this, Dr Heath resigned immediately from the Register but continued as a pathologist.

Two forensic pathologists were called by the prosecution during the trial – Dr Heath, who had conducted the first post-mortem, and Dr Jerreat, who had carried out a second post-mortem on behalf of HM Coroner. Due to the fact that, at the time, there was no known defendant and, as such, no defence post-mortem.

There was no effective challenge to Dr Heath's evidence concerning the first and fatal stab wound. Dr Heath's evidence concerned the depth of the second wound, which he stated was 18cm, contrary to Dr Jerreat's view – that the depth was 16cm. Yet a third forensic pathologist, Dr Djurovic, agreed with Dr Jerreat's view. The discrepancy in views between the pathologists meant this: in Dr Heath's description, the second wound was caused by 'considerable force', whereas according to the other pathologists' view, the wound was caused by 'reasonable force'. The jury were already fully aware of this dispute. The issue regarding the bruising was described as 'trivial', since it had been accepted that Mr Cameron did indeed punch the defendant. Despite trying to use every opportunity to get released, it was understood that the grounds for Noye's appeal were deeply flawed. At the end of the hearing, the conclusion was: 'Appeal is Dismissed'.

Noye remained in custody, despite his incessant applications to the parole board up until May 2019, when the parole board announced that Noye was 'Suitable for return to the community.' He was released from prison on 6 June 2019, then aged 72, after having served twenty years for the murder of Stephen Cameron.

For me, this case was finally over. Already two lives lost – those of Stephen and Alan Decabral – but the tragedy did not end there. In 2022, whilst writing my account of the M25 Road Rage killing of Stephen Cameron, I learnt that Stephen's mother, Toni, had died back in 2016, having caught septicaemia following an accident in her garden. Her ashes were buried with those of her son and, tragically, Ken, who could no longer carry on with the loss of his beloved son and wife, took his own life. All four were victims of a terrible crime, and all four faces will live, as clear as crystal, in my memory.

My thoughts are, and always will be, with those to whom Stephen remained dear. I attended Ken's funeral in April 2022, as did my two former SIOs in this case, Nic Biddiss and John Grace, together with Terry Gabriel and several other former colleagues who had worked on the investigation. It says a lot for the Police Service throughout the UK that, despite having retired from Kent Police, we were all present. It just goes to show that I am not alone, none of us in the force can ever forget, we spend a lifetime living with the memory of such faces.

By 16 June 2000, I had completed almost twenty-eight years' service with Kent Police and was readying myself for retirement in two years' time. I didn't anticipate having to deal with another high-profile investigation in that time. I had plenty of work to keep me busy, reviewing an unnatural death for the Metropolitan Police Service and overseeing numerous other major crimes in my own force area. I was also spending more time than expected, training officers of all ranks around the country.

I was the duty senior detective 'on call' for the force over the following weekend, and assumed (for some reason!) that things would stay quiet and I'd get to spend my Sunday evening at home watching television before settling down for a good night's sleep. That's what I'd hoped would happen in any case. Hmm …

My home telephone rang just after midnight. I'd only been asleep for ten minutes!

The fresh face of the author as a new recruit to the Kent County Constabulary in August 1972. (Author's collection)

Noye had been living at a villa - 21 Atlantara in Zahara, about an hours drive from Gibraltar.

Known locally as "Mick the Builder" he had a new alias of "ALAN EDWARD GREEN."

Passport Passeport

P   GBR   025140857

GREEN

ALAN EDWARD

BRITISH CITIZEN

27 JAN /JAN 56   O

M   GRAVESEND

03 DEC /DEC 96   UNITED KINGDOM

PASSPORT AGENCY

03 DEC /DEC 06

Major Crime Department

Kenneth Noye's doctored passport, used by him for fake identification. (Author's collection)

Me arriving at the Central Criminal Court in London for the trial of Noye. (PA/Alamy)

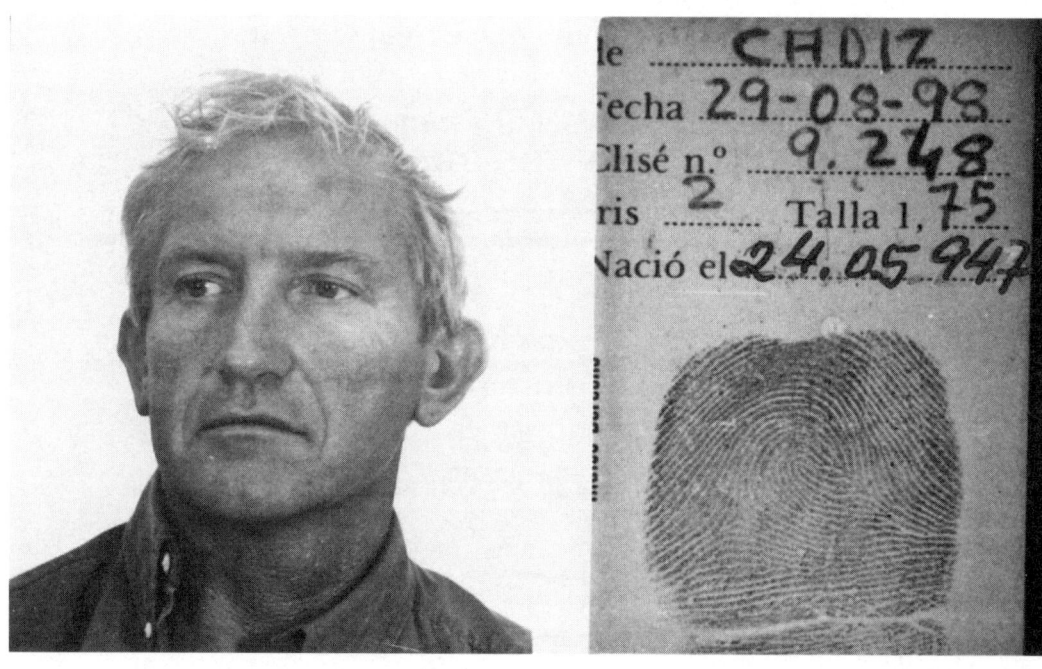

Spanish Police's photograph and fingerprints of Kenneth Noye following his arrest for the murder of Stephen Cameron. (PA/Alamy)

Stephen Cameron, the victim of Noye's road rage attack, on 19 May 1996. (PA/Alamy)

Me opening the post conviction press conference after the conviction of Kenneth Noye. (PA/Alamy)

Me with Ken and Toni Cameron outside the Central Criminal Court after Noye's conviction for the murder of Stephen Cameron. (Roger Allen/Mirrorpix)

Me conducting an appeal for information during an interview on a national news report on Chinese television, following the death of fifty-eight Chinese nationals at Dover Dock. (PA/Alamy)

The memorial stone in the village of West Kingsdown, Kent, laid in memory of Detective Constable John Fordham, who was killed nearby by Kenneth Noye. (Marathon/Geograph.org.uk)

An aerial view of Orchard House, showing the construction of a new indoor swimming pool. (Author's collection)

6

DOVER TRAGEDY: FIFTY-EIGHT DEAD

It ought to concern every person, because it is a debasement of our common humanity. It ought to concern every community, because it tears at our social fabric. It ought to concern every business, because it distorts markets. It ought to concern every nation, because it endangers public health and fuels violence and organised crime. I'm talking about the injustice, the outrage, of human trafficking, which must be called by its true name - modern slavery.

Barack Obama (25 September 2012)

The words of the former President of the United States of America are a fitting introduction to this story, which deals with the tragic deaths of fifty-eight Chinese nationals who were found dead in the back of a lorry at Dover Docks, Kent, England on the night of Sunday, 18 June 2000. It was the largest fatal human smuggling offence in the UK.

Only two young Chinese men survived this tragedy and their stories show the lengths to which organised criminals will go for monetary gain, with little to no regard for human lives.

Gangs sell the idea of settling in Europe for big money, in exchange for falsified work permits to work in what is now known as the former Yugoslavia, and passports. (It is not illegal in China to apply for a passport, but it is illegal to apply for a passport if it is to enable an illegal purpose.)

It begins in their home city, Fuzhou, the capital of the province of Fujian, which is located on China's south-eastern coast and faces the island province of Taiwan, east of the Taiwan Strait. It is from there that people embark on their long journeys firstly to the former Yugoslavia, then onward across Hungary, Austria, Paris and Rotterdam, before being placed in lorries which enable them to travel across the Channel.

These Chinese people travel in the hope that they will be successful in gaining secret entry into the United Kingdom. When they do succeed, they are dispersed throughout Chinese communities across the United Kingdom and their fate is unknown. If they are intercepted by HM Immigration Service, however, then they live in the hope that they will be permitted to stay in the United Kingdom where they then endeavour to build enough wealth to send money back to their families in China, who usually fund their perilous journey to the 'promised land' in exchange for this very promise.

The story which I am about to tell, on how events unfolded in one unprecedented case regarding the now infamous trade of people-smuggling, will reveal how the discovery of their bodies, the quest to identify them, the subsequent criminal investigation and the ultimate arrest of those responsible was made possible.

None of the victims in this tragic story had any means of identification upon them when they were found, and that only made us more determined to find out who they were and return them to their families, so they could say their own goodbyes.

The investigation was led by Kent Police, and involved numerous UK agencies, including HM Coroner for the County of Kent (East Kent District), the Embassy of the People's Republic of China in London, the Ministry of Public Security in Beijing and Fujian, the Foreign and Commonwealth Office, HM Immigration Service, Dover Harbour Board Authority and the British Embassy in Beijing.

The one group of people who were not involved in the investigation but should have been involved were the families of those who died. Investigators travelled to China but Chinese authorities would not permit them to meet or speak to the families.

❖

Sunday, 18 June 2000. Unbeknown to the authorities, and whilst many ordinary folk across the UK were settling down to watch their favourite Sunday evening television soaps, sixty people were struggling to breathe inside a container lorry, aboard a ferry bound for Dover. By the time the ferry had reached English shores and been directed to the customs search, fifty-eight of those had perished.

It had just gone midnight, my weekend as the duty senior detective on-call for the force had been relatively quiet. Little did I know that at that very point in time, a rescue operation was unfolding inside the perimeter walls of Dover Docks, located in the south-east area of Kent and often referred to as the 'Gateway to Europe'.

I had barely been asleep ten minutes when my home telephone rang. The caller identified herself as the force Control Room Supervisor. I vividly recall how careful she was to make sure I was compos mentis enough (at such an hour of the night) to understand what she was about to tell me. I assured her that I was awake and she told me there had been an incident at Dover Docks in which at least two people were dead.

Several illegal immigrants had been found inside a stopped lorry. Two of them had died. My mind started racing and as she spoke, I recall wondering why she was referring this matter to me specifically. Each area in the force had its own DI on-call and their training meant they were each capable of dealing with two deaths of this type. Before I questioned the Supervisor, however, she explained that the number of dead was now five. Within seconds, she apologised and corrected herself again – she had just been told that there were now eight dead, and that number was likely to rise.

I asked her to make sure that the on-call Chief Officer for the force was informed of this information, that I had been notified and was making my way to Dover Docks at once. I told her I would be available on my car phone within ten minutes. I jumped out of bed and jumped into the shower – it was going to be a long night and, as experience had taught me, I would have a reasonably comfortable night if I had showered and shaved, at the very least.

Once dressed, I called my colleague DCI Bob Nelson, who I knew was due to return to duty that Monday morning, after a short period of leave. I requested that he meet me at Dover Docks. I then telephoned our Head of Crime Scene Investigations, Lorraine Harris. She had also been called to attend, as had her team. We arranged to meet at the docks to review the scene and plan the forensic strategy.

My mind worked overtime on the hour-long journey to Dover. Very few detectives in the country would have experienced what me and my team were, potentially, about to face – mass fatalities.

There had recently been a report published called the *Thames Safety Inquiry* by Lord Justice Clarke, which examined the details of a collision between the pleasure cruiser called *The Marchioness* and a river dredger, called *Bowbelle*. The accident had taken place upon the River Thames in 1989 and resulted in fifty-one deaths. I bore in mind that some of the evidence from this case had called into question how some of the bodies of the deceased had been treated. Hands had been removed from the bodies of twenty-five of the victims as part of the fingerprint identification process. There was outrage when it was discovered that the bodies had been mutilated in the name of identification. This inquiry eventually led to a Public Inquiry, after which, changes were implemented when dealing with mass disasters.

My thoughts were interrupted by an incoming call on my hands-free facility. It was the FCR Supervisor who gave me the update – at least twelve people had now died. I thanked her, asking that she log the fact that I had phoned DCI Nelson and Lorraine Harris. We had no sooner ended our conversation, when my phone rang again. This time it was my colleague, Ian Humphries, who had been the former Head of the CID in the county but was now acting as a Chief Officer. We had a brief conversation about what was happening. I assured him that I would deal with everything once I arrived at the scene. Ian reminded me that he was due to start a new job at the Home Office that very morning, but he would still meet me at the docks. I had one more conversation with our FCR supervisor. The death toll had now risen to thirty-five and was likely to grow even higher.

The remainder of my journey seemed to pass in a flash. There did not appear to be much activity along the A20 approach road into Dover and down towards the docks' entrance, and I began to wonder if there had been a mistake. I was to discover soon that was not the case. Within seconds I was producing my warrant card at the security gates and being directed to a large HM Customs warehouse which stood approximately 100yd in front of me. A young Police Constable stood at the door to the warehouse. I identified myself, and asked him if he had been briefed as my mind flashed to a former image of myself, all those years ago as the young uniformed Constable who had once been left to guard a murder scene for which no one had briefed me. It was a relief to hear that the Duty Uniformed Inspector had instructed him to ask everyone to show their official identification before letting them enter the warehouse.

The first thing I saw upon entering the warehouse was a large articulated lorry, neatly parked and facing the outer doors of the warehouse. The blue Mercedes cab displayed a foreign number-plate and the attached articulated unit had the name *Sea Land* printed on its side.

I walked further into the warehouse. The Duty Uniform Inspector recognised me at once. We had a very brief conversation before he escorted me to the back of the lorry. Several bodies were lying in the back of the container. The Inspector assured me that they had all been certified dead and were about to be recovered. More bodies were laid out side-by-side upon a raised ramp area along the length of that side of the building. The bodies were in a state of undress. My initial thought was that they appeared to be of Chinese origin. I looked on as the remaining bodies were gently removed one-by-one and placed neatly beside the others. The duty Inspector then told me that once all the bodies had been certified dead, he had delayed the removal process so an evidential video could be obtained. In view of the complications which had arisen from the aforementioned Marchioness Public Inquiry, I felt this was an excellent decision.

The forensic team were already dealing with the lorry as a crime scene, which meant that work would be required in both the container and the cab. Numerous items were recovered from the cab in an attempt to link the driver to the lorry's macabre load. Photographs were taken to show the driver's position and whether he had been able to view the ventilation flap in the closed position, as he drove the vehicle off the ferry. The container itself had a dummy partition, in front of which there had been crates of tomatoes. The victims had been instructed to sit quietly behind that partition. There were piles of clothes scattered within the container. It would later transpire that, as the victims were not allowed to carry any luggage, they had layered their clothing. The discarded clothing could prove vital down the line when the investigation linked the victims to the human trafficking organisation in the UK.

Most of the victims appeared so young, and I found it sad that the only items they had with them were small funereal tokens of their ancestors since the traffickers must have taken their money and identity papers.

Soon after, the Duty Inspector and I were joined by the Duty DI for the area, Rob Vincent, and the on-call SIO for the force, David Gutsell, together with DCI Nelson and Lorraine Harris. I asked that the Police Surgeon join us as well, only to be told that he had left the scene after certifying all the bodies as dead.

Fifty-eight expense claims from the doctor requesting a payment for each one of the deceased was then placed before me. To say that I was shocked by this would be an understatement, especially given that, upon reading the claims, I discovered that all fifty-eight victims had been certified dead at exactly the same time. Needless to say, I gave instruction that if the doctor wanted his expenses paid, he would need to return to the scene and certify the death of each of the deceased again whilst they were being numbered and photographed for the identification process.

I released Rob Vincent and David Gutsell from their duties, since I knew they would be expected to return to their day jobs later that morning and, as such, it was unfair to keep them there.

Lorraine Harris, Bob Nelson and myself approached the fifty-eight bodies. None of us could quite believe what we were dealing with here. I thought my colleagues were both just behind me as I walked between the rows of bodies – some were face-up, some were lying on their sides, as if in the first-aid recovery position. It was a surreal scene to take in.

I recall saying, 'They look like they are just sleeping, don't you think?' as I looked at these figures on the ground. 'I feel like we should tell them to wake up, that everything will be fine and we will look after them.'

There was no response from Lorraine and Bob, only silence behind me, so I turned around to see why they had not answered me and found that they were not behind me at all – they had not moved down the line of bodies with me – they were already planning the linking of the criminal and the forensic strategy.

It was eerie to find myself, all of a sudden, standing alone amongst these dead people in the semi-darkness of a warehouse in this bizarre silence, the likes of which I had never experienced, and which was amplified by the cold weight of death. Very little air was circulating, since the doors of the warehouse were closed, and the stillness caught me entirely off-guard. It truly was a shuddery feeling which trembled through me as I discreetly, but swiftly, made my way back to the comfort and company of my colleagues.

The heat which had been generated from the back of the container grew uncomfortably high as I approached a large pile of discarded clothing stacked up at the entrance to the container. I couldn't imagine how high the temperature must have been inside that vehicle when these individuals had lost consciousness one by one and eventually died. It was utterly morbid to even try to imagine it.

When any senior officer attends a major crime scene, they are given a verbal briefing. This is not usually in a nice meeting room, but on arrival at the outskirts of the scene. The information outlines the discovery, any arrests, any back story that has been gathered. Sometimes there is a lot of information, the accuracy of which is unknown but which serves as a starting point. Other times, there is very little information. I was informed that the lorry had travelled from Zeebruger by ferry. It had been subject to a routine customs check as there was no customs seal on the doors. Once the rear doors were opened, two young men were visible. They were in medical distress and the customs officials were able to pull them from the lorry and call for the emergency services. The customs officials recalled seeing numerous faces in the vehicle, at that time, without realising that the people those faces belonged to were deceased. They instructed the driver to move the vehicle to a nearby customs rummage shed, which turned out to be an incredibly helpful move (unknowingly at the time) because it neatly enclosed the crime scene, shielding the lorry from the world's press when it descended. It allowed the victims' bodies to be moved and placed, with dignity, away from prying eyes.

I was told that two survivors had been conveyed to hospital and a police team, deployed with the ambulance, was awaiting permission from medical staff before they could speak with the victims.

The driver had been arrested and conveyed to Dover police station.

I was joined by Ian Humphries, who asked me if there was anything specific he could do to assist me (he clearly needed some sleep before he had to start his new job in several hours' time). I assured him that we were in control of the situation and that the lorry driver had been arrested and was in custody at Dover police station. All he needed to do was update the Chief Constable at an appropriate hour – my team and I would do the rest. We were joined by members of HM Customs and Excise, HM Immigration Service and the Port of Dover Authority (PDA) and Port of Dover Police, all of whom were following the discovery of these tragic events.

The Port of Dover Police is owned, operated and funded by the PDA. As a non-Home Office police force, the Port of Dover Police do not have a 'police area'. Kent Police are responsible for policing the whole of Kent, including the Port of Dover. The Dover Harbour Board, however, choose to fund their own police force to cover the port area. There may be occasions when Kent Police seek their assistance in dealing with local issues, but the jurisdiction of Port of Dover Police restricts the area in which their Constables can operate to within 1 mile of the property of Dover Harbour Board boundary.

Prior to having our first inter-agency briefing, I left Lorraine Harris to manage the forensic strategy. In the first instance this was to identify and ensure scenes were secure. She would then deploy teams of experienced scene of crime officers to deal with each scene. There was the initial process of photographing and searching the victims' bodies in the presence of the Police Surgeon, who gave an individual time of death for each victim. I made the decision that the deceased be given a number from one to fifty-eight, and that this unique number remain with the body until they left the jurisdiction of the UK Government. Of the fifty-eight victims, fifty-four were male and four were female. Other scenes were the lorry, the lorry driver and the clothing removed from the container. It was evident that post-mortem examinations would need to be held and Lorraine arranged the post-mortem teams. This would involve photography, examination, disaster victim recording and fingerprint teams. In the meantime, Lorraine identified an area just behind the rummage shed that was a cold room. That was usually the place where goods were stored prior to onward transfer. A number of wooden pallets were arranged in order that the victims' bodies could be stored there.

The initial interagency briefing, which I chaired, took place around 0400 hrs. I asked for any further details regarding the circumstances behind the vehicle and its driver. The interagency briefing included Dover Harbour Board Authority, Dover Harbour Board Police, HM Customs and Excise and HM Immigration Service. I requested details of all the agents involved.

I was informed that the lorry was a Dutch registered vehicle, bearing the registration number VT-31-TS. It had travelled on the P&O ferry, *European Pathway*, from the Port of Zeebrugge in Belgium, and had arrived in Dover around 2330 hrs. When the vehicle had been stopped at the HM Customs terminal and checked by Custom Officers, it was discovered that the seal on the rear door had been cut. The driver of the lorry was identified as a Dutch national, named Perry Wacker, aged 32 years.

An initial search of the rear of the vehicle was made and, when the rear doors were opened, two young Asian men were pulled out of the container. Neither man could speak English and they appeared to be in a poor physical condition. Thankfully, the Kent Ambulance Service had arrived on the scene and the two survivors received treatment and were transported to a local hospital. I gave the instruction that the term 'local hospital' should be used, as I did not want anyone to disclose which hospital they were in at the time, because, even at this very early stage of the investigation, I was concerned for their safety. This would be an investigation involving police forces in Europe, and if my initial thoughts were correct, and the victims came all the way from China, then the roots of this investigation would be in China. I can now disclose, however, that it was the Kent and Canterbury Hospital, which is located on the outskirts of Canterbury.

Organised crime syndicates were most probably behind the illegal smuggling of people, and since the two survivors were our key witnesses, their lives could very well be at risk. With this in mind, I asked the uniform Inspector to make arrangement for the two witnesses to have armed police protection in the hospital.

I was briefed about how the vehicle was moved to the rummage shed. After recovering the two survivors, the Custom Officers, a Dover Harbour Board police officer and several HM Immigration staff were startled by the sight of a large number of people found lying behind several boxes of tomatoes on the floor of the lorry. The driver of the vehicle was ordered to park the vehicle in a warehouse next to the HM Customs terminal, where he was arrested on suspicion of conspiracy to smuggle immigrants into the UK.

It was only as the tomato boxes were unloaded that the full extent of this incident started to unfold. Emergency services were called to the scene and a major incident was declared by the duty Police Inspector.

> A major incident is defined by the College of Policing as an event or situation requiring a response under one, or more, of the emergency services' major incident plans. This will usually include involving large numbers of people, either directly or indirectly.
>
> College of Policing*

Despite being declared a major incident it was, in fact, a mass fatality incident. The College of Policing advises that the decision to declare a mass fatality incident lies jointly with HM Coroner for the area where the incident has occurred, and the Police Gold Commander. The college advises that a fatality coordination group (MFCG) should be formed as soon as the decision is made to declare a mass fatality incident. In this incident, however, these formalities were delayed until later in the morning.

Where police respond to a mass fatality incident, the Gold Commander assumes overall command and has ultimate responsibility and accountability for the police response. The strategic commander chairs the strategic coordination group (SCG). Technically the on-call senior officer performs this role, but because I was the senior officer at the scene, it was I who took on this role. I was later joined by my colleague, Superintendent Chris Eyre, who was the local Area Commander, so we shared this responsibility. (Later in his career, Chris became the Chief Constable of Nottinghamshire Police and on retirement he was appointed as the Chief Police Officer for the Sovereign Base Area Police in Cyprus.)

---

* www.college.police.uk/app/civil-emergencies/disaster-victim-identification/definitions

The decision to form an MFCG was justified by a number of factors, including: the number of deceased (actual or potential); whether the nature of the incident was likely to make identifying the deceased difficult; whether the incident was as a result of terrorist or criminal activity; and whether suitable and sustainable mortuary capacity was available for as long as is likely to be required.

When a body is discovered, it lies under the jurisdiction of HM Coroner. The police must liaise with the Coroner regarding anything to do with the body. If there is to be a criminal inquiry, HM Coroner is responsible for authorisation of any examination – s/he tends to adjourn any inquest, however, until the outcome of a criminal investigation. Part of a Senior Investigator Officer's role is to liaise with the Coroner, seek authorisation for any decisions, and to keep them updated on the progress of the investigation.

The cold room's use as a temporary holding area for the victims was discussed with HM Customs and Excise. This was excellent news since the one thing I did not want was for the bodies to be transported to different mortuaries around the force area and beyond. At that time, mortuaries were at local hospitals, and many had less than a twenty-person capacity.

The next issue I raised was the media. I knew that an incident like this would not only make local and national news but become international news very quickly, and that, within the next twenty-four hours, television crews and reporters would descend on Dover Port in their hordes. Thankfully, the Dover Ports Authority was well-equipped for such an event and immediately offered to house the media in a conference room, away from the warehouse where the victims were located.

At the end of this initial meeting, I reminded each of the agency representatives that each agency needed to consider the welfare of the members of staff who were involved in the recovery of the victims. I also reminded my colleagues that the bodies were now the responsibility of HM Coroner, Mr Richard Sturt, and that I would be speaking with him at around 0600 hrs. Once our meeting finished, I returned to the scene in the warehouse to speak with Lorraine Harris so that she could update me on the Forensic Strategy together.

Our Forensic Strategy was:

- To secure all physical evidence at the lorry crime scene in order to enable any potential material recovered to be maximised for the purpose of assisting in the interview of suspects
- To test the reliability of any accounts given by the suspect
- To identify the fifty-eight victims
- To assist the SIO in prioritising lines of enquiry, or submitting particular items for further examination.

The deceased's clothing was searched and the bodies photographed, and Lorraine Harris updated me on the progress of the search. It suddenly dawned on me that, technically, we had all overlooked another crime scene – the ferry that had transported the vehicle into Dover Port.

It was possible that other vehicles had been used to transport this illegal cargo. Where were those vehicles now? With this in mind, I instructed a member of my staff to make sure the ferry did not leave the port until it was thoroughly searched, and all crew aboard had been identified. This instruction was immediately actioned and the result came back to me quite quickly.

It was not good news. The ferry had already reloaded and was in the process of leaving the harbour area and entering the English Channel. Upon receiving this update, I was approached by a gentleman who introduced himself to me as HM Coroner's Officer. I was in the process of explaining to him that I would be speaking to Mr Sturt later in the morning, but he told me this would not be necessary since he had all the necessary details required by the Coroner.

I realised the importance of a good liaison with the Coroner and politely informed his officer that I would speak with Mr Sturt directly. It is not unusual for the investigating officer to adopt the role of Coroner's Officer but I had the foresight to acknowledge that this would be one such occasion.

At this point, I realised that the Coroner's Officer was holding a camera. Any evidence gathering must be completely controlled. This ensures continuity and adherence to the 'law'.

'Have you been taking photographs?' I asked him.

'Yes, I have a photograph of each of the victims,' he replied.

He did not realise the implications of such an action. 'Well, you will be handing that camera over to me immediately,' I told him.

'What? Why?' he asked.

'The contents will, obviously, now become an exhibit in this investigation.'

Clearly, from the look on his face, he still did not understand but he handed it over to me.

I took myself away from the scene for a few minutes, in order to sit quietly in my car and prepare a media statement. It was up to me to set out the facts and circumstances regarding the incident as far as we knew them at that point in time and, given the enormity of the crime and the impact the death of fifty-eight victims would have on so many families, this had to be done in a sensitive manner.

I was able to confirm that fifty-eight unidentified foreign nationals had been found dead in a foreign, registered lorry and that a major police investigation was under way and one individual was in custody on suspicion of human smuggling and manslaughter. I deliberately avoided revealing that person's nationality or any details of the vehicle involved. I then dictated the media report to our FCR for onward transmission to our Media Services Department and requested that a member of that department either phone me when they came in to work, or travel down to Dover Port in person.

Soon after this, I held a mini conference so Bob Nelson and Lorraine Harris could update me on their progress. The forensic recovery work was ongoing and likely to be time consuming. Bob had organised the MIR and staff for our support facility at Nackington, which is located just off the Dover Road in nearby Canterbury.

A message from the FCR informed us that the Chief Constable had been notified and he would visit the scene with HM Coroner, Mr Sturt, later in the morning. Superintendent Chris Eyre and I agreed to meet Mr Sturt and our Chief Constable, Sir David Phillips, who had just received his Knighthood in the Queen's Birthday Honours that weekend.

We needed to progress the victims' identification process as a matter of priority, which required the assistance of a forensic pathologist, or possibly two taking into account the number of victims involved. In view of this, I had an initial telephone conversation with Mr Sturt at 0600 hrs that morning, to discuss both the forensic pathologist/s and the use of a temporary mortuary. Without hesitation, Mr Sturt gave me his permission to use a forensic pathologist. He was not keen, however, to set up a temporary mortuary. He had previously encountered issues with a temporary mortuary, when dealing with the victims of the *Herald of Free Enterprise* ferry disaster, which saw 193 staff and passengers perish, on the night of 6 March 1987.

After this conversation I telephoned Dr Michael Heath, one of our regular forensic pathologists. I reminded him who I was as soon as he took the call.

'What have we got?' he asked.

'Fifty-eight dead foreign nationals at Dover,' I stated.

'I'm on my way,' he said.

'Hold on, hold on,' I said. 'How much is all of this going to cost me?' As callous as it sounds, budget control is a major part of crime investigation. It is imperative that every manager in control of a budget can justify the decisions on how and where money is spent.

'Oh, don't worry about that now. We'll work it out later.' I had worked with Mike on many occasions and knew from this comment that he would not try to make any unnecessary monetary gain, or exploit such an awful situation.

He then suggested that we use his colleague, Dr David Rouse, another one of our recognised forensic pathologists. I agreed to this and instructed them to meet me at Dover Port so they could see the victims in situ. He anticipated they would arrive around midday, which afforded me time to sort out the mortuary issues.

I spoke to Bob Nelson and together we examined the matter of staffing from our already stretched department. Despite the unprecedented demands of this particular incident, I still had to be mindful of the fact that there were other major crimes at various stages of investigation which required our staff resources. After the scene of crime staff had completed searching the clothing the victims had removed during transit, as well as clothing they were still wearing at the time of their deaths, it would be necessary to provide extra staff members to coordinate the identification process. Lorraine had already identified teams of scene of crime officers to work in the mortuary, alongside the police who would also be dealing with the Disaster Victim Identification process. In addition to this, the police officers and civilian colleagues working for us were under a great deal of pressure, and their day to day welfare was of primary concern. With all these issues needing attention, I was grateful to Chris Eyre, who had taken control of the extensive staffing needed for guarding the scene, and liaised with the Port of Dover Authority who were very helpful, allowing our staff to use their facilities around the port area.

Later in the morning, Sir David Phillips and Mr Sturt arrived at the scene, and Chris and I met them. After an initial discussion, we took them to visit the warehouse where the victims were still being photographed and searched. Various boxes of tomatoes had been removed from the lorry and were now in the background – I realised at once that those boxes would have to be fingerprinted, and tomato samples would need to be examined in case some type of chemical had kept them fresh in transit, and been inhaled by the victims, possibly causing their deaths.

Together with Sir David and Mr Sturt, we discussed the initial arrangements for storing the bodies within the port area in the customs cold facility. This was agreed. Mr Sturt then told us that the mortuary at Dover Hospital was not suitable, and that the post-mortems would have to be carried out at the mortuary at the William Harvey Hospital at Ashford, which was some 23 miles away. Another logistics problem we would have to overcome.

After this initial meeting, Sir David took me aside to discuss the management structure which had been put in place during the initial response to this incident. Sir David took the view that the policing arrangement was yet to be clarified and DCI Nelson would be the SIO for the criminal investigation – which was bound to require his full commitment – along with significant liaising with the Dutch police and the Belgian authorities.

My role and responsibilities as Head of the Major Crime Department would remain, but Sir David made it very clear that, as the Identification Commissioner on behalf of Mr Sturt, I was personally responsible for all aspects of the identification and repatriation of the victims. All liaising with foreign embassies and government departments was also my personal responsibility. No pressure on me then!

The next challenge for Lorraine Harris and me was to prepare for the arrival of the forensic pathologists. We needed to be extremely organised on this score, so I appointed DI Gerry Smith from our Detective Training School to the position of mortuary manager. He was to deal with the following complex tasks:

- Identifying and briefing mortuary teams
- Identifying and organising a funeral director to deliver the victims to and from the mortuary
- Locating fifty-eight Interpol Body Identification documents which, in these circumstances especially, were of significant importance.

Gerry's excellent management and communication skills made him the perfect officer for what would inevitably be a very demanding task. He made contact with a major funeral director in Dover, who agreed to transport the victims to and from the mortuary. They were scheduled to start this process in the early afternoon. Our Coroner's Officer, Mr Steve Perrin, notified me that the mortuary technicians were on standby and ready for the arrival of the first victims. Slowly but surely, everything which needed to be done was being done.

Mr Sturt's secretary phoned me to tell me that Mr Sturt was concerned about a number of other funeral directors who had found out that the transportation of the victims was being taken care of by one company. They felt this was unfair. Mr Sturt asked me if I could resolve this matter. I assured him that I would do so at once, even though business matters are of little concern to the police and, in truth, I found it a little distasteful. In any case, I was able to resolve the matter and did not let it affect me. I appointed Sergeant Dave Weller as my office manager and his first job was to coordinate each of the Dover funeral directors who wanted to get involved in the transportation of the victims. Dave was a Training School Sergeant with a very cool head and his amenable temperament made him perfect for this role.

I appointed the remainder of my Identification Commission team, bringing in DI Steve Corbishley as my deputy; my expert researcher

PC Bob Kelly and DC Stuart Rush, who was an Area detective from Canterbury and was to be responsible for coordinating all the telephone numbers we would (hopefully) find in the victim's clothing; of course, Mr Perrin was also in our team.

By late morning, a large gathering of representatives from the press, together with television news crews (both local and national), were gathering in the port area. We had our force Media Services Manager and his staff housed away from the warehouse and the cold storage facility.

When I returned to the warehouse to await the arrival of our pathologists, I had quite a turn of luck. I was standing close to the door of the warehouse when the door opened and our Media Manager walked in with several people in tow. I stopped them at once and demanded to know what on earth he thought he was doing.

'I'm just letting a few photographers through to photograph the lorry the victims died in,' he said. 'They'll be out of the way in a few minutes.'

'Get out immediately!' I said. 'Don't you ever bring anyone into a crime scene without the express permission of the SIO.'

Apparently, the individual had told the Police Constable who was guarding the door that he was the force Media Services Manager and had the authority to enter. Unbelievable behaviour!

Once we were outside, I took the Media Services Manager aside and (not for the first time in his career) told him that he was totally out of order. I had to explain to him that if photographs of that lorry had reached the press then it would have been broadcast around the world within minutes, and potentially jeopardised not only the criminal investigation but the safety of our two witnesses.

In the midst of all this tragedy, our pathologist arrived. I briefed them on the nature of the work ahead of them. They were totally professional when they saw the victims; after all, this is their day-to-day work. Soon after, they travelled to the mortuary to join the mortuary teams and await the arrival of the first victims. It had been agreed that the mortuary would receive four bodies at a time in order not to overwhelm the process.

I had decided that each victim be accompanied by a police officer. That officer was to be responsible for all the paperwork and forensic samples generated during each post-mortem. I had called on the force's Support Group – a section of experienced uniformed officers who support their colleagues as they perform routine, daily policing matters, specially trained to carry out numerous tasks such as: searches, execution of warrants and public order. On this particular day, they had the most unusual task of escorting our victims to and from their post-mortems. The first post-mortems commenced at approximately 1500 hrs.

I called a meeting with Bob Nelson, Lorraine Harris and our deputies. Bob gave us an initial account of the first interview with the driver, who denied any knowledge of the contents of the container, claiming that his paperwork said 'Tomatoes' and so that was what he believed he was carrying. Bob then gave us the first account from one of our survivors, whom I shall refer to as 'Soi' and who was 21 years of age.

Soi was first interviewed at Canterbury Hospital during the early hours of the morning. He informed the interviewing officers that he had come from the Fujian province in China with his friend, whom I shall refer to as 'Lee'. Their families had paid a lot of money to a local 'snakehead gang', who were to organise their illegal travel arrangements to England.

> The term 'snakehead' is a word which dates back to around the 1800s. It is the name given to members of a Chinese criminal network, chiefly engaged in smuggling immigrants to the Western world. At the time of this incident, Interpol estimated that it would have cost a family around £18,000 to get a member of their family into the UK.
>
> Interpol (its proper title is The International Criminal Police Organisation) fights international crime. It was created in 1923 in Vienna, Austria, with a membership of 194 countries. Interpol facilitates worldwide police co-operation and crime control.

Gang members of the snakehead operation show families in China photographs of young Chinese men and women sitting in expensive cars outside popular tourist spots all around London, such as the Houses of Parliament and Buckingham Palace. This encourages families to believe that their own family member could potentially become very rich in the UK, which would mean they could eventually send money back to them in China.

Individuals who pay to travel are told to apply for a Chinese passport on the basis that they are applying to work in Belgrade, in former Yugoslavia (this part of a nation later to be called Serbia). Our two survivors were then flown to Beijing, where they were escorted by 'snakehead' members to another group of thirteen young Chinese men and women. Their passports were stamped with forged work permits which permitted them to leave China and enter Yugoslavia. On arrival in Belgrade, the group and the two snakeheads members were driven away from the city in two minibuses which crossed the border into a country which he believed was Hungary. They travelled deep into the country, when both minibuses stopped in an isolated area. They were ordered out of the minibuses and told to stand in a line. They were physically searched by the gang members, at which point their passports, identification cards and all personal possessions were taken from them. (None of these items have ever been recovered.) They were then ordered back onto the minibuses and carried on with their journey. They crossed over the border into Austria and travelled north to Vienna International Airport, where one of the snakeheads issued them with forged North Korean passports. They then boarded a flight to Paris, where the forged documents were taken from them. None of these documents have ever been recovered.

According to Soi, there were no immigration checks upon their arrival in Paris. They were escorted by the snakeheads to the main railway station, where they boarded a train to Brussels and then Rotterdam.

They arrived in Rotterdam just before midnight on Friday, 16 June 2000. Together with the two snakeheads, they all took a tram into the city centre, where the group was split into two. One group turned right outside the tram terminal, whilst the other group turned left. Soi's group (along with one of the snakeheads) was joined by another man who was Chinese but spoke Dutch. His group was, once again, split into two and his new group was joined by three more gang members – two men and a woman. These three people were also Chinese but spoke Dutch. Soi recognised one of these men as coming from his home town in Fujian. He was named Ke Hang. Soi, Lee and two females who had travelled from China with them were then driven away in a private car by the female snakehead. One of the male snakeheads told them his name was Ka Lang.

They drove through the city to a large house where they were placed in a second-floor room. The room contained two men, whom Soi did not know, but he did hear one of them mention that he had been in Holland for four years. They stayed in the house that night and all of Saturday, during which time approximately fifty more Chinese nationals arrived at the property.

Soi also recalled some extremely important information which helped us immensely in the investigation. Whilst everyone was waiting in the house in Rotterdam, apparently, the snakehead who referred to himself as Ka Lang gave them a piece of paper with a telephone number on it. He told them that if they were arrested, they should ring a lady on that number and that she would immediately get them bailed out.

Soi also said that when they were preparing for their journey, people advised him to hide money, along with family telephone numbers, in the lining of their clothes because their pockets would probably be searched by the snakeheads.

This was an excellent start to both the criminal investigation and the identification process. Bob was able to share this information with our colleagues in Holland, in order to assist them in identifying the locations being used to accommodate these immigrants, and from that they would, hopefully, be able to identify the individuals who had access to those premises.

The information regarding the hiding of money and numbers in the clothing was relayed back to Lorraine. She then had to arrange for the scene of crimes officers to examine every item of clothing, and unpick every seam and pocket in search of such items. It was a mammoth task.

At around 1000 hrs on the Sunday morning, the snakeheads began taking groups of four away from the house in various cars. Soi and Lee were in one of the last groups to leave. They were driven to another house about seven minutes away. They remained at this property with approximately ten others until lunchtime, after which they were all taken in a white van to a yard about a twenty-minute drive away, where they were ushered into the back of the container on the lorry.

This was the start of their living nightmare.

Soi described the inside of the container and how cramped it was. He had spotted a window covered with a net, in the top left-hand corner of the container which was, in fact, the air-vent. As the boxes of tomatoes were being stacked at the back of the container, a Chinese man in a black T-shirt who was working with the snakeheads explained to Soi in English that when the window was open they were permitted to talk in a low voice, but when it was shut it meant they were crossing a border so they had to stay completely quiet. Those who could not speak English were communicated with hand-gestures to remain quiet when the vent was shut.

Once the tomato boxes were stacked, the doors of the container were closed and, although it became dark, Soi could still see his watch – the time was 1500 hrs. The lorry started up and drove off. It did not stop for three and a half hours. Soi had kept his eyes on his wristwatch during the journey, so he knew it was 1830 hrs when he saw the window in the corner of the container being closed from outside the container by a hand belonging to a white man. The journey continued for another thirty to forty minutes, then the lorry stopped and the engine was turned off. His watch showed 1910 hrs. About forty minutes later, the lorry started up and slowly moved on to what he thought was a ramp. He believed that was when they went on to the ferry. After twenty to thirty minutes everyone started to feel uncomfortable. The temperature in the container was increasing, and at around 2100 hrs people started to find breathing difficult. One portly man at the front of the container near the window started to bang the window. Someone told him that if he could not stand it at the front, he should move to the back. The man made his way to the back of the container and stood beside Soi.

'I'm dying, I'm dying,' the man told Soi, before lying down beside him. Both Soi and Lee tried to comfort the man, telling him to breathe slowly and not to panic, since there was fresh air at the back. Soi explained to us, however, that he was well aware there was no fresh air at the back, they only told the man this to comfort him.

About ten minutes later, some people at the front of the container started to panic. Some were crying, some were shouting in Chinese and English and banging on the side of the container.

'We're dying,' they called out, 'we can't wait.'

This went on for twenty to thirty minutes, by which time everyone who could shout and bang the walls, did so. Some people made their way to the back of the container, where Soi was, and tried pulling at the boxes to get to the doors, but they were locked from the outside.

As time went on, and people grew weaker and weaker, fewer and fewer of them were capable of shouting. Soi and Lee thought they were dying too. They held hands to encourage one other for a few minutes. After another few minutes, Lee started to grab tomatoes from the floor of the container and eat them very quickly. A Chinese superstition says that it is better to die full, than hungry. Others in the container had taken mouthfuls of the tomatoes, knowing they were dying; the fact that Lee recounts doing this demonstrates that he had resigned himself to the fact he was going to die.

It grew very quiet in the container – everyone was on the brink of death. Soi then lost consciousness.

The next thing Soi remembered was someone shouting at him, and rousing him from his unconscious state. The back doors of the container were open, so he struggled to his feet and moved towards the doors where he was then helped off the lorry. Lee was behind him and he too was pulled from the container. That ended Soi's account of his journey to England as best he could remember it.

From the identification point of view, it appeared that I had been correct when I surmised that the majority of our victims were Chinese. This meant that my first action the following day would be to contact the Chinese Embassy.

I confirmed with Lorraine Harris that any telephone numbers found in the clothing should be logged and passed on to the Identification Team – initially for research, and afterwards to be shared with the criminal investigation team, for formal disclosure and in order to avoid duplicated actions being raised by the criminal investigation team and the Identification Commission.

I felt pleased with our progress to date, but then I received a message to call our Mortuary Manager as a matter of urgency.

What could possibly have gone wrong at the mortuary? I wondered.

I telephoned Gerry Smith. He was as calm and in control as he had been before, but he seemed to have a serious problem on his hands. Whilst the first four post-mortems had been completed, and all necessary forensic samples and photographs taken, the completion of the Interpol Disaster Victim Identification (DVI) forms was slowing the entire process down. The problem was that literally every inch of a body, including body-cavities, had to be examined for any identifying feature a family member might recognise the victim by – birthmarks, scars, tattoos, etc.

It seemed to me that the only possible course of action we could take to resolve this problem was to abandon the competition of the DVI forms at the mortuary, and have them completed after the victims had been returned to the cold storage facility at Dover Docks. I knew from past experience that examining, in detail, a body which has already been subjected to a post-mortem is not the most pleasant of tasks. It was imperative that the DVI be completed, however, and completed accurately. I asked Gerry to pre-warn the officers who had ownership of each of the victims about my decision, and to let them know that I would arrange for police surgeons to assist them in examining the bodies once the victims were returned.

Once again, my mind focused on the welfare of all my staff, so I sought the assistance of our force Welfare Department on this matter. They were very helpful and suggested that, unless a member of staff needed support right away, it might be best to offer everyone the opportunity to attend a group meeting in a few days' time. I assured them that every supervisor would be made aware of this, and be updated with the date, time and location of the meeting once it was set.

The afternoon was passing quicker than I had realised and, having spoken to the Welfare Department, I thought it best I set a time for everyone to finish work that evening, particularly considering some of them had been involved in this incident since around midnight. It was evident there were weeks of work ahead of us.

I gave the instruction to the team leaders that anyone who had been called out during the night should finish work no later than 1900 hrs, and those working from that morning should finish no later than 2100 hrs. All scenes were guarded overnight.

I required time now, to complete my Policy File regarding the disturbing and exhausting events of that day, which was a lot to process.

The purpose of maintaining a policy book is to provide a written account of the decision-making process including important decisions made, and the rationale supporting those decisions. In this incident, Policy Files were kept for the criminal investigation, the forensic work to be carried out and the identification process. In addition to this, I needed to maintain an Administration Policy File in regards to welfare, community issues, hours of work, expenses and any other general issues which were likely to arise. I was about to start writing when my phone rang. It was a member of our Media Services Department, who told me the Chief Constable had approved the go-ahead of a Media Conference in the conference facility at the dock, to take place the following morning at 1100 hrs.

'The world press will be there,' she told me.

'That's good,' I replied. 'Which Chief Officer is going to front-up the conference?'

'There is no Chief Officer available,' she replied, politely. 'The Chief Constable said you would handle it.'

'Thanks a lot for that,' I said.

In view of this decision, I thought it best to prepare a media strategy which covered questions which might be asked about either the identification process and/or the criminal investigation itself. I would need to complete it before I finished for the day.

I began with the 'Aims of a Media Strategy' Powerpoint presentation I had used on detective training courses, from which all other activities or actions could stem. So, what I finally came up with, in fact, was simply a long-term plan for this major investigation:

- To maintain public interest in both the criminal investigation and the identification of the victims, in a manner which encourages any information which arises in response to developing events, to flow continuously and directly to the investigation teams
- To ensure the attention of the media is managed in a positive and appropriate manner

- To minimise disruption to crime scenes, to Investigating Officers' activities and to local communities, in particular, to the families of victims
- To safeguard the position of Kent Police, Kent Police Authority (now known as Police, Fire and Crime Commissioner) and HM Coroner for East Kent District, in relation to what information is released and taking into account any potential impact on future judicial proceedings.

These were to be my basic guidelines for the forthcoming press conference. Although no one knew the true identity of all sixty victims (two surviving victims) I was aware that those behind this evil trade might very well know the victims' families – even if they were on the other side of the world. The policing strategy did not need to be altered, although actions coming from it might change in the coming hours, days or weeks ahead, depending on what obstacles arose throughout the investigation.

By early evening, it was time to head home, and though I longed to switch off after one of the most daunting days in my police career, I was concerned that I had not yet visited the mortuary to check on how things were progressing, and to thank everyone involved in this stressful process. Needs must. I headed up the A20 to Ashford and the William Harvey Hospital. I had visited this mortuary many times in my role as a SIO, so I knew exactly where to go.

As I approached the entrance to the mortuary, I was greeted by several of the uniformed Constables who had escorted the victims; they were all wearing their white, crime-scene suits and seated on the ground having refreshments.

'Why are you sitting outside, rather than in the hospital facilities?' I asked.

'The hospital is happy to supply food to the teams,' one of the officers explained, 'but we are not permitted to walk through the hospital after having been deployed to the mortuary.'

Though I was none too pleased to hear this, the officers did not seem to mind. On reflection, I understood the decision made by the hospital management, which was made due to hygiene concerns and the requirement of the officers to continually move back and forth between the mortuary and the canteen.

On entering the mortuary, I was offered a white suit to wear. I declined, as I was now feeling tired and knew I would not be staying long.

Despite the gravity of the work ahead of us and the heavy nature of this gruesome scene, everyone greeted me warmly – being used to having me visit post-mortems – including the pathologists, the two mortuary technicians, our S/SOCOs, Martin Pope, Stephen Griffiths and, of course, my mortuary manager and colleague, Gerry Smith, and all the officers escorting the victims. I took the opportunity to thank them for their work and briefly updated them on what was happening back at the docks.

The pathologists told me that they anticipated completing the examination of all fifty-eight victims by the following evening. On hearing this, I couldn't help but notice that two of the technicians looked quizzically at one another. The following morning, I discovered that those technicians told the pathologists they were not prepared to work all the way into the evening of the following day. Apparently, they were keen supporters of the England international football team. England were playing that evening and nothing was going to stop them from watching the game.

I said my goodbyes to everyone and headed home, at long last, for a hot shower, a change of clothing and a large glass of whiskey – which I think I deserved after the events of the last twenty-one hours.

As I sat at home reflecting on the events at Dover, my thoughts turned to the extended communities who would inevitably be affected by the tragedy – the families and communities back in China, those who helped in the rescue operation, other workers at the port and, of course, my own staff.

I couldn't help but think of an even bigger picture, and wondered how many Chinese communities around England might also be affected by these events. (I initially, and wrongly, dismissed this as being a priority.) I realised, there and then, that as the international media gathered in the morning, this incident would be headline news all around the world – most especially back in China. I couldn't possibly sleep with these endless concerns running around in my head, so I put pen to paper to set out my Community Impact Assessment (CIA).

> The purpose of a community impact assessment (CIA) is to identify issues that may affect a community's confidence in the ability of the police to respond effectively to their needs, thereby enhancing the police response. It helps to inform forces about long-term plans to rebuild community confidence and learn lessons for the future.
>
> College of Policing*

I decided that the upcoming media conference would form the basis of my initial CIA and that I would:

- Share the basic details about the discovery of all the victims in the lorry, including the fact that there were fifty-eight deceased and two survivors, who were in hospital away from the scene
- Provide brief details about the victims' journey from China to Holland and onwards to Zeebrugge and then Dover
- Give credit to the response of staff from various agencies who had assisted in both the rescue and the ongoing police investigation
- Share the fact that a Dutch national was in custody (although no details of the suspect or the vehicle would be released)
- Make an appeal for witnesses who may have been expecting a family member or friend to arrive in the UK, to contact our MIR using a dedicated telephone number.

I was acutely aware that families of all the victims were likely to feel at risk themselves back in China since, technically, they may have committed a criminal offence by encouraging and paying for their family member to leave China in the first place.

After completing this work, I slept well that night and was back on the road to Dover at 0700 hrs the following morning. I rang the Nackington MIR at 0800 hrs and told my team that I would join them straight after the press conference. I met a member of our Media Services Department who advised me that members of the media were already setting up in

---

* www.college.police.uk/app/engagement-and-communication/engagement

the conference room, and that she was expecting an extremely large turn-out of reporters and film crews, including several from Holland, Belgium and even a crew from a London-based Chinese news agency. This colleague would stay close-at-hand throughout, as the television companies wanted this to go live worldwide on the 1100 hrs broadcast.

I entered the conference room at exactly 1058 hrs to be confronted by the flashing of cameras and the noise of commentators presenting their live reports of this event. I walked briskly to the front and surveyed the audience – they were from every branch of media and appeared from every nationality. Human smuggling was a worldwide problem.

There were a few uncomfortable seconds before my media services assistant gave me the thumbs-up to start. I gave my press statement exactly as I had planned to and it lasted for four to five minutes, after which, I took questions. I can honestly say that I don't remember a single one of those questions asked, possibly because I was so relieved to have completed the media briefing without a hitch. When I ended the conference, I was asked, through my media services assistant, to do approximately twelve one-to-one interviews, and merely ended up repeating everything I had said in the original statement.

Once the conference was over, I made my way back to the MIR at Nackington, first to liaise with Bob Nelson, and then with the Identification Team. The most pressing issue which came up was that we had no Chinese-speaking members on either of our teams. We had reached out to Chinese communities, asking that they contact us if they believed they knew any of the victims, so it was imperative we find translators – we desperately needed some assistance on this – and urgently.

I telephoned our DCC Ayling and explained our difficulty to him. I requested his permission to approach the MPS for assistance finding Chinese-speaking officers, because there is a large Chinese community in London. He granted me permission, but the MPS could not spare any officers and so I was forced to take my problem back to DCC Ayling, who advised me to speak with the Chief Constable of Hampshire Police, Mr Paul Kernaghan QPM, who had the portfolio for overseas investigations on behalf to the Association of Chief Police Officers (which is now called the Chief Constables Council). Mr Kernaghan was very helpful, and immediately arranged for two of his officers, who were fluent in Chinese, to be seconded to our investigation. It was a great pleasure to welcome Sergeant Joe Hon and Constable Andy Lau to our team. They were to prove vital throughout the whole of the investigation.

It was now time to speak with the Chinese Embassy in London and seek their assistance. My call was eventually answered, after a very long wait. I explained who I was, and that I needed their cooperation. Unfortunately, my request fell on deaf ears. Whoever it was that I spoke to hung up on me.

I refused to be defeated, however, and contacted the Police Service in China to see if they would be willing to assist us in trying to identify our fifty-eight victims. Normal protocol would have been to submit a report outlining our request for assistance to Interpol for onward transmission to the Police Service in China (which is correctly named the Ministry of Public Security). I knew from my experience dealing with Interpol in the past, however, that it would likely be several months before I received a reply, so I searched the internet and found a telephone number for the headquarters of the Ministry of Public Security in Beijing.

I dialled the number. My phone call was answered and I asked if they spoke English. The recipient immediately replied in English, with an American accent. I introduced myself and told him the purpose of my call. He replied that he was aware of the incident in Dover and that an investigation was already under way in China to identify those responsible for the crimes. He told me that the person I needed to speak with was his boss, Mr Zhen Jeng Hua. His boss could not speak English, however, and so he would act as interpreter for us.

I had an informative conversation with Mr Hua, and I asked him if he could assist me and whether he was willing to send a team of his officers to Kent. He agreed. The only thing he asked of me was to provide his team with the necessary visas to gain entry to the UK, to which I agreed. We then exchanged addresses, facsimile and telephone numbers, and agreed to keep in contact in order to confirm all necessary arrangements for their visit.

Having secured the services of the Chinese police, I decided to make contact with the China/Hong Kong desk at the Foreign and Commonwealth Office in London. I got through to the China/Hong Kong desk straight away and a very helpful gentleman arranged for me to visit his office the following afternoon, promising me as much assistance as possible. I then returned to my office in the MIR and was just about to have a coffee when my phone rang. It was my secretary, Julie, at Force Headquarters, and she told me that she had an MPS Commander on the telephone demanding to speak with me. I asked her to put the caller through and, whilst I was introducing myself, the MPS Commander interrupted me, telling me that he was from Special Branch and (in a rather rude and aggressive tone) demanding to know what right I had phoning China and inviting the Chinese police to the UK.

I was slightly taken aback by the attitude of this individual but I was also surprised – how on earth did he know that I had been on the telephone to China?

In any case, I was not prepared to be spoken to like this by anyone, no matter what their position or reasoning.

'Excuse me,' I said calmly, 'but may I ask you a question?'

'What?' the individual asked.

'Have you got fifty-eight unidentified, dead Chinese people in front of you?'

'Obviously not,' he said.

I stayed as calm as I had been up to that point and simply said, 'Well, old chap, I have. So I shall call whoever I like.' Then I hung up and went to have my coffee.

No sooner had I finished my coffee than my office telephone rang again. It was an old friend and colleague, Bob McCaughan, who was in charge of Special Branch in our force. After exchanging pleasantries, Bob mentioned that he had just had a phone call from an MPS Commander regarding my request to the Chinese police to travel to Kent. He told me that I really should not have done that without the authority of the Metropolitan Police Special Branch.

I asked Bob where such rules were written down, and he told me it was simply protocol.

I was very pleasant to my old friend but I informed him that it was too late and that the Chinese police were coming. We ended the conversation with me thinking, *That is surely not the last I am going to hear about this.* Thankfully, though, it was.

Now I had to find a way of getting their visas issued.

Around lunchtime on the second day of the investigation, I received a telephone call from Gerry Smith at the mortuary. This was when he informed me about the mortuary technicians who were refusing to work late that evening because of the football. He asked me to contact someone of seniority, who was able to impel them to work. I assured him that I would do my best and get back to him.

I then rang Mr Sturt, to see if he had the authority, or if he at least knew someone at the William Harvey Hospital who had the authority to make the technicians work late. Alas, however, the technicians were well within their rights to finish work at 1700 hrs each day. I rang Gerry back and (much to the chagrin of the pathologists) everybody finished work at the mortuary at 1700 hrs, so the technicians went off to watch the football.

I do hope they enjoyed their night's football despite their inevitable disappointment at the result, which had England losing 3-2 to Romania.

I spent the following day in London. I visited the Chinese Embassy and although they opened their door to me, they would not let me enter. In what seemed an utterly bizarre ten minutes, I was made to stand on the steps outside and hold a conversation about my requirements. I was permitted to speak with their 'media adviser'. He was aware, before I even mentioned it, that I had invited the Chinese police to the UK and volunteered the information that their visas had been granted. This was a pleasant surprise – I had assumed that I would be the one to have to arrange this.

After this visit, I attended my appointment at the Foreign and Commonwealth Office, where I discussed the identification issues we were facing and explained my planned approach to resolve this matter. We also spoke about the two survivors. I informed my colleagues that I had a meeting with HM Immigration Service the following day. They then rebuked me for having gone to the Chinese Embassy earlier that day, and informed me that, in future, a member of the Chinese/Hong Kong department would accompany me.

I am still to this day not privy as to how they knew I went to the embassy in the first place. I have my own thoughts on this matter but I think those thoughts should remain with me!

It was mid-afternoon by the time I returned to the MIR, and the news came in that the post-mortem examination on all fifty-eight victims had been completed. It confirmed that each victim had died from irreversible cerebral anoxia which, in layman's terms, means a lack of oxygen to the brain. All the bodies had now been returned to the temporary mortuary and were being re-examined for the completion of the DVI forms. I then received a message telling me that the Chinese Ambassador to the UK would visit Dover Port the following morning, together with several members of his staff. I thought it appropriate to inform Mr Sturt and the Chief Constable, but neither one of them was available to meet the Ambassador.

Now that all the victims had been photographed and their property had been searched and inventoried, I authorised copies of each of the victim's fingerprints, including those of the two survivors, to be sent to HM Immigration Service in order that they be checked against database records. I also had copies of these prints forwarded to the Dutch police and Interpol, for circulation across Europe. Whilst I did not expect many of the victims to be identified this way, I did at the very least hope that some of the victims might be snakeheads who were guarding the immigrants and might have previously come to the attention of police or immigration services.

To round off the day, we briefed our staff in the MIR at Nackington. I had arranged for photographs of the fifty-eight deceased victims to be made available and began the briefing by explaining that the photographs were to be displayed in the briefing room on white boards, so that we could place any information we received regarding the victims alongside their photograph, for everyone's viewing. I also informed our cleaning staff that these photographs would be on display. Despite not being part of the investigation, the cleaners took a keen interest in each and every victim. The was a stark reminder that it is not only the police who work in this environment – every person has a role and it is the combination of those roles that makes a team.

Bob Nelson provided an update on the lorry driver, Perry Wacker. He still denied any knowledge about his illegal cargo, but had difficulty explaining how his fingerprints ended up on several of the tomato boxes and on the inside of the walls of the container, which made up a dummy partition. We had been keen to find a way to confirm that Wacker had knowledge of his cargo, and the fantastic discovery of fingerprints on the loaded boxes did just that. Wacker was charged with conspiracy to facilitate human smuggling, as well as fifty-eight counts of manslaughter, and was remanded in custody. Bob also told us that a solicitor called Ying Guo and her boyfriend had been arrested for the aforementioned conspiracy offence on the basis that her telephone number was found on eighteen different pieces of paper amongst the victims' clothing. Again, the diligence of the forensic teams, who had discovered these links whilst searching the mounds of clothing, had paid off. She was later to be charged with conspiracy and remanded in custody. Her boyfriend was initially charged with this offence but the Crown Prosecution Service subsequently discontinued the charge against him because, although he was living with her at the time, there was no direct evidence against him.

On the morning of 23 June 2000, Mr Sturt opened the inquest into the deaths of the fifty-eight victims. He took evidence of the cause of death and the brief circumstances of the incident from his Coroner's Officer, then he adjourned the inquest in order to allow the criminal investigation and identification of the victims to continue.

Our collaboration with the Dutch police and the judicial authorities in Belgium was going well. One body of opinion maintained that the Belgian authorities should lead the investigation, since the ferry had departed from the port of Zeebrugge. To rectify this position, I arranged for the judge for the Court of Assizes, which covers Zeebrugge, to visit our MIR together with the Head of the Crown Prosecution Service (CPS) for Kent, Miss Elizabeth Howe. This meeting took place on the forthcoming Friday. Bob Nelson and I met with them and it was quickly established that the Belgian authorities were not all that keen to get involved in the investigation, since the vehicle only drove through Belgium and then directly on to the ferry to Dover. Miss Howe agreed that there was no necessity for them to be involved, as she was already reviewing the evidence against Wacker and Guo on behalf of the CPS. At the end of the meeting, we treated our guests to lunch and our dealings with the Belgian authorities ended there.

Our dealings with the Dutch authorities were entirely different, however. A direct link with their People Smuggling investigation team in Rotterdam was established from early on in the investigation and we shared intelligence and evidence from our investigation and from the crime scenes. They, in turn, shared their intelligence with us, and after pinpointing the locations where the immigrants had stayed in Rotterdam, we formed joint scene of crime teams. In order to facilitate this work, they sent their own police aeroplane to Kent to collect our S/SOCO, Mr Steve Griffiths.

Steve had a rather amusing moment on that flight across the Channel. Apparently, after landing at Lydd Airport, the pilot invited Steve to sit up front with him. Steve was thrilled by the idea of sitting in the front seat and headed there with great enthusiasm whilst the pilot left the cockpit for a moment, to check on the safety of the aircraft. When the pilot returned to the cockpit, he politely told Steve he could not sit there.

Confused, Steve reminded the pilot that only moments ago, he had told Steve he was welcome to sit up front with him.

'Yes,' the pilot replied, 'but not in the pilot's seat, just move across.'

Moving on in the criminal investigation, a decision had to be made regarding the two survivors, which required me to meet HM Immigration Service (HMIS) later that day at their headquarters in Croydon.

We discussed the legal position the survivors were in. Namely, that they fell into a combination of three categories: victims, witnesses and illegal immigrants. To resolve this conflictual matter, the HMIS agreed that the two survivors would be granted Temporary Leave to Remain Orders, which would cover them, at least for the duration of the criminal investigations and subsequent criminal trials, in both England and Holland. After this, their position would require a second review.

This was the best of both worlds for everyone involved in these investigations and, as an additional measure, we arranged witness protection for both survivors. We called upon the services of the MPS Witness Protection Team and, whilst this is an expensive service, we needed to ensure that they would be 100 per cent safe. Both survivors agreed to this. They also agreed to travel to Holland with the Dutch Police, in order to identify the properties where they had stayed following their arrival in Holland.

As we approached the end of the first week of the criminal investigation and the identification of the victims, I felt pleased with the work our teams had carried out. The Chinese police officers were scheduled to arrive the following week and the DVI forms had all been forwarded to Interpol.

Despite things progressing well, I received a phone call which put additional pressure on the situation. The chief officer in charge of HM Customs and Excise at Dover Port called to inform me that the temporary mortuary facility at the port was urgently required for their own purposes. He needed all the victims removed as soon as practicable. I gave him my word that I would deal with it within the next twenty-four hours. I shared this matter with Dover Harbour Board and they agreed to supply us with a cold storage container in which the victims could be stored, and which could be placed at an isolated position in the docks area. This was good news.

I, in turn, had agreed to purchase racking for the container, so the next dilemma I was faced with was: *Where on earth do I find racking for a container?* I passed this problem on to Sergeant Dave Weller and, within one hour, he came back to me with a smile on his face.

'Your racking will be delivered on Monday,' he said, 'and the company will fit it for us too.'

Excellent news.

My telephone rang again. It was my colleague at Dover Harbour Board. The offer for the use of a container had been confirmed but, unfortunately, it could not be stored in the area of the docks. They had shared the information regarding the container with their staff, who complained to their trade union representatives, who threatened to close down the entire port if the victims were stored in the docks area. I gave thought to this. I could fully understand that people found it distasteful. I was in a situation where I was trying to treat these people with respect until we were able to identify them, but nobody seemed to want to provide a safe location in which they could lie.

I called Dave back into my office to hand him his second problem for the day.

Over the weekend, and in consultation with Mr Sturt, we came up with a solution. We would ask the Commander in Chief at the local military barracks if the fully loaded container could be kept at their barracks. They agreed to this, but needed our assurance that we were able to come up with a contingency plan in order to keep the container secure.

It was subsequently decided that the container would have to be kept locked and alarmed, only able to be opened by a member of the Identification Team. A generator would have to run twenty-four hours a day to keep the contents preserved, and would be checked every eight hours by the local police. I also agreed that we would pay the electricity used by the generator.

I insisted that each member of the teams have one day off over the weekend and Bob Nelson and myself agreed to a similar arrangement. I worked on the Saturday of that week and, when I arrived at the MIR, I was greeted with: 'You want the good news or the bad news first?'

I chose the good.

The Dutch Immigration Authority had confirmed four fingerprint identifications.

The bad news was that they were all for the same individual. Victim number 6, believed to be Kam Kwun Cheng, aged 33 years, originally from China. He had initially been arrested in Hong Kong in July 1997, for being in possession of forged travel documents for which he received six months' imprisonment. After being released from prison, he was arrested in Holland for illegally entering the country. He gave the same name and date of birth, on this occasion, as the one he had given in Hong

Kong. He was then released on bail and promptly disappeared. He was arrested by immigration teams in Holland on three more occasions and gave a different name, date of birth and address each time. Clearly, their fingerprint system did not have the capability to match all the identities he had used.

Kam Kwun Cheng remained a thorn in my side throughout the entire identification process, since we were unable to trace his next of kin and it was my fear that, if we ever received the Chinese Government's approval to repatriate the victims to their families in China, that they may not accept No. 6.

We received four more fingerprint identifications for four other victims during that day. Our research indicated that they were either snakeheads or working for the snakeheads team. Of the sixty, I was confident that five were traffickers and the remaining fifty-five were victims of their crime. I found it sad that it was the snakeheads who were identified first.

The first of these was Victim number 4. The German authorities identified him, through his fingerprints, as Chen Xang Lin. He had been arrested on 22 May 2000, for violating the aliens' law in Germany, and was subsequently deported to the Czech Republic. We had not received any passport details to confirm the name, so I could not accept this as an identification, but I did feel that we were, at least, well under way to confirming that this was his true name.

The second identification made in Germany related to Victim No. 27. He had been arrested in Germany on five occasions and had provided a different name to the authorities on each occasion. The first name he gave was Zheng Guang Li, which matched a name given to the Identification Team from an unidentified female who telephoned the MIR early in the investigation, asking if there was someone by that name amongst the victims. The description she gave of the male did not match this victim and, unfortunately, with so many aliases, I could not accept this as a confirmed identification. I would have to decide later what the best course of action would be to resolve the issue of his identification.

The third identification related to Victim 35 who, like the others, had been arrested in Germany for alien offences a few weeks earlier, on 25 May 2000, and subsequently released. This victim was one of the four females, and she was believed to be called Yue Ru Gao, aged 32 years. My decision to accept this as a confirmed identification would also have to be delayed, since there was an intelligence report in Germany indicating that she may have gone by the name of Yue Ying Zhen.

The fourth German identification that day was made, once again, through fingerprints, and related to Victim 55, who was believed to be a male called Long Zhong You, aged 42 years. He had been arrested in Germany on three previous occasions, dating back to January 1993. This looked like a positive identification but I still required additional confirmation, which I hoped to obtain from a family member.

We had more good news over the remainder of that weekend. A Dutch-issued immigration card was found in a pocket of one of the last items of clothing which had been discarded inside the container by a victim when the ferry crossed the English Channel. A closer examination of all the male victims indicated that there was a strong possibility it was Victim number 36, whose name, it seemed, may well have been Xiao Xiang Li. I could not accept this as a confirmed identification, at this stage, but at least it was another step in the right direction.

I was looking forward to making progress with our colleagues from China, who were due to arrive in the UK the following week. I was aware that their presence was likely to attract some media attention, so I started thinking in line with my media strategy, and how to turn this to our advantage.

I decided we should appeal to Chinese communities, requesting that they contact us if a family member or friend they had expected to arrive in the UK had not in fact arrived. It was during this time that it occurred to me to contact the Chinese TV company which had been at the initial press conference, to ask them if they were willing to record and transmit an interview with me regarding our appeal for families back in China to get in touch. I had the team arrange Chinese interpreters to be available for a one-off twenty-four-hour hotline and I kept my fingers firmly crossed, in the hope that a deluge of information would pour into our MIR.

I also hoped some Chinese citizens who resided in the UK might come forward and request a visual viewing of one of the victims and perhaps make an initial identification from a photograph. With this in mind, I realised that we would require a decent facility to use as a Chapel of Rest and, in order to demonstrate our respect for the victims, I decided to convert a mobile police office into a Chapel of Rest in keeping with the specific traditional customs which the Chinese community follows when someone has died.

One such rite demands that no red flower be displayed, since they are a symbol of celebration in China. I also insisted that any plainclothes officer dealing with the Chinese community refrain from wearing a red tie.

We had the chapel blessed by the local police Padre and did our best to follow compassionate guidelines to make sure nothing inappropriate was done or said in any way that might upset the Chinese community as a whole.

We installed a traditional fire-bin, where incense could be burnt, as well as some US dollars, as we were told that, traditionally, burning money enriches a victim's soul.

We managed all of this on several occasions, but I was later advised that we had made a couple of errors. Not only was the fire-bin the wrong colour (it should have been white) but, instead of burning US dollars (which I have since come to learn is considered a federal offence in America), we should have purchased (for just a few pence) special paper which is only sold in Chinese supermarkets – you don't burn real money!

Ultimately, the appeal we made via the UK media and the Chinese news agency worked reasonably well. Once the twenty-four-hour hotline was opened, the team covered those twenty-four hours with an interpreter. Unfortunately, this did not turn out to be such a good idea – we received no phone calls from China. The appeal did, however, generate some interest in the UK's Chinese communities, resulting in four positive facial identifications:

- Victim number 18 was identified by his brother as being Chang Ming He, aged 35 years
- Victim number 34 was identified by his brother-in-law as being Ti Di Dong, aged 31 years
- Victim number 46 was identified by his uncle as being Xin Xuan Yang, aged 22 years
- Victim number 57 was identified by his brother as being Zhen Chun Li, aged 24 years.

As we entered the second week of the criminal investigation and the identification process, the Chinese Embassy and the Foreign and Commonwealth Office confirmed that the Chinese officers and their interpreters would be with us by mid-morning that Wednesday.

I was also told that later in the week, Mr Charles Clarke, who was a UK government minister at the Home Office, would chair a meeting in our conference room regarding illegal human smuggling and that I would be required to brief him about our work. The national head of the Regional Crime Squads (now referred to as the National Crime Agency) would also be in attendance, since they were the lead agency responsible for the criminal investigation into this illegal trade. I had assumed that a Chief Officer of the force would wish to attend this event, but was later told that a relatively new Assistant Chief Constable would be instructed to attend.

Our force Welfare Department also called a meeting that week, which I agreed they could hold in our briefing room. Every member of staff (both police officers and civilian staff) were invited to attend this meeting, including the uniformed officers who had attended the scene on that Sunday night. I explicitly encouraged all officers who had attended that initial night to attend this meeting, even if they were not part of the ongoing investigation teams. Many officers and staff, including scene of crime officers, politely declined, but some were grateful to attend.

I made a special effort to be there myself, of course. It took place at 1530 hrs on the Thursday afternoon. A female member of the welfare team stopped me as soon as I approached the room. She addressed me pleasantly enough and asked me where I was going. I told her I was going into the welfare debriefing. She then informed me that I was not invited. Apparently, my presence might prevent certain staff from speaking out on issues which concerned them.

I was somewhat taken aback by this but, nonetheless, I politely told the lady that I understood her concerns. As she turned away from me, I asked, 'Excuse me, but who actually cares about *my* welfare?'

She made no reply and I'm still waiting for that question to be answered.

The Chinese contingent consisted of two members of the Chinese Embassy staff and four police officers. They arrived as expected and were later joined by a forensic pathologist who was a member of the Ministry of Public Security, seconded to Interpol in Lyon, France. We were formally introduced and then went on to discuss the protocols for information sharing. In essence, the Chinese wanted a copy of everything we had, without offering us anything by way of information in exchange. I agreed to them having copies of the photographs of the fifty-eight victims but they wanted photographs of the post-mortems as well, which to this day, I do not understand. Why would they have wanted those?

Nonetheless, I agreed to this request as well, with the clear understanding that the post-mortem photographs should not be made public and that families in China should only view them if they specifically asked for them. This was agreed.

Next, before they would work at trying to identify the victims, they demanded access to the two survivors. I told them that the two survivors were in hospital and that it was not possible for them to be interviewed. They were not happy about this at all and demanded that we hand over personal details of the two survivors. Again, I told them that this was not possible, unless each survivor agreed to have their information shared. We were at a stalemate there, so we adjourned for coffee and several members of their team got busy making phone calls. I had no idea who they were talking to, nor what they were discussing (they were, of course, speaking in Chinese) but, if I am not mistaken, there was a sense of urgency and panic in their tone. While I was content for details of evidence to be handed over, I was determined to make sure the survivors were not identified to them.

Whilst we waited for the Chinese team to sort themselves out, two colleagues from Hampshire Police, along with the rest of my team, Bob Nelson and a few members of his team were with me. I couldn't help but notice how one member of the Chinese team took a particular interest in the first few photographs of the victims on display in our conference room. This individual had his back to the rest of his colleagues and to our team, but I could see that he was continually bending his head down, as if inspecting something hidden in his jacket.

I walked towards him and, as I approached him, he surreptitiously tried to hide something in his jacket. It was only then that I realised it was a photograph he had hidden in his jacket; he was checking it against our photos, to see if it was one of our victims. I did not say anything to him, as I was not sure he would understand me. When we did eventually restart the discussions, I asked our visitors directly, how many photographs of possible victims had they brought with them.

This started a frenzy of discussions between them in Chinese.

They eventually told us that they had brought copies of passport photographs of every person who had applied for a passport in Fujian during the first six months of the year. This was good news for us and gave me the opportunity to let them know that I felt we might work well together to some extent. They agreed.

After this initial delay, we deployed my team and the Chinese police officers to begin the slow process of checking passport photographs against those of our victims. We ate a Chinese meal from a local take-away and washed it down with cans of Coca Cola. After lunch, I was pleased to see that the embassy staff were also keen to get involved in the work. It turned out to be a long afternoon, as it was an extremely slow process, but it had to be done. By mid-afternoon, our Chinese colleagues appeared to be growing restless. Next thing I knew, they decided they had done enough work for the day. I invited them to join our team for a welcome drink in a nearby country pub but they declined, subsequently left us, and returned to London. We agreed to meet with them again the following morning.

When they arrived the following day, I expected they would continue where they left off the previous afternoon, but that was not the case. They insisted on seeing the two survivors before they would continue helping us. I informed them that the survivors had declined to meet either the Chinese police, or representatives from the embassy. They were not happy with this, so I had a flash of inspiration. I told them that the two survivors were no longer the responsibility of the police – that they were now in the hands of HM Immigration Service, who had refused to let anyone see them. Surprisingly, the Chinese accepted this and started to get on with the work at hand.

The next few days were fairly similar. The Chinese arrived mid-morning and left mid-afternoon. Slowly but surely, they made progress with our team and, face by face, we started to put names to our victims. This was good but I required more fact-based information before I could confirm each victim's identity with 100 per cent surety. The type of confirmation I required could only come from DNA being matched from each victim to a blood relative, all of whom were most likely back in China.

For the first time, I broached the subject with the embassy staff and the senior police officer regarding the possibility of a team of my staff travelling to China in order to meet the victims' relatives on behalf of HM Coroner and, where appropriate, to obtain DNA samples. This suggestion was initially accepted but the Chinese team working with us could not confirm whether it would, ultimately, be permitted by the Chinese Government.

The following morning, I had to attend a meeting at Police Headquarters, which meant that I was unable to travel to the MIR until just before midday. As I was about to turn into the car park at the back of the MIR, I had to give way to a minibus which was leaving the MIR. I recognised it, at once, as the Chinese minibus and, much to my surprise (and consternation), all the Chinese staff were in it. I parked up and walked into the MIR, where Dave Weller and some of my team were working away.

'Where has the Chinese team gone?' I asked Dave.

'They're in the next room along, boss,' he replied.

'Oh no they're not,' I said.

He looked surprised. 'Yes, they are.'

'Really?' I asked. 'Please, go and check.'

He looked at me in total confusion as he got off his seat, walked out of the room and down the corridor towards the next office.

He returned quick-smart. 'They are not there,' he declared.

'Yes,' I agreed. 'Did you do something to upset them?'

He pleaded not guilty and we laughed.

I then tasked him to find out why they had gone.

After a phone call to the China/Hong Kong desk at the Foreign and Commonwealth Office, we established that they had been ordered back to their embassy because the Chinese Government had closed the embassy and consulate offices as a protest against the UK Government having invited the newly elected President of Taiwan to visit the UK. We found it incredulous that they did not feel the need to tell us this before they left. Due to this protest, we did not see them again until the protest had been lifted and the embassy reopened three days later. A frustrating hold-up for our progress, I must say.

By the start of the following week, we had made excellent progress and there were only a few victims left to provisionally identify. We gave the Chinese team all the photographs they had requested and they, in turn, gave us copied passport photographs of the people they believed were victims.

In the end, we came to an agreement, through the Chinese Embassy and the Foreign and Commonwealth Office, to make formal arrangements for myself and members of my team to travel to China to meet families and obtain DNA samples. Prior to the departure of the Chinese team, I invited them again to have a farewell drink with our team but this was also declined.

Over the following week, several major issues had to be addressed in respect of the fifty-eight victims. I received information from the Metropolitan Police Service that a number of memorial rallies were to be held for the victims in Chinese communities around the UK. These rallies were planned to be held every thirty days, until all the victims had been repatriated back to their families in China.

As part of our Community Impact Assessment, I sent officers to London, Manchester, Bristol, Birmingham, Glasgow and Edinburgh, where rallies were to be held. The officers were briefed to liaise with senior officers in those forces, not only so that they could properly police the rallies, but also to provide updates on our progress identifying victims and our efforts to persuade the Chinese Government (via their London embassy) to allow the repatriation.

I, in turn, visited the embassy with a colleague from the China/ Hong Kong Desk to speak with the Chinese Ambassador over this matter. At the outset, these meetings were not very successful, but at least they let us into the building this time – although a request to use the lavatory was refused!

On our second visit, we were just about to open our discussions when an embassy official started blaming me for an unfortunate situation which was taking place at the immigration desks at Heathrow Airport. Upon entering the UK, Chinese students were being harassed, insulted and overly scrutinised by immigration officials. Despite my efforts, and those of my colleague, to explain that I had nothing to do with the airport nor any of the airport staff, the official stormed out of the meeting and we were asked to leave the building.

After this incident we decided, together with the Foreign and Commonwealth Office, that we would not return to the embassy until after our planned trip to China.

Back in the MIR, we had collated a large number of mobile telephone numbers which had been found hidden in the clothing of the victims. Subscriber checks on the majority of these numbers determined that they belonged to Chinese restaurants and takeaway shops in the UK. This indicated to me that many of the victims had intended to make their way to friends or families who were already in the UK, which meant that they would have been readily accepted into Chinese communities here. At the time of the investigation, it was our view that these people were to enter the UK and try to make lives for themselves by working, not to be a burden to the benefits system. It is only years later, however, that the full extent of human smuggling has been revealed and I am mindful of the fact that many of these people may have ended up in human slavery.

We had to liaise with immigration authorities and local police before visiting any of the premises of these friends and relatives, in order to ensure that in doing so, we didn't stumble into ongoing investigative operations they were running at the time. Furthermore, giving due consideration to grouping all these addresses into different geographic areas saved any unnecessary repeat journeys around the country. Each team went out with an album of photographs of the fifty-eight victims, and showed the occupants of the telephone subscriber's address. We provided additional albums to the investigative teams on the criminal investigation side, so that any potential witness could try and identify the victim. Every team was made aware that the photographs were only to be shown in the appropriate locations and must be presented in a sensitive manner. The teams were also given details of a Chinese branch of Victim Support, which they were to share with the subscribers and their families and staff.

The presence of our two Chinese-speaking colleagues who worked with these teams was of significant assistance to us. I later discovered that Andy Lau had taught members of the Identification Team to refer to me, out of my earshot, as *Di Lo Ban*, which translates into English as Number One Boss. Quite pleasing on the ear, I think.

In regards to the DNA, we liaised with the Forensic Science Service who, in turn, established via scientists in Beijing that the process of analysing DNA samples was significantly different in China than it was in the UK. Together, they agreed that, since the UK had more advanced DNA techniques, the analysis should be carried out in the UK.

To aid integrity, and as a sign of goodwill, we agreed to supply the Chinese authorities with samples of blood from each of the victims, in order that they be able to do their own analysis. These blood samples, which were obtained during the post-mortems, were delivered to the Chinese authorities on KM (Kastle Meyer) paper – a technique which complemented the Chinese method of analysing blood.

During these discussions about the DNA, the Chinese Embassy informed myself and the Foreign and Commonwealth Office that, whilst we were able to visit China and collect sample from the relatives of the victims, we were not permitted to meet with the families, or speak with the Chinese media. (They did however, assure us that they would deal with the families of the victims in a sensitive manner.) This meant that my plans to train a team of police officers and civilian colleagues to take blood for DNA analysis had to be abandoned.

❖

Our visas to enter China were issued by their embassy, and Mr Sturt and our Chief Officers agreed that I would travel to China on 4 September 2000, accompanied by my deputy, Steve Corbishley, with Sergeant Joe Hon as our interpreter.

After a ten-hour flight from Heathrow, London, to Beijing, we were met at the airport by Chinese police officers who accompanied us to our accommodation in the centre of Beijing. Our itinerary included a visit to the British Embassy that afternoon at 1600 hrs – it was only a short taxi-ride from our hotel and we were greeted by an embassy staff member who introduced himself as a media officer. I had expected to meet the ambassador, Sir Anthony Galsworthy, but was told that he was currently on leave and fishing in Mongolia.

The senior diplomat at the embassy rushed into the room, said a brief hello and shook our hands before telling us he was sorry, but he could not stop to talk, as he was late for a drinks reception and had to go. He left as quickly as he had come in. Not long after this, we ourselves left to return to our hotel.

The three of us spent the evening enjoying a traditional Chinese meal and walking around the city. The Metropolitan Police Special Branch had told me in advance that the Chinese security service would follow us everywhere we went, but if they were following us that night then they must have been very bored.

We returned to the hotel bar and enjoyed a beer called Tiger – a brand which is now world famous but in 2000 was certainly a new one for us.

We were up bright and early the next morning to enjoy a typical, western-style breakfast in preparation for our meeting with senior members of the Public Security Ministry of the People's Republic of China at their headquarters in the centre of Beijing. The Deputy Director of the CID, Xue Dongzheng, chaired the meeting in the main conference room at the headquarters building. Representatives of their Forensic Science Department, the Foreign Affairs Ministry and their Immigration Department were also present.

After initial introductions via our respective interpreters, I expressed two important concerns from the British point of view. Firstly, I asked what the official Chinese view on the return of the victims to China was. Secondly, I raised the issue regarding my colleagues and myself not being permitted to liaise with the families of the victims on behalf of HM Coroner. Xue Dongzheng explained that neither he nor the police were responsible for making decisions regarding the return of the victims and that such a matter should be taken up with the Chinese Embassy in London. In regards to liaising with families of the victims, he said that most of the families had been identified and he assured us that his officers had dealt with them in a caring and sensitive manner. They were too widely spread out over the country to make it possible for us to visit them, but when we travelled to Fujian Province, he assured us, the matter would be resolved.

My next task was to give them an insight into the roles of HM Coroners in England and Wales and of the Identification Commission, as well as to provide them with an update on the criminal investigations in both England and Holland.

After the meeting, we had a light lunch together, before confirming our travel arrangements for the next day when we were due to fly to Fujian City. I was asked to record an interview for the BBC World Service and the BBC Radio Four morning news programme, which would be broadcast the next morning UK time. Aside from that, we were free for the remainder of the day and so we did some sightseeing. We visited the Great Wall of China, the Forbidden City, Tiananmen Square and the Summer Palace. It was truly an amazing experience, but in the back of our minds we were always aware that we were in this country for the most sombre of reasons.

The following day, we flew south to Fujian with our colleague from the Chinese Forensic Science Service, where we were met by the familiar faces of those same Chinese police officers who had travelled to Kent. We were taken to our new hotel and later that evening were treated to an evening meal with our Chinese colleagues. It may have been easier to eat with us than to have us followed everywhere!

The following morning, we were collected by minibus and taken to the Fujian police headquarters where we met with members of the Fujian Public Security CID and two members of the Chinese Embassy who had travelled separately from London, especially for this meeting. The meeting was chaired by Zhen Jing Hua, who was the Vice Director of the Fujian Public Security CID. I explained the role of HM Coroner and how imperative it was to ensure that the identification of each victim was 100 per cent correct. We discussed facial mapping as a possible means of assisting in the identification, and the Chinese police agreed to supply us with albums of photographs of each of the victims but, this time, we would be looking at photographs from their actual families.

They supplied us with statements from victims' family members, giving evidential continuity that they had provided their blood for DNA analysis, the samples of which had been retained on KM paper.

> KM stands for Kastle and Meyer, the surnames of two scientists who, in the early 1900s, discovered a formula that could be used to identify the presence of blood impregnated on paper. This is now commonly referred to as 'a KM test'.

We went through the painstaking process of cutting each of their KM Paper samples in half, in order that the Chinese retain one half and we took possession of the other half. We then individually recorded and safely packed them for transport back to the UK.

After this process was completed, I raised the issue of Family Liaison again and, to my surprise, they were quite open to the discussion this time. They even went as far as sharing a video with us which demonstrated how they dealt with identification issues concerning our fifty-eight victims. It had been recorded in some kind of village or community hall, where families were invited to look at albums of photographs. When someone recognised a family member, one of the plainclothes police officers who was managing the process took them aside and obtained both a statement and a DNA blood sample from them. To my horror, the video showed photographs (which had also been included in their albums) of several victims as they lay naked in the mortuary. At the end of the video, they all appeared pleased with what they had achieved. I did not share my sense of dismay with them, I did my best to hide my true feelings in fact, because in honesty, I was shocked by what I regarded as an extremely poor standard of victim care.

The formalities of the conference drew to an end. We were invited to lunch and then treated to a tour of Fujian city and the surrounding countryside, including the smaller city of Xiamen and the South

Puto Temple, which is one of the area's most famous tourist attractions, despite being located halfway up a mountain.

The following morning, we returned to our Beijing hotel with a copy of the video of the victims' relatives, the blood samples and the album of photographs. A note had been left at the hotel reception desk for me from the British Embassy, inviting the three of us to meet the British Ambassador, Sir Anthony Galsworthy, at 1600 hrs that afternoon.

The British Embassy was established on 26 March 1861 in the former palace of Duke I-liang when Sir Frederick Bruce became the first Envoy Extraordinary and Minister Plenipotentiary to Imperial China to reside in Beijing (formerly known as Peking). In 1959, the Chinese authorities required the British to vacate their location because they wanted to redevelop the land and use it for the Supreme People's Court. In exchange for vacating their old premises, the Chinese authorities built and offered the British their current embassy and residence in the diplomatic district. The embassy consists of two two-storey houses set in walled gardens.

Upon our arrival at the embassy, we were greeted by same man we had initially met when we arrived in Beijing. He informed us that Sir Anthony was ready for us and escorted us up a flight of stairs to a first-floor landing. The man then explained that we were to go to the next floor but that he was not permitted in that part of the building. Just as he said this, I heard an electric-lock device being activated and saw what looked like an ordinary door opening beside us. This was no ordinary door, however, it was approximately 10in-thick and appeared to be built of solid metal.

We were greeted by a Royal Marine, who invited us to follow him up the next flight of stairs where we were greeted by Sir Anthony in his private office, which was more like a country house sitting room. Sir Anthony invited us to sit down and we proceeded to take afternoon tea with him. Before we began our general discussion about our work, he told us about his fishing trip to Mongolia. He was pleased with the relationship we had established with the officers of the Ministry of Security. When he asked me if there was anything which might have made our work easier, I suggested that a UK liaison officer of senior police rank would have made our task easier. That was exactly what he had wanted, he told me, and asked me to share my thoughts and recommendation with the Foreign and Commonwealth Office once we returned to the UK. I agreed to make the recommendation and, in the fullness of time, this recommendation was actioned in that a new position of Police Liaison Officer at the embassy was eventually established.

The meeting came to an end. We finished our tea and cakes, and he shook each of our hands upon wishing us a safe journey back home. Another pleasant and interesting experience, with a backdrop of sadness.

We spent the remainder of the afternoon shopping, after which we prepared for an evening meal with the Director General of the Ministry of Public Security and all his senior officials, at one of Beijing's most famous restaurants. This restaurant was the very one their Government had used when the former President of the United States of America, the late President H. W. Bush, visited back in February 1989.

It was a meal I will never forget. I had always been taught that a guest must accept, with good grace, whatever food is placed on the table. I should have realised this meal would be like no other when it began with seafood soup made from sea horses! After this, we enjoyed several more traditional dishes. It appeared to take a long time to finish the meal but I believe this had more to do with myself and Steve Corbishley not being as quick with the chopsticks as our Chinese counterparts were.

The time came for the after-dinner speeches and I was the first to be invited to address the gathering. I had prepared in advance and, after the initial greeting and thanks for a wonderful meal and evening, I shared a few traditional Irish jokes. I must say, I was disappointed that they did not seem to appreciate my jokes as much as I had hoped they would. Afterwards, I presented the Director General, the Deputy Director General and the Vice Director General with neatly wrapped gifts of one-litre bottles of twenty-year-old Scotch whisky.

The next thing I knew, and without so much as an introduction, a gentleman I did not know started a speech of his own. Several minutes into his speech, I noticed the entire senior staff looking over in my direction. They smiled and nodded. It took a moment before it eventually dawned on me – this man was not making a speech – he was repeating my speech in Chinese! All at once, there was an outcry of laughter and I was so relieved to hear it – they must have arrived at the Irish jokes.

The Director General gave his formal reply in English, thanking us for all the work we had done and presenting each of us with a wrapped gift. I found it peculiar (and slightly awkward) that I received the largest gift. Steve was presented with a medium-sized parcel and Joe, the smallest one. We did not open the presents until we were safely back in our hotel, where we discovered they had given us Chinese vases. Although grateful for the gesture, I still look upon those vases as a symbol of what the trip represented – trying to identify victims in the hope of eventually returning their bodies to their loved ones.

We were taken to the airport the following day, feeling very pleased to be returning home having completed an important part of the identification side of this investigation.

Back in the MIR, I updated all our staff, in both the identification and the criminal investigation teams, on the progress we had made in China. All the blood samples obtained in China were then sent to the Forensic Science Service to be analysed against the samples of blood obtained from the victims in the mortuary. This process would take several weeks to complete, during which time, we focused our research on the facial mapping process, as we now had good, clear facial photographs of the victims from their families.

> Facial Mapping is the objective comparison of questioned facial images, with known reference imagery, in order to determine whether the two faces under comparison may be excluded from being the same person, and if not, the likelihood of them being the same person.
> RJB Forensics Limited*

Canterbury University was one of the leading authorities in the scientific development of facial mapping. The history of facial mapping, however, dates back several thousand years to the days of ancient

---

* www.forensic-science.uk.com/facial-mapping-2/

Chinese medicine. How ironic is that? As an experiment, we supplied the scientists with photographs of a random sample of twelve of the male victims, together with ten passport photographs which we believed to have been correctly matched. We also selected two other passport photographs from two victims who were certainly not in that group. The results confirmed that ten of the twelve victims matched ten of the passport photographs. The remaining two could not be confirmed, which proved that the technique they were using was 100 per cent accurate. This was very helpful to our investigation.

We did a similar exercise with a forensic pathologist at Glasgow University, using all fifty-eight victim photographs and the family photographs. Whilst their overall results were good, there were several errors in the matching. Whilst this supported some of the identifications, it was not satisfactorily accurate so it was discarded from an evidential point of view.

After this, we did all fifty-eight with Canterbury University and the results were entirely accurate.

Over the following days, the work required from both the criminal investigation team and the Identification Team eased up somewhat, and staff was redeployed to other major crime investigations around the county. The teams (which were made up of officers and civilian colleagues) would re-form, when necessary, down the line, in order to complete the identification process, the victim repatriation and the criminal trial of the lorry driver and Chinese solicitor.

We received the final DNA results from the Forensic Science Service by mid-September 2000, and I chaired a meeting with my original team in order to methodically examine the identification evidence available for each of the fifty-eight victims.

By the end of this process, I was satisfied that I had enough evidence to confirm the identification of each of the deceased. I did, however, still have concerns about Victim No. 27, who we believed to be Zheng Guang Li. I discussed this victim with Mr Sturt and he was reasonably comfortable with the identification. Mr Sturt then fixed 18 September 2000 as the date to reopen the inquest into the tragic events at Dover Port on the night of 18 June 2000.

I attended the inquest and agreed that members of the identification team could also attend. I had anticipated that I might be required to give the names, so I prepared the list in advance, numbered one to fifty-eight, and handed a copy to Mr Sturt. I also produced copies for the media representatives, assuming that would suffice. Unfortunately, it did not. As I was the only witness, Mr Sturt asked me to read out the names of the victims for the public record and for the benefit of the media who were in attendance.

In order to give every victim their due respect, I tried to pause between each name but I still felt like each name ran straight into the next. Reading through those Chinese names was not as easy as it may have sounded to my colleagues, and I almost tripped myself up over my own tongue several times. The situation was not helped by my team's evident enjoyment as they watched their *Di Lo Ban* struggle with the pronunciation but I got there in the end.

Mr Sturt then commended the Identification Commission in the following terms:

> This has been a superb example of the way in which a disaster ought to be managed and, hopefully, other people who are faced with similar problems in the future will learn lessons from them. It has been quite a formidable achievement by DSU McGookin and his team, given all the potential difficulties.

The next challenge was to get the Chinese Government to permit and to facilitate the return of the victims to their families through their embassy. This required me and my colleague from the China/Hong Kong Desk to visit the embassy on several occasions. Certain conditions had to be met before any formal agreement could be made but, in principle, they agreed that the deceased could be returned to China. They first insisted that the bodies of the victims be examined by their own forensic pathologists and that all international rules for transporting bodies be adhered to. The agreement I eventually made with the Consul General, Dr Sun Dali, which was endorsed by Mr Sturt, covered the following:

- Each victim would still be identified by the number with which they were allocated after they had been pronounced dead. My reasoning behind this was that their names should not go on the coffin because any slight error in translation might cause unnecessary hurt to families.

- Each victim would be embalmed. In addition to this, their faces would be treated, in order to delay the decaying process. This is a process often referred to in embalming as 'Kalo Form'. A massaging cream is mixed with the chemical formaldehyde to form a pale, coloured paste which is gently massaged into the face. Due to the toxic nature of formaldehyde, a notice printed in English and Chinese would be placed in each coffin, to warn anyone opening the coffin to inspect the body of the deceased, as toxic fumes may be present.
- A copy of the identification process relating to the victim would be placed in their coffin, to give the family proof of the identification if they decided to open the coffin.
- Each coffin would be lead-lined and individually wrapped in hessian cloth.
- A copy of the Identification Commissioner's Report to HM Coroner would be given to the Chinese Government.
- The UK Government would pay for the victims' transportation to China. Initially, I wanted the Chinese Government to pay the cost of the transportation of their citizens, but their embassy staff were adamant that their government would not pay these costs. Since it was taxpayers' money, Mr Sturt raised this matter with the County Council, and they agreed to pay.
- China Eastern Airlines would collect and transport the victims. This was not my original plan, I would have preferred to use Swiss Air as the carrier, but again, the Chinese Embassy staff would not consider any other airline, so we had to accept this decision. That was not the end of the matter, however, as we later established that this airline did not possess an Air Worthiness Certificate to fly in UK airspace. The aircraft was permitted to enter European airspace and regularly flew to Paris, but this still did not permit it to fly to the UK. We asked the Civil Aviation Authority how we could resolve this matter, and they very helpfully informed us that if the carrier landed in Paris then they would permit it to fly to the nearest UK airport, which was Stansted Airport in Essex, on the condition that it was the last flight into

the airport, on a date to be confirmed, and that it was the first aircraft to leave that same airport the following morning. This was good news for us and the Chinese Embassy agreed.

- HM Coroner would require a letter from the Chinese Ambassador in London stating that the Chinese Government would take full responsibility for the fifty-eight deceased, once the bodies had arrived in China, and that the bodies would be handed over to the families. This was agreed.

- Details of a named Chinese official would be required, to sign for the bodies after the Chinese pathologists had viewed them and they had been sealed in a coffin. This was agreed.

- No clothing or personal property would be placed in the coffin of each victim. This was based on security and health and safety issues.

All we had to do now was get the bodies examined by the Chinese forensic pathologists, after which we could get on with the preparation to transport the victims back to China. Thankfully, no issues were raised in respect to Victim No. 6, who had no known relatives in China.

After consulting with Mr Sturt, I had a member of our team contact a company called Global Partnership, who specialise in dealing with disaster body identification and world-wide body repatriation. The director of this company, Mr Phil Lewis, visited our headquarters in Maidstone where I chaired a meeting with him and my team. This was already mid-December 2000, and my aim had been to acquire final confirmation that the Chinese Embassy would be willing receive the bodies as early in the new year as possible.

I agreed that Mr Lewis should take the lead in preparing the victims' bodies and to ensure all aspects of coffining were dealt with in the correct manner. This was to take place at Gore Brother Funeral Directors in Dover after they had been collected, under the supervision of a member of the Identification Commission from the Parachute Regiment's Barracks.

Along with details of the identification of each victim, we agreed that each coffin would include the following certifications:

- Interim Death Certificate, as to the fact of death
- A Form 103, signed by HM Coroner, which is required when exporting a body outside the UK

- A Certificate of Embalming
- A Freedom from Infection Certificate, signed by our forensic pathologist.

There was still one victim whose identity I had concerns about, Victim No. 27, since this victim was initially identified by a Chinese lady who declined to give her details but did give a physical description of this person, saying that he had three piercings in his left ear. She said that he had been arrested in Germany for violating alien law on five occasions and was now on his sixth alias. One of the names she gave was Zheng Guang Li. On examining his body, there were indeed three piercings in his left ear.

It was on that basis, of her giving information without imparting her own information, that I decided the only way to resolve it was to send two officers to Germany, in an effort to prove or disprove this identification. Bob Kelly and Dave Weller had not been selected to visit China with me so they were my first choice to travel to Frankfurt. They decided to drive to Frankfurt, and I allowed them to make their own travel arrangements but I double-checked that: they had the necessary documents with them, they had made initial contact with the German police, and that their accommodation was booked. Their families had my contact details if they had any concerns whilst Bob and Dave were abroad. They left on 20 December 2000 and I was satisfied they would be back home safely before Christmas Eve.

All went well with their visit to Frankfurt, but I later heard that when their German colleagues had asked them which hotel had they booked themselves into, they innocently informed their colleagues that they had booked into a certain Kaiser Hof Hotel in the Wiesbaden Strasato district. Apparently, this response elicited a roar of laughter from every-one in their office. They had booked into a notorious red-light district hotel which was, in fact, a renowned brothel and due to be raided by the police vice squad that exact week. How embarrassing that would have been! Thankfully, the German police sorted out a more appropriate hotel for the boys.

The following day, with the assistance of a German police officer, they made enquires with a solicitor who had previously represented Victim number 27. He confirmed that, when he represented the victim, he had used the name Zheng Li. The solicitor could not be 100 per cent certain, however, that this was his correct name. The solicitor then suggested to confirm his identification via medical records.

They subsequently visited a local doctor, and after a heated exchange between the police officer and the female doctor, she confirmed that the victim was indeed Zheng Guang Li. It was established from records at the solicitor's office and from medical notes that Li had fled China after he had assaulted a police officer. He had allegedly challenged the police office whilst distributing leaflets promoting the Roman Catholic faith. His mother had been aware that he was in Germany and might very well make his way to the UK, but she was frightened to tell the Chinese police, in case she got into trouble. This was very useful information – I was now satisfied that Victim No. 27 had been positively identified. (I must admit, I was also relieved that Bob and Dave returned home safely.)

PC Bob Kelly collected the Chinese pathologists, and a member of the Chinese Embassy staff who was entrusted signing documents, asserting that everything had been managed correctly, and that each coffin had been sealed in their presence. They examined the bodies over the weekend, before finally agreeing to return them to China. Jo was present to do all the interpretation whilst Bob looked after the Chinese during this visit.

I authorised a budget to provide the officials with a nice Sunday lunch after they had finished this work. I later discovered that the visitors had selected a particularly strong beer during the meal and were not in an altogether healthy state when they were returned to the embassy later that day.

The new year passed and on Wednesday, 16 January 2001, Mr Sturt and I were invited to attend the Chinese Embassy in order to confirm the repatriation arrangements and receive the Chinese Government's official correspondence on the matter.

Mr Sturt very kindly offered to collect me in his chauffeur-driven Jaguar, so we certainly travelled to the embassy in style. We received a warm welcome (significantly different from my first visit there!) and, after being served Chinese tea, the day's formalities began. Mr Sturt was presented with the official document concerning China's acceptance of the fifty-eight bodies, along with the undertaking of repatriating them to their next of kin after their arrival in the People's Republic of China. On leaving the embassy, Mr Sturt suggested that we visit his private club nearby, to enjoy some refreshments before travelling back to Kent. I have always felt this was a particularly kind gesture.

Back in my office, I was pleased to hear that my team had arranged for the China Air Eastern flight, which was currently in Paris, to arrive at Stansted Airport in Essex late the following evening, and that transport for the victims to the airport, the following afternoon, was in hand. Since, technically, the bodies were going to be lying in another Coroner's jurisdiction, Mr Sturt requested and was granted permission from HM Coroner for Essex, Mrs Beasley-Murray OBE, for them to lie in her jurisdiction.

The bodies were safely transported to the airport the following day and I arrived at the airport later that evening, together with Steve Corbishley, Dave Weller and Bob Kelly. The bodies had been unloaded and the airport staff were getting them ready to load onto the heavy-duty lift which was to be used to place them in the cargo section of the aeroplane.

Despite the thick fog, which weighed the cold deep into my bones that night, the flight arrived safely. *What could possibly go wrong?* I asked myself. *My team has covered everything.*

Hmmn. Indeed, what could possibly go wrong?

Soon after, we were informed that the loading was about to take place, so we went outside to watch. The heavy-duty lifting device had rollers, which moved in several different directions so that a load could be manoeuvred into the correct position on the plane. There was only one member of staff operating it. I felt like applauding him whilst watching our victims go through the loading-hatch.

At long last, I thought. *They are going 'home'.*

Within minutes, I watched, horrified, as the cargo came back out, the same way it went in. My heart sprung up into my mouth, I swear it did. All I could think of was that something 'political' had occurred, in that moment, and the Chinese were now refusing to take the victims back to their homeland.

Thankfully, however, it was just one manoeuvre, a necessary step to correctly balancing the load in the aeroplane.

Phew.

I received a telephone call around midnight from the airport manager, who informed me that the captain of the aircraft had requested refuelling. The captain expected us to pay the bill for this, otherwise he would not take the bodies on board but would, instead, return to Paris to refuel. I could hardly believe such a request was being made, but I dispatched Dave and Bob to go and sort it out. They returned about forty minutes later, smiling, and told me that the aircraft was now refuelling. They had told the airport manager to forward the bill to me at Police Headquarters. What else could I do but laugh.

As the night wore on, the temperature dropped even more substantially. A heavy mist fell, bringing with it a damp cold, the likes of which I had never known – it was absolutely freezing! And it only grew colder. Still, I was certain nothing else could go wrong and trusted that, in a few hours' time, the aeroplane would depart and we would all return home.

We tried to sleep in the airport lounge but it was too cold even to sleep.

At around 0500 hrs, the airport manager contacted me once again. The aeroplane would not be able to depart early, as scheduled – it needed to be de-iced before it could take off and the pilot was not able to pay for this facility.

Dave was still awake, so I dispatched him to go and get the matter resolved. He returned soon after, smiling. Sure enough, he had organised the de-icing, and that bill would also be sent to me.

Well, if I'm paying for this, I'm going to see how the de-icing is done.

In the freezing fog of morning, the four of us went outside to watch the de-icing spectacle take place. The de-icing of an aircraft is not dissimilar to de-icing a car windscreen only on a much larger scale. De-icing fluid for an aircraft is a mixture of a chemical called glycol and water, which is heated and sprayed at high pressure, to remove ice and snow on an aircraft. This fluid also contains an additive to help it adhere to aircraft surfaces whilst it speeds down the runway during take-off.

After this, we watched dawn break whilst taking in an early coffee. Airport security informed me that the Chinese Ambassador and his entourage were arriving at the airport soon and would be permitted to drive airside, to pay their respect to the 'Dover fifty-eight'. On hearing this, I decided we should greet them, so we went airside and liaised with airport security staff to ascertain where we should all stand.

Soon after, at around 0725 hrs, the China Air Eastern aircraft started moving, just as two cars from the Chinese Embassy appeared airside and drove up close to where we stood. In total there were eight individuals form the embassy in attendance but I only recognised the Consular General. The aeroplane moved onto the runway and as its engines revved up, the doors of the embassy cars opened, the occupants alighted, and stood in a line, with their heads bowed, some twenty feet away from the three of us. The aeroplane moved along the runway, gathered speed and, at 0738 precisely, the China Air Eastern aircraft took off. As the plane climbed up into the sky over Essex, my thoughts went straight to the victims, who were all going home.

I turned towards the Consular General with the intention of shaking hands but as I did this, he turned in the opposite direction, walked to his car and got into the rear of his vehicle, followed by his staff. Within seconds their doors were shut and both cars drove off at speed. We then left the airport and headed back to Kent.

I telephoned our Media Services en route and gave them an official statement for immediate release, stating that 'The fifty-eight victims of the tragedy in Dover on 20 June 2000 were this morning flown out of the UK, on their way home to their relatives in China.'

I telephoned Mr Sturt to confirm the news before listening to the car radio at 0800 hrs to tune in to Radio 4 News. I was pleased to hear our press release read as the headline news.

Back in Kent, life started to get back to normal for myself and our Identification Team. The criminal investigation trials in England and in Holland, however, were only weeks away now.

In mid-February, the lorry-driver Perry Wacker and the Chinese solicitor Ying Gou appeared at Maidstone Crown Court and pleaded not guilty to charges of conspiracy to smuggle illegal immigrants and Wacker's additional charges, of fifty-eight counts of manslaughter. The trial lasted six weeks. Evidence from the two survivors, along with the host of forensic evidence from the lorry and telephone numbers found in various item of clothing, was compelling. The jury returned a verdict of guilty to all counts against both defendants. Wacker was sentenced to fourteen years' imprisonment, and Gou to six. The court record shows that the trial judge, Mr Justice Moses, described how Wacker had treated the victims and the two survivors as 'cargo'.

Meanwhile, over in Holland on 19 April 2001, the trial began for the eight people charged with human-trafficking-related charges, and the manslaughter of the fifty-eight victims at Dover. This trial lasted several weeks and, at its conclusion, all eight were convicted of the human trafficking offence. They were acquitted of manslaughter but the prosecution appealed the acquittal under Dutch law, and the two main ringleaders were convicted of fifty-eight counts of manslaughter. On 11 May 2001, Gursel Ozcan and Haci Demir were each sentenced to nine years' imprisonment for these offences.

These convictions, together with the convictions of Wacker and Gou in the UK, brought this very sad sequence of events to a close ... almost.

I received a message from the Chief Constable's office telling me that the Chief Constable wished to commend the key individuals in both the Identification and Criminal Investigation teams. I was to nominate who should be commended and prepare the citations for each nominee. This was not as straightforward as one may think, but eventually (and somewhat ironically), fifty-eight members of staff were commended. The Chief Constable also commended the Dover Harbour Board Police for their involvement in the case, but unfortunately, offers to commend individuals from HM Customs and Excise and HM Immigration Service were declined. A special award was made to HM Coroner Mr Sturt to recognise his services to the community over many years.

From a personal point of view, I was extremely pleased to receive a letter for my personal attention, addressed to the Chief Constable, from the then Home Secretary, Mr Jack Straw, which stated that my report on the tragic deaths of the fifty-eight Chinese immigrants at Dover demonstrated a thorough, yet sensitive, investigation into the tragedy.

I also received a letter addressed to the Chief Constable from HM Coroner, Mr Sturt, in which he congratulated the force for a 'highly professional police operation'. At the conclusion of the letter, he gave me a personal mention, stating: 'Finally, I think the service rendered by Dennis McGookin was simply outstanding and he deserves the highest commendation, I am not sure what an appropriate award for him would be, but I would think that a Queen's Police Medal has been well merited.'

A lovely comment, but I did not receive the QPM.

Wacker appealed and his trial has made case law with regard to gross negligence manslaughter. In truth I felt he deserved far longer than the term of imprisonment he received.

Meanwhile, I worked so well with Lorraine, the Head of Crime Scene Investigation, that I decided to marry her.

EPILOGUE

The target events at Dover finally came to an end for me in mid-January 2001 and life did get back to normal, if investigating murders and other serious crimes can be regarded as 'normal'.

Later in the year, as I entered my twenty-ninth year in the Police Service, I started to think about my retirement from the force the following summer – surely there would not be another crime that would surpass the cases I had already dealt with!

Sadly, there were. Having previously travelled to Pitcairn Island and dealt with a sexual assault, other allegations of sexual abuse had now been made against several island men. I had to co-ordinate this investigation with the Foreign & Commonwealth Office, but I was grateful to my colleagues Peter George and Rob Vinson who did all the work on these cases, which led to numerous successful prosecutions.

After Pitcairn, there was yet another case that required my direct attention. This occurred on a cold winter night in Kent when a little 10-year-old girl was abducted and seriously assaulted. I initially appointed my colleague DCI Colin Murray to investigate this case, but when a second offence in another force area was linked forensically to our investigation, I had to take on the role of the 'Officer in Overall Command' (OIOC) of these two crimes. Eventually, six police forces became involved in this investigation, banding together to find the suspect that the media had dubbed 'The M25 Trophy Rapist'.

I eventually retired from Kent Police on 31 November 2002 and I am pleased to say that the offender for these attacks was arrested soon after and charged with each of these offences. He was later sentenced to life imprisonment.

In my retirement, I started a new adventure as an Investigative Consultant, specialising in the management of major disasters and the training of detective officers in all ranks of the Police Service. I was also appointed as an Associate Tutor at the Police Staff College at Bramshill (now known as the Police College) and at the Netherlands Police Academy in Apeldoorn. Through my work with the Police College, I represented the Police Service in ongoing training projects in Lebanon, the Philippines and throughout the UK. In a more private capacity, colleague and friend Malcolm Ross (retired West Midlands Detective Superintendent) and I developed and delivered a full detective training program for the Police Service of Bermuda.

During this same period of time, I was invited to undertake a research project in Northern Ireland with my friend and colleague Graham Driscoll (retired Kent Police Detective Sergeant). This was initially projected to take around twelve months but would eventually take almost five years to complete. It was quite ironic for me to return to work in Northern Ireland, but it gave me the wonderful opportunity to spend some quality time with my mother before she passed away at the age of 89 years.

My training role eventually took me to Abu Dhabi, capital of the United Arab Emirates, where I led a training exercise with the Abu Dhabi Police Service alongside Richard Silver, a former colleague at the Police College. We delivered a one-week Major Crime Investigators Course to a variety of officers of different ranks. Twenty-four officers attended and registered for the course, but only eighteen officers actually attended; as each day passed, more and more officers dropped out, despite my insistence that they all had to complete it.

On the fifth and final day I delivered my presentation on the Dover Tragedy to twelve officers and an interpreter (even though all the students could speak good English). The presentation was being well received, and as we broke for coffee, I asked all the officers to return at exactly 1030 hrs. At the agreed time I was in the classroom and was joined by the interpreter and only one of the officers, who I shall refer to as 'Mohammed'. After a few minutes I asked Mohammed where his colleagues were.

He replied, and I quote, 'They have all gone to the camel sales.'

'What?!' I asked, sounding like a cat squealing.

Mohammed explained to me that these sales, which were similar to those of thoroughbred racehorses in the UK, could quite simply not be missed.

'Why are you not at the sales?' I tried to stay calm as I asked him.

'Mister Dennis, when you own the best camels in your country you do not need to go to the sales. *Liakun*.'*

Somewhat shocked at all of this, I offered Mohammed the opportunity to terminate the course there and then.

'No no, Mister Dennis,' he declined. 'I want to know what happened at Dover.'

'*Liakun*,' I said, and proceeded to finish the presentation to him and the interpreter.

After Mohammed and the interpreter had left the room, I started to pack up and go in search of Richard. As I left the classroom, a member of the administration team handed me twenty-four certificates to sign. I protested, but the young lady said very politely to me '*La tawqie, la mal*' – 'No signature, no money.'

This was the point when I decided it was finally the right time to retire. So that was exactly what I did.

Barak allah lakum jamiean – may God bless you all.

---

* Arabic for 'so be it'.

INDEX

Locations in pictures and tables are in *italics*.